UNIVERSITY
CHALLENGE

QUIZ BOOK

University Challenge

Quiz Book

OVER 2,000 QUESTIONS
FROM TELEVISION'S TOUGHEST
QUIZ SHOW

GRANADA

University Challenge is a Granada Television Production

First published in Great Britain in 2001
by Granada Media, an imprint of André Deutsch Limited
20 Mortimer Street
London W1T 3JW

In association with Granada Media Group

A catalogue record for this book is available from
the British Library

ISBN 0 233 99947 7

Typeset by Derek Doyle & Associates, Liverpool
Printed and bound in the UK by
Mackays of Chatham plc

10 9 8 7 6 5 4 3 2 1

CONTENTS

INTRODUCTION

September 21, 1962. Harold Macmillan is in Downing Street. The USA, still reeling from the news of Marilyn Monroe's death, finds itself in a face-off with Khrushchev over Soviet missile bases on Cuba. In Pretoria, an African nationalist called Nelson Mandela is facing trial.

This is how the world looked on the day *University Challenge* first appeared on the UK's television screens.

Few people watching that first edition could have predicted that, along with *The Sky at Night* and *Coronation Street*, the series would still be transmitting in the next millennium, and in much the same shape as it started out. The format has remained constant, the rules are still the same, and we still use our signature split-screen shot – by now, surely, the oldest special effect in television – which makes it appear that one team sits on top of the other. This one image is so much a part of the programme's identity that our studio audiences are still disconcerted to see that the teams' desks actually sit side by side on the studio floor.

With television schedules as they currently stand, *University Challenge* has a slightly anachronistic appeal. Other programmes, on other channels, can offer quiz-show contestants a cash prize in seven figures, but our students are still tempted into months of swotting and pre-show jitters by nothing more than the fun and honour of competing, and the icy thrill of an encounter with Jeremy Paxman. As viewers, we can choose programmes in which contestants endure having their every moment scrutinised by hidden cameras, but millions of us still get a kick out of watching teams of students struggling to define Olber's Paradox, or remember which of Rossetti's models married William Morris, or list all the original companions of Scooby Doo.

Anachronistic or not, when we have two evenly-matched teams only a few points apart in the closing minutes, both of them dazzlingly well-informed and almost psychic in their ability to anticipate questions, the programme can deliver as much excitement, drama and intellectual fireworks as anything else on screen.

This is not to say the programme hasn't changed at all over the years. Originally running on the ITV network, it has now found its place on BBC2. It has been exceptionally fortunate in its presenters, both of whom have been fundamental to its enduring success. Watching the programme as a child, I viewed Bamber Gascoigne as a personification of academic achievement, apparently steeped in the pursuit of knowledge for its own sake. Jeremy Paxman's style is more robust and combative. He won't pull his punches when teams fall short of the mark, and is genuinely admiring when they shine. The questions are about as hard as they have ever been, but we now include far more on the sciences. We also like to throw in a few questions on popular culture to tempt our teams into revealing, for example, just how much they know about winners of the Eurovision Song Contest. We always warn our students: it's not just what you know, it's also what you're prepared to *admit* you know.

What today's students do or do not know, and whether they are as bright a bunch of people as the students of past decades, is a theme frequently debated in the press, and very often the standard of questions on *University Challenge* is claimed to prove the argument either way. As programme-makers, we're reluctant to make any such claims. Of all the societal changes the programme is claimed to illustrate, there's only one to which we feel it genuinely bears witness, and that is the vast improvement in the personal hygiene of the young British male. Granada Television's redoubtable make-up team, who now list the transformations on *Stars In Their Eyes* among their many achievements, report that the skin and hair of young male students have improved beyond all recognition since the Sixties and Seventies, and they are now a pleasure to deal with. No longer do they privately refer to the programme as 'The Spots Show'.

So how do these fresh-complexioned, well-informed people come to be on the programme? We leave it to them to form themselves into teams and elect a captain. We ask them to return an application form to us with a completed general knowledge test. These forms frequently reveal more about them than they realise, and from some, it's clear their test-papers owe more to alcohol-fuelled guesswork than academic excellence. A hastily scribbled cartoon of four faces in the space reserved for their team photograph makes us wonder how seriously they are taking their application but, oddly, this often proves to be a good sign. Teams who are relaxed about taking part, and who are out to have a good time, are more likely to entertain viewers, and may surprise themselves with what they can dredge from the dimmer recesses of their minds when under pressure.

Teams with a reasonable score on their application test paper will be asked to attend an interview session around the Easter vacation, in which members of the production time will invigilate a second, much tougher test. The twenty-eight teams with the highest scores in this second test will be invited to compete in the series.

Once they've made it onto the programme, teams have different strategies for preparation. Some of them can be found flicking through encyclopaedias until the last moment before they go on set. One team psyched themselves by dancing to Abba tracks, another team passed around a photo of their patron, the Queen Mother, which each of them would kiss in turn.

As we watch the contests over the years, patterns begin to emerge. One is that the early stages of each series will often by dominated by teams who notch up dramatically high scores. Very often, though, these are not the teams who make it through to the final. The ones to watch out for are the quieter, more thoughtful teams who score solidly and consistently well. They'll confer well together, and they'll have an unflappable captain who knows which team member to listen to on a given subject. They'll have a scientist on board, or at least a player who took some sciences at A-level. They won't be thrown by being fifty points down at the half-way mark. And they'll secretly enjoy being told off by an incredulous presenter when their answers are embarrassingly off beam.

Among so many television quiz programmes, I suspect *University Challenge* has survived because it offers unique pleasures. There's something very reassuring in being shown that the student population includes a good number of astonishingly well-informed and charming people. There's something pleasantly old-fashioned in a quiz programme entered for the fun of it, for no prize other than a trophy and the honour of having taken part. And if there's one explanation our viewers offer more than any other for why they enjoy the programme, it's because, with the standard of questions at a respectably high level, getting two or three right every week proves to us that our brains are still functioning.

And on that note: Olber's Paradox asks why, if the number of stars in the sky is infinite, is it dark at night? William Morris married Jane Burden. Scooby Doo's companions in the original Hanna-Barbera series were Fred, Shaggy, Velma and Daphne.

How to Play the Game

Like most successful television quizzes, *University Challenge* has a very simple format, and lends itself to being played outside the television studio, without bells and buzzers. The basics are very few: you'll need someone to ask the questions, and two teams to answer them. An extra, non-partisan pair of hands to keep track of the scoring helps enormously but, at a pinch, this can be done by the Questioner or by the teams themselves.

The rules are simple. We ask two types of questions: starters and bonuses. Players must answer starter questions on their own, without conferring with team members. A correct answer gets ten points.

If you can set up a version of the bell-and-buzzer system, you'll need the rule that says if a player interrupts the asking of a starter question and gives the wrong answer, the team will lose five points and the entire question will be offered to the opposing team. You will also need to remind players that once they have signalled to answer, they must give the answer promptly.

If you are playing without any mechanical means of showing who thinks they've got the answer first, we suggest simply addressing starter questions to individual team members in turn. Your players will feel under much more pressure but this game is meant to be a challenge.

For each correctly answered starter, that team gets the chance to answer a set of three bonus questions, and on these they can and should confer. Each of the three bonuses is worth five points, so fifteen points are on offer for each set. Incorrectly answered bonus questions are not handed over to the opposing team.

Simple though the rules are, anyone who fancies the role of Questioner might want to think about the practicalities of applying themselves. For instance, you'll occasionally have to judge whether too much information has been given, or not enough. If, when interrupting a starter question, a player gives *more* information than the question demands, as long as the answer is given promptly and contains the specific information required, points will be awarded.

We usually allow contestants to give only the minimum amount of correct information to earn points. Surnames, rather than full names, will usually suffice, except in cases where contestants need to make clear they understand the difference between, for instance, the two American presidents with the surname Roosevelt. In such an instance, the Questioner can insist on a more specific answer being given.

For some of the questions in this book, parts of the answer will appear in brackets. The information outside the brackets is what we consider the minimum amount of information we need for points to be awarded.

In very rare cases, a starter question will be answered incorrectly in such a way that the right answer becomes obvious to the opposing team, who otherwise would not have known it and can therefore pick up points without doing any work. It is down to the Questioner's judgement whether or not the question is still offered across to the opponents. A strict interpretation of the rules will say that it should be; the spirit of fair play might suggest that the question simply be dropped.

It is also down to the Questioner's judgement how much time will be allowed for teams to confer on bonuses. By all means use a clock, but remember that questions which require players to make mental calculations should be allowed a little more time.

Be ruthless with teams who, finding themselves in the lead in the closing moments, spend too long conferring on bonuses, or ask for their questions to be repeated, as a tactic to deny their opponents a few extra questions.

Never be lenient towards a team just because they are doing very badly. If there is a chance they may recover and catch up with their opponents, you will want to be sure that all your judgements have been as fair as possible throughout the match.

When answering bonus questions, we strongly recommend the entire team confer, agree on the answer, and then let the answer be given by the team captain, or by another player clearly nominated by the captain. If any team member gives an answer clearly and directly to the Questioner before the team have had a chance to confer, we take that as the team's offered answer, and award or deny points accordingly.

You'll need a means of sounding the moment when time is up. On the programme we use a rather portentous gong, but an alarm clock set to ring thirty minutes after you begin playing will serve just as well. The rules state that a player must have completed the answer to a question before the 'time up' signal is heard, if they are to be given points.

If both teams are tied on the same number of points when 'time up' sounds, the Questioner will continue to ask starter questions until one is answered correctly.

If you play the game at the same pace as we do in studio, you'll probably find you need to allocate about thirty-five starter questions and twenty-five sets of bonuses to each game. If you want to rate yourselves against the teams who appear on screen, this is our rule of thumb: scores below one hundred are best glossed over; anything between one and two hundred is creditable, and a score over two hundred is impressive. If you can get yourselves over the three hundred mark, you can congratulate yourselves on being a match for any of the brightest teams to appear on the programme.

I hope you enjoy playing the game as much as we enjoy playing it in studio. And remember, if you do score well and you're a team of students, the programme wants to hear from you!

First Round

1 STARTER

Q. The 1913 'Prisoners (temporary discharge for ill health) Act', otherwise known as 'the cat and mouse Act', was particularly directed against which group of activists?

BONUS QUESTIONS

Three questions on names of flightless birds:

Q. Which flightless bird of the genus *apteryx* gets its name from the local indigenous people's imitation of its cry?

Q. Which flightless bird gets its name from the Portuguese for ostrich?

Q. Which flightless bird shares its name with, and is thought to be named after, the daughter of Uranus and Gaea and sister of Kronos, in Greek mythology?

2 STARTER

Q. Born in 1955, at the age of 15 he constructed a device to control traffic patterns in his native Seattle; he dropped out of his applied mathematics course at Harvard in 1975, yet has been called 'the Thomas Edison and Henry Ford of his age'. Who is he?

BONUS QUESTIONS

Three questions on the River Wye:

Q. The River Wye empties into the estuary of which river, near Chepstow?

Q. Which ecclesiastical ruin on the banks of the River Wye is the subject of a poem by William Wordsworth?

Q. The town of Hay-on-Wye is particularly famous for shops selling what?

3 STARTER

Q. What is the fundamental difference between magma and lava?

BONUS QUESTIONS

Three questions on serpents:

Q. Which creature of classical mythology was half-woman and half-serpent, and was said to have given birth to the sphinx, the hydra, Cerberus and the chimera?

Q. Which fairy of French folklore was condemned to change into a serpent from the waist down every Saturday, disappearing once her husband broke his promise never to visit her on that day?

Q. In which of Shakespeare's plays does a wife advise her husband: 'bear welcome in your eye,/your hand, your tongue: look the innocent flower/but be the serpent under't'?

4 STARTER

Q. Brew, mash, draw and scald are all dialect words for making which beverage?

BONUS QUESTIONS

Three questions on secretions:

Q. Which oily substance is secreted through hair follicles, forming the thin layer of fat over the skin that slows the evaporation of water and produces an antiseptic effect?

Q. The secretion cerumen is commonly known by which name?

Q. The parotid glands, sublingual glands and submandibular glands all secrete which alkaline fluid?

5 STARTER

Q. If 'p' is a positive integer and 'p' is not equal to one and its only positive divisors are one and itself, then 'p' is known as what?

BONUS QUESTIONS

Q. 'Sambo' in Russia, 'kushti' in Iran, 'glima' in Iceland and 'yagli' in Turkey are among the styles developed from which sport, contested at the ancient Olympic Games?

Q. In which novel of 1921 does Rupert Birkin wrestle with Gerald Crich?

Q. In Genesis, who wrestled with a mysterious messenger from God at a ford of the River Jaboc, a tributary of the Jordan?

6 STARTER

Q. Which two-word French term is the name of a character equivalent to the English 'Mister Punch', and was formerly the name of a Parisian Theatre, the term now being applied to a sensational and horrific style of entertainment?

BONUS QUESTIONS

Three questions linked by a name:

Q. Voiced by the ballet teacher Judith Gibbons in her second and third stories, who is the star of the *Tomb Raiders* adventures?

Q. Who starred as 'Lara' in the 1965 film *Doctor Zhivago*?

Q. The Test cricketer Brian Lara was born on which West Indian island?

7 STARTER

Q. Which device was developed in the 1950s by Ian Donald, then Professor of Midwifery at Glasgow University, and used the naval echo-sounding technique known as sonar to become an important aid to diagnosing foetal progress during pregnancy?

BONUS QUESTIONS

Three questions on fictional governesses:

Q. Which literary heroine made a secret marriage to Rawdon Crawley, son of Sir Pitt Crawley, to whose children she had been a governess?

Q. Which governess begins the last chapter of her story with the words, 'reader, I married him'?

Q. The villainous governess Miss Slighcarp appears in which novel by Joan Aiken, where England under James III in the 1830s is overrun by wolves that have strayed through the newly opened Channel tunnel?

8 STARTER

Q. In April 1998, which Arsenal striker became only the second foreign footballer to be voted 'player of the year' by his fellow professionals?

BONUS QUESTIONS

Complete the following sayings attributed to Voltaire:

Q. 'I disapprove of what you say, but I will defend to the death...'

Q. 'If god did not exist, it would be necessary...'

Q. 'It is one of the superstitions of the human mind to have imagined that – ' what ' – could be virtue'?

9 STARTER

Q. 'The unlawful killing of a reasonable creature under the Queen's peace ...'; which three words complete this definition of murder?

BONUS QUESTIONS

Three questions on beef dishes:

Q. A dish of a fillet of beef with liver pâté, baked in puff pastry, is named after which military leader?

Q. Which nineteenth-century Russian diplomat has given his name to a dish of thinly sliced beef fillet, served with mushrooms and sour cream?

Q. A very thick slice of fillet steak, generally served with a *béarnaise* sauce, is said to have been named after which French writer and statesman?

10 STARTER

Q. In which commonwealth country will you find the regions of Malborough, West Coast and Thames Valley?

BONUS QUESTIONS

Q. Indicated by the symbol 'Sv', what is the SI unit of radiation dose equivalent?

Q. Hans Sievert of Germany, in 1934 with 8790.46 points, became the last world record holder in the original method of scoring which athletics event?

Q. Which American railway engineer became famous after he was popularized in a vaudeville song written in 1909 by Lawrence Siebert and Eddie Newton?

11 STARTER

Q. Which Italian word, meaning 'detached', is used in music to indicate a method of playing a note so that it is shortened and is signified by a dot over the note?

BONUS QUESTIONS

Q. Which warrior queen was at one time erroneously thought to have been buried under platform nine at Kings Cross Station?

Q. Boudicca's husband, Prasutagus, was king of which tribe?

Q. Reflecting the fact that Boudicca's actual name is uncertain, which contemporary of Shakespeare described her in *The Masque of Queenes* as 'our own honour, Voadicea, or Boodicia, by some Bunduica and Bunduca, Queene of the Iceni'?

12 STARTER

Q. What is the name of Gianni Versace's sister, who succeeded her late brother as head of the fashion house in 1997?

BONUS QUESTIONS

Three questions on railways:

Q. Inspired by George Pullman, what was the name of the company founded by the Belgian Georges Nagelmackers in 1876, to provide luxury dining and sleeping accommodation on trains?

Q. Which train service was born out of a conference in 1883, when Nagelmackers met representatives from eight different railway companies in Constantinople?

Q. Who, as commander of the Allied forces during the closing months of World War I, received the surrender of the German forces in wagon-lit car number 2419?

13 STARTER

Q. What name is given to the payment made for the right to use someone else's property, including intellectual property, for gain?

BONUS QUESTIONS

Three questions linked by a film:

Q. Which classic film title appeared on an anti-nuclear poster of the 1980s, which showed Margaret Thatcher in Ronald Reagan's arms with the mushroom cloud of an exploding atom bomb in the background?

Q. Which city is burned to the ground in *Gone With The Wind*?

Q. Hattie McDaniel won a best supporting actress Oscar for her role as 'Mammy' in *Gone With The Wind*; in terms of screen history, what was the particular significance of her award?

14 STARTER

Q. Which group of people are known as the *hiba kusha* in Japan?

BONUS QUESTIONS

Q. Which distorted form of art is usually credited to, and takes its name from, the sixteenth-century painter Annibale Carracci, who saw it as a counterpart to idealization?

Q. Which German Expressionist painter and illustrator was born in Berlin in 1893, and created many caricatured depictions of social evils in Germany between the wars, including 'the faces of the ruling class' in 1921?

Q. Which wizened clergyman was created by the eighteenth and nineteenth century English caricaturist Thomas Rowlandson, and appeared in a series of books that began with his *Tour ... in Search of the Picturesque*?

15 STARTER

Q. What is being described? An oval-shaped, anticyclonic circulation system centered at about latitude 23 degrees south, its north-south extent is about equal to the diameter of the Earth. Discovered in 1665, its colour varies from brick-red to brown?

BONUS QUESTIONS

Three questions on the Epistles of St Paul:

Q. Arguably attributed to Paul, the pastoral Epistles are three New Testament writings, one of which was addressed to Titus and the other two to which close companion of Paul?

Q. Written while Paul was in prison, the shortest of his extant letters is an appeal to whom, begging him to be merciful to the runaway slave Onesimus?

Q. Which of Paul's Epistles has a biblical position immediately after his letter to the Romans?

16 STARTER

Q. The world's oldest surviving example of which musical instrument is housed in New York's Metropolitan Museum, having been made by Bartolomeo Cristofori in 1720?

BONUS QUESTIONS

Three questions on biochemistry:

Q. What term is used specifically for the emission of light by a living organism, such as the light produced by fireflies to attract other fireflies, and by deep-sea fish to lure prey?

Q. In biochemistry, what name is given to the organic compound whose oxidization in the presence of a certain enzyme produces light?

Q. What name is used for the light-emitting organ present in fireflies and certain other bioluminescent creatures, such as the lantern-fish?

17 STARTER

Q. 'Spank the children darling, I'm too tired', were words reputedly spoken to her husband by the mother of which expert in baby care, who died in March 1998 at the age of 94?

BONUS QUESTIONS

Three questions on the abbreviation i.e.:

Q. When used to mean 'that is', what do the letters i.e. stand for?

Q. The capital letters I.E. are used by philologists to refer to which group of languages?

Q. To computer users, what does the abbreviation i.e. represent?

18 STARTER

Q. The title of poems by both Chapelain and Voltaire, who was 'La Pucelle'?

BONUS QUESTIONS

Three questions on general election years:

Q. There were two general elections in the 1960s; in which years did they occur?

Q. There were four general elections in the 1970s; in which years did they occur?

Q. There were two general elections in the 1980s; in which years did they occur?

19 STARTER

Q. Which external architectural feature of a building may be hipped, gambrel, saddleback, mansard or gabled?

BONUS QUESTIONS

Q. 'No Woman No Cry' in 1975 was the first UK singles chart entry for which performer?

Q. Chris Ofili, who won the Turner Prize in 1998 with works such as 'No Woman, No Cry', used what substance, coated with resin and decorated with coloured map-pins, to ornament his paintings?

Q. In which eponymous American state was the corn 'as high as an elephant's eye'?

20 STARTER

Q. Which four-letter word can precede all of the following words to make a longer word or phrase: bell, blood, print and ribbon?

BONUS QUESTIONS

Three questions on women's firsts in sport:

Q. How did Wendy Toms make football league history at Torquay United's Plainmoor Ground, on 20 August 1994?

Q. In 1996, Alex Greaves became the first woman to ride in which race, coming last on the five-hundred-to-one shot Portuguese Lil?

Q. In November 1998 Jane Couch, the self-styled 'Fleetwood Assassin', beat Germany's Simone Lukic in which sport, in the first officially licensed contest for women in Britain?

21 STARTER

Q. Among vertebrates, which hormone is involved in reproductive behaviour and is secreted by the pineal gland, the blood containing higher levels during darkness than in the light?

BONUS QUESTIONS

Three questions on British currency:

Q. Which coin, first minted in gold by Henry VIII, finally ceased to be legal tender in its cupro-nickel version on January 1st 1970?

Q. Which British coin had a lifespan of just 13 years, being introduced when Britain went decimal in 1971, and ceasing to be legal tender on 31 December 1984?

Q. The United Kingdom's 'bronze' coins, made between September 1992 and April 1997, were actually made from which metal, plated in copper?

22 STARTER

Q. Which rum-producing district of Cuba gives its name to a cocktail, originally made with rum and lime juice, often with the addition of fruit?

BONUS QUESTIONS

Three questions on botany:

Q. It was announced in 1998 that scientists at Kew Gardens had discovered new relationships between plants by comparing them not by appearance but by – what?

Q. Under the new system, the lotus *nelumbo nucifera*, was revealed to resemble which tree, *platanus hybrida*, which had grown in cities where no other trees would grow until the introduction of the clean air act?

Q. Which botanist invented the system of binomial nomenclature, the system of using two Latin names to describe plants and animals?

23 STARTER

Q. What word describes a figure of speech which substitutes for a word an attribute of that word? For example, the use of 'the stage' for the theatre, or 'the White House' for the US presidency?

BONUS QUESTIONS

Three questions on mounts and mountains:

Q. Which mountain in Spain lies about 25 miles north-west of Barcelona, and is the site of the monastery which houses the carved wooden statue of the madonna and child, popularly known as 'La Moreneta', or 'the little dark one'?

Q. Mount Vernon, a Georgian mansion overlooking the Potomac river 15 miles south of Washington DC, was the home and burial place of which famous American?

Q. Mount Cook National Park, on New Zealand's South Island, extends for approximately 40 miles along the crest of which mountain range?

24 STARTER

Q. Established in the UK in the early 1930s, which form of inexpensive accommodation was based on the German *Jugendherbergen*, founded in 1909 by Richard Schirrmann?

BONUS QUESTIONS

Q. In his poem 'Jerusalem', William Blake wrote the line: 'bring me my bow of burning gold!' what was his request in the next line?

Q. Which director, noted for the violence of his films, was responsible for *Bring Me The Head of Alfredo Garcia*, a 1974 effort notable for even more slow-motion violence than usual?

Q. In a parody of the film's title, Channel 5 introduced *Bring Me The Head of Light Entertainment*, a comedy panel game first presented by which comedian and actor?

25 STARTER

Q. What word is being described? Said to be originally a university slang expression, it derived from the Greek for 'of long standing', and ultimately for 'time', and is now a somewhat pejorative term for an intimate companion?

BONUS QUESTIONS

Three questions on fields:

Q. What name is generally given to the field which saw the ceremonial meeting between Henry VIII and Francis I of France in June 1520, the name referring to the splendour of the occasion?

Q. Referred to in the title of the 1984 film directed by Roland Joffé, in which country did the *The Killing Fields* occur?

Q. Which artist painted several 'field' studies in 1890, the last year of his life, including *Wheat Field Under Cloudy Skies* and *Wheat Field With Crows*?

26 STARTER

Q. Which gland is situated at the base of the brain, and has a major influence on growth?

BONUS QUESTIONS

Three questions on famous people mentioned in songs:

Q. The name of which American architect was used in the title of a track on Simon and Garfunkel's *Bridge Over Troubled Water* album?

Q. Which pop group recorded the track 'Dreaming Of The Queen', in which the singer dreams about an invitation to Buckingham Palace for tea with Her Majesty and the late Princess Diana?

Q. A track by the group Space featured a vocal performance by Cerys Matthews, and described a quarrelling couple who were prevented from killing each other by hearing the greatest hits of which recording artist?

27 STARTER

Q. The writer born Adeline Virginia Stephen in 1882 committed suicide in 1941. By what name was she better known?

BONUS QUESTIONS

Q. What name is given to any double sulphate of a monovalent metal or radical, such as sodium, potassium or ammonium, and a trivalent metal, such as aluminium or iron?

Q. Alum Bay in the Isle of Wight is particularly noted for its multi-coloured – what?

Q. The latin term 'alumnus' is used today to mean what?

28 STARTER

Q. Launched in 1998, 'the Silver Seraph' is the first new model for 15 years to be produced by which motor company?

BONUS QUESTIONS

Three questions on Indian cities:

Q. Which Indian city is now officially known as Mumbai?

Q. Which city is the capital of Tamil Nadu State, and is now offically known by its Tamil name, Cennai?

Q. How was the Indian city of Pune better known, when it was a summer retreat for the British in India?

29 STARTER

Q. On Earth, where can the abyssal plains be found?

BONUS QUESTIONS

Three questions on the same name in different states:

Q. Springfield, Illinois, is the state capital and the burial place of which American president, who lived there from 1837 until he took office in 1861?

Q. Springfield, Massachusetts, is the site of which game's hall of fame, the game having been devised in the city by James Naismith in 1891?

Q. Springfield, Missouri is an agricultural and tourist centre in which wooded upland region, lying between the Arkansas and Missouri rivers?

30 STARTER

Q. The availability of what became a statutory obligation in the nineteenth century, culminating in an Act of Parliament in 1908; their numbers temporarily increased during both world wars, each one covering a quarter of an acre, rented from a local authority?

BONUS QUESTIONS

Three questions on the films of Robin Williams:

Q. After the success of *Good Morning Vietnam* in 1987, which anti-war film of 1992 was also directed by Barry Levinson and starred Robin Williams, this time alongside Joan Cusack?

Q. In *Awakenings*, Robin Williams played Dr Malcolm Sayer, who revived stricken victims of the great 'sleeping sickness' of the 1920s; which real life doctor wrote the book of his experiences on which the film was based?

Q. Believing that 'laughter is the best medicine', what is the name of the doctor played by Robin Williams in a film first released in 1998?

31 STARTER

Q. Which device alters the amount of resistance in an electrical circuit, thus regulating the flow of current?

BONUS QUESTIONS

Three questions on unfinished romantic poems:

Q. Which epic poem by Keats, about Jove's defeat of Saturn and the Titans, did he abandon because he thought his writing was 'too Miltonic'?

Q. Which poet wrote 'The Triumph of Life' in the village of Lerici on the Bay of Spezia in 1822, but left it unfinished on his death in that year?

Q. Which poem in nine books by Wordsworth was published in 1814, and was the middle section of a projected three-part poem on 'man, nature and human life'?

32 STARTER

Q. In the Bible, the Hexameron is an account of what?

BONUS QUESTIONS

Three questions on chemicals used in beauty products:

Q. Also known as rutile, which chemical is used in the cosmetics industry in its crystal form, because its light-scattering properties makes facial imperfections less obvious?

Q. For what purpose are aluminium chloride and hexachlorophene used in the field of personal hygiene, although the first one, marketed in 1888, consisted of a zinc compound in a cream base?

Q. Dihydroxyacetone, or DHA, which has a characteristic smell, is used in which products?

33 STARTER

Q. Which organization was founded in 1905, when its chief aim was to warn members of policemen lurking behind bushes to uphold speed limits, the agreed signal at one time being a failure to salute the member's car?

BONUS QUESTIONS

Three questions on European kings:

Q. Which country has been ruled by 18 kings called Louis?

Q. Which country has been ruled by 16 kings called Charles, or Carl?

Q. Which country has been ruled by 10 kings called Christian?

34 STARTER

Q. What name is given to the painting technique in which opaque, water-based colours are thickened with gum, or glue and honey before application to the surface?

BONUS QUESTIONS

Q. Which two metals make up the alloy, brass?

Q. On whose death, in Shakespeare's *Henry VIII*, does Griffith remark 'men's evil manners live in brass: their virtues we write in water'?

Q. According to some versions of the Greek myth, Talus, or 'the man of brass', was the guardian of Crete. What was his novel method of killing his victims?

35 STARTER

Q. Which play by Neil Simon was successfully adapted for the screen, and has as its central characters the ageing vaudeville performers Al Lewis and Willie Clarke?

BONUS QUESTIONS

Three questions on spies and espionage:

Q. Which sixteenth century statesman was effectively the first head of England's secret service? He collected intelligence for Lord Burghley, uncovered the Ridolfi conspiracy, secured the convictions of Babington and Mary Queen of Scots, and vainly urged Elizabeth to prepare for the Armada in 1587.

Q. Born in 1660, which journalist, satirist and novelist carried out several spying missions for the government in a varied career that included several prison terms?

Q. Created by John Le Carre, which secret agent made his first appearance in print in the 1961 novel *Call For The Dead*?

36 STARTER

Q. For what purpose would an angler employ a brandling?

BONUS QUESTIONS

Q. Which British scientist was awarded the 1921 Nobel Prize for chemistry for his work on isotopes, a term he coined.

Q. Frederick Soddy also worked alongside Sir William Ramsay in showing that which noble gas is a product of radioactive decay?

Q. In which other academic field did Soddy write, producing his main work on the subject in 1922?

37 STARTER

Q. Much employed by nomadic herdsmen of the Gobi Desert, what is a yurt?

BONUS QUESTIONS

Q. Which life-size mechanical tiger, named after an eighteenth-century Sultan of Mysore for whom it was made, is exhibited in the Victoria and Albert Museum where it is seen to be devouring a prostrate European?

Q. 'The tiger' was the soubriquet of which French statesman who presided over the peace conference of 1919, although it is thought his hatred of Germany may have contributed towards World War II?

Q. Which British Prime Minister once spoke of dictators as 'riding to and fro upon tigers which they dare not dismount. And the tigers are getting hungry'?

38 STARTER

Q. What is the name of the rural pressure group which organized a mass protest against government policies in March 1998?

BONUS QUESTIONS

Three questions on prisoners in Dickens' novels:

Q. Which character in *A Tale Of Two Cities*, when asked for his name replies, 'one hundred and five, north tower' on account of having been a prisoner in the Bastille for 18 years?

Q. In which Dickens novel does Mr Creakle the magistrate visit a prison and ask, 'well, twenty seven, how do you find yourself today?' the prisoner stating that he is 'very 'umble'?

Q. In *The Pickwick Papers* an inmate of which debtors' prison is addressed as 'twenty' because he carries a calling card which bears no name, simply his 'address' within the prison, no.20 coffee-room flight?

39 STARTER

Q. Which large sea-bird is sometimes known as the solan goose?

BONUS QUESTIONS

Q. What is the alternative name for a wide 'batwing' sleeve cut in one piece with the bodice, creating a deep armhole that reaches from the waist to a narrowed wrist?

Q. What type of pleat consists of two parallel creases turned inwards towards each other?

Q. What name is given to either the fitted portion of a garment covering the back between the shoulders, or an extended waistband curving downwards?

40 STARTER

Q. In the standard seating arrangement in a symphony orchestra, which instruments would be sited immediately in front of the conductor?

BONUS QUESTION

Six US states constitute the area known as New England.

Q. Name three for 5 points, five for 10 points and all six for the full 15.

41 STARTER

Q. Which complex carbohydrate substance serves to strengthen the tough outer cuticle of insects and crustaceans and the cell walls of many fungi?

BONUS QUESTIONS

Q. Elected since 1866, the lower house of the Tynwald, the Isle of Man Parliament, is known by what name thought to derive from a Norse word for 'chosen'?

Q. *The House Of The Seven Gables*, Nathaniel Hawthorne's novel of a jinxed family, is said to have been inspired by his own family history as his great-grandfather allegedly presided over what proceedings and was cursed by one of his victims?

Q. 'House of Fun' reached number one in Britain in 1982 for which group?

42 STARTER

Q. What name is given to the theory held by many American administrators, which supposes that if one small nation were to fall to communism then its neighbours would surely follow?

BONUS QUESTIONS

Q. The lustre and surface colour of which precious objects are called their 'orient'?

Q. Which major Chinese city is situated just upstream of the head of the Pearl River estuary?

Q. Which novel by Pearl Buck about Chinese peasant life won a Pulitzer Prize in 1932?

43 STARTER

Q. Which craggy Scottish headland is the extreme northwest point of the British mainland?

BONUS QUESTIONS

Q. What did Hesiod define as the primeval state of emptiness, although according to Ovid it was a mass of muddled forms and elements which separated out into the universe?

Q. The concept of chaos was applied to the interpretation of which event by the early church fathers?

Q. In 1961, which meteorologist accidentally found the first mathematical system with chaotic behaviour in a computer model of how the atmosphere behaves?

44 STARTER

Q. What name is the Greek for 'goddess loving her father', and has been given to several Egyptian queens, including the second daughter of Ptolomy XII, who committed suicide in 30 BC?

BONUS QUESTIONS

Three questions on voting systems:

Q. Also known as 'first past the post', what is the two word name for the voting system whereby the party gaining the majority of votes cast secures all the available seats?

Q. Which system allows the voter to cast two votes, one for the party and one for the candidate, so that half the assembly is elected on a simple plurality basis while the other half, using party lists, is chosen to accurately reflect the national vote?

Q. The European polls of June 1999 saw people in the UK voting for the first time in an election whose outcome was based on which system?

45 STARTER

Q. Rifle shooting and cross-country skiing together form the Olympic biathlon event, but which sport is twinned with cross-country skiing in the Nordic combination?

BONUS QUESTIONS

Three questions on architects who trained in other disciplines:

Q. Which Swiss-born architect originally trained as a metal engraver, his work in metal winning a prize at the Turin international exhibition in 1902?

Q. Which architect was born in Aachen in 1886, and first worked as a stonemason in the family business; from the mid 1920s, his chairs became classics of twentieth-century furniture?

Q. Which architect trained as an engineer at the University of Wisconsin from 1885 to 1887?

46 STARTER

Q. What is the English name for the city that Italians call Livorno?

BONUS QUESTIONS

Three questions on football grounds:

Q. Which Scottish football league club has its home ground in England?

Q. Which English football club's home ground has one goal in England and the other in Wales?

Q. Which club play in the Irish Republic's football league, although their home is in Northern Ireland?

47 STARTER

Q. Mythologically associated with evil, which creature is mentioned in several passages of the Old Testament, and has been variously interpreted as referring to the crocodile or whale?

BONUS QUESTIONS

In each case, identify the Shakespeare play from its opening words:

Q. 'In sooth, I know not why I am so sad.'

Q. 'Hence! Home, you idle creatures, get you home : is this a holiday?'

Q. 'In delivering my son from me, I bury a second husband'.

48 STARTER

Q. If an item previously advertised for sale at £24 has a 12.5 per cent discount, what is the new price?

BONUS QUESTIONS

Q. A corroboree is a type of ceremonial dance amongst which indigenous people?

Q. William Lanney, who died in March 1869, was the last male tribal aborigine in which Australian state?

Q. Of aboriginal descent, which daughter of a sheep-shearer became a top sportswoman who reached her peak in the 1970s?

49 STARTER

Q. What name is given to the person who chants the liturgy and leads the congregation in prayer in a synagogue?

BONUS QUESTIONS

Three questions on fabrics:

Q. What name was formerly used for a fabric made partly from the wool of a South American mammal related to the llama and today describes a rayon crêpe material?

Q. Also called Persian lamb, what alternative name is given to what was originally the fleece of the karakul lamb of Russia, used as a trimming until the late nineteenth century?

Q. Made of silk, rayon, cotton or wool, which fabric takes its name from the French for 'caterpillar' because of its protruding velvety tufts?

50 STARTER

Q. Which word derives from the middle Dutch for 'to groan', and originally meant to sing softly to a baby, but since the 1930s has come to mean to sing in a soft and sentimental style, often with a dance band?

BONUS QUESTIONS

Q. Which social and educational organization began in Canada in 1897, with classes on domestic science at Stoney Creek, Ontario?

Q. The first Women's Institute in Britain was founded in 1915 in a village whose name means 'St Mary's church in the hollow of the white hazel near the rapid whirlpool of Llantysilio of the red cave'. How is this place name more usually abbreviated?

Q. How did members of North Yorkshire's Rylstone and District branch of the WI hit the headlines in April 1999?

51 STARTER

Q. What term is used for the direct change of state from a solid to a gas?

BONUS QUESTIONS

Three questions on circumcision:

Q. According to Genesis, circumcision of male Jewish babies on the eighth day after birth represents part of which patriarch's convenant with God?

Q. Which English dramatist wrote the line, in a play first performed in 1967: 'every luxury was lavished on you – atheism, breast-feeding, circumcision'?

Q. About which of his former colleagues, who was leader of the Liberal Party from 1931 to 35, did Lloyd George say that when they circumcised him: 'they threw away the wrong bit'?

52 STARTER

Q. Which Italian word, meaning 'shore' or 'coast', was originally applied to the area around Genoa, but was later used for the coast from Marseilles in France to Spezia in Italy, and has come to be a generic term for a coastal resort area?

BONUS QUESTIONS

Three questions on the manufacture of tyres:

Q. Which American inventor, whose surname is still used in the tyre industry, accidentally discovered the vulcanizing process for hardening rubber when he dropped a mass of rubber and sulphur on to a hot stove and noted that the mixture did not melt?

Q. Which Scottish vet invented the pneumatic tyre when his nine-year-old son complained of the rough ride his tricycle gave him over the cobbles of Belfast?

Q. Which European company was the first to use pneumatic tyres on cars, and introduced the steel-belted radial tyre in 1948?

53 STARTER

Q. Wladimir Koppen, at the beginning of the twentieth century, devised a classification system for what, according to their associated major vegetation types?

BONUS QUESTIONS

Three questions on brewing terms:

Q. What name is given to Isinglass, usually made from the swim bladders of sturgeon and other substances, which is used to clarify beer?

Q. Related to the cannabis plant, 'fuggles', 'goldings' and 'saaz' are examples of which plant, used to flavour and preserve beer?

Q. What name is given to the liquid resulting from the mashing process, which is rich in malt sugars?

54 STARTER

Q. The date of the Scottish devolution referendum coincided exactly with the 700th anniversary of which battle, when William Wallace's supporters routed the English forces?

BONUS QUESTIONS

Q. Reputedly created in the town by Elizabeth Raffald in the eighteenth century, which is the main filling of an eccles cake?

Q. Who created the character 'Eccles', a stalwart of the *Goon Show* radio programmes?

Q. Which letter of the alphabet did Spike Milligan use for the title of his television comedy series, beginning with 5 in 1969 and ending with 9?

55 STARTER

Q. Which field of study has two branches: the 'natural', concerned mainly with observation and theory; and the 'judicial', which involves foretelling events in individual lives?

BONUS QUESTIONS

Q. Which dance was popularized in the early 1940s and performed primarily to boogie-woogie and swing music, its name being a slang term also applied to a nervous or alarmist person?

Q. What letter and number designation was given to the World War II rockets, also known as flying bombs or doodlebugs?

Q. In *Gulliver's Travels*, with what were the Struldbrugs endowed? Instead of finding it a boon, it made them the most miserable of mankind.

56 STARTER

Q. Sergei Prokofiev's *Symphony No. 1 in D*, 'the classical', was written in parody of the style of which eighteenth century Austrian composer?

BONUS QUESTIONS

Q. By what must the mass, 'm', of a body be multiplied, to obtain its weight, 'w'?

Q. To the nearest whole number, what, in metres per second squared, is the acceleration due to gravity at the earth's surface?

Q. Assuming the Earth to be a rotating ellipsoid of uniform density, where on the Earth's surface is the acceleration due to gravity greatest?

57 STARTER

Q. How is a church architect called Querry described in the title of Graham Greene's novel of 1961, because he is devoid of desires or ambitions?

BONUS QUESTIONS

Q. In Hindu mythology, the primeval goddess Aditi who supports the sky, sustains all existence and nourishes the earth, is often represented as which animal?

Q. In Norse mythology, what was the name of the giant, the first being, who was nourished by the cow, Audumla?

Q. *The Book Of The Dun Cow* is the oldest surviving miscellaneous manuscript in which country's literature?

58 STARTER

Q. Issued in France as currency from 1789 to 1797, which paper bills were a financial expedient on the part of the revolutionary government, although their increasing availability resulted in inflation?

BONUS QUESTIONS

Three questions on films:

Q. Based on a play by Alexandre Breffort, which film was directed by Billy Wilder in 1963, and starred Shirley Maclaine as a Paris streetwalker exploited by the pimp, Hippolyte?

Q. In the 1987 film *Personal Services*, Julie Walters appeared as 'Christine Painter', a character based loosely on which Streatham 'hostess'?

Q. Directed by Colin Higgins, which film musical of 1982 starred Dolly Parton and Burt Reynolds, and is said to have been inspired by the American 'madam' Polly Adler, who died in 1962?

59 STARTER

Q. If the numbers 1 to 10 are written as words and arranged in alphabetical order, which will come first?

BONUS QUESTIONS

Three questions on popular music:

Q. Which musician was born at Itta Bena in Mississippi, used the nickname 'blues boy' early in his career, and christened his guitar 'Lucille'?

Q. Ben E. King was signed by George Treadwell, along with fellow members of The Crowns, to replace the former line-up of which singing group, disbanded in 1959?

Q. The Drifters' 'Up On The Roof' is one of the best-known compositions of which American-born singer-songwriter, who was herself the subject of a song by Neil Sedaka?

60 STARTER

Q. From the Gaelic for 'large sword', which two-edged broadsword was traditionally used by Scottish highlanders?

BONUS QUESTIONS

Three questions on medical terms:

Q. Long-sightedness, in which an image is focused beyond the retina, is a condition of the eye more properly known by which medical term?

Q. What term is used for a level of blood sugar above the upper limit of the normal range, and is a characteristic of diabetes mellitus?

Q. Hyperthyroidism, which is an overactivity of the thyroid gland, sometimes results from an exophthalmic goitre, a condition otherwise known by which name?

61 STARTER

Q. In inflected languages such as Latin, which term denotes the case used for the subject of a verb?

BONUS QUESTIONS

Three questions on tombs in English cathedrals:

Q. Which English cathedral houses two royal tombs; that of Robert of Normandy, heir to the conqueror who was disinherited by his father, and that of Edward II, who was murdered nearby at Berkeley Castle?

Q. In which cathedral are the tombs of four kings: Egbert, his son Ethelwulf, Canute and William II?

Q. Which English cathedral houses the body of King John, and the ashes of Stanley Baldwin?

62 STARTER

Q. According to the title of a song by Ray Davies of The Kinks, what explanation is given for the fact that 'one week he's in polka dots, the next week he's in stripes'?

BONUS QUESTIONS

Three questions on Greek islands:

Q. According to classical mythology, of which island was Ulysses, or Odysseus, the king?

Q. Which of the Ionian islands has the Greek name Kerkyra?

Q. Which British poet and novelist lived for many years on the Greek islands, and wrote several travel books on the subject, including *Prospero's Cell* about Corfu, and *Reflections On A Marine Venus* about Rhodes?

63 STARTER

Q. Mechanics, the science that studies the effects of forces on bodies at rest or in motion, has two branches, one of which is dynamics; name the other.

BONUS QUESTIONS

Three questions on European languages:

Q. Which language group has three main branches, Polish being an example of the western branch, Bulgarian the southern branch and Russian the eastern branch?

Q. Which language had replaced the native language of the transcaucasian region by the seventh century BC? It has its own alphabet of 38 characters, which dates from 400 AD, and has approximately five and a half million speakers today?

Q. Which Germanic language was widely spoken throughout central and eastern Europe for centuries, although it was never a national language? At the outbreak of World War II it had 11 million speakers, but now under five million speakers survive.

64 STARTER

Q. In bridge, what term means to play a card of another suit while holding a card of the suit that was led, resulting in a penalty?

BONUS QUESTIONS

Q. At which event of 1999 did the Queen deliver a speech that began, 'it is a great privilege to be here today at a notable moment in our nation's long history'?

Q. Who, in 1999, became First Secretary of the Welsh Assembly?

Q. According to a report in *The Times*, to whom did Lord Ellis Thomas, Speaker of the Welsh Assembly, address the words: 'There are no honourable gentlemen in this chamber'?

65 STARTER

Q. Which device first came into use during World War I, and was designed to detonate by means of a hydrostatic valve; early forms consisted of large cylinders of TNT that were rolled or catapulted from a ship's stern?

BONUS QUESTIONS

Q. Published in 1998, *By Design* is the comic first novel of which British actor?

Q. What is the title of comedian Sean Hughes' first novel that centres around a successful yet frustrated Dublin antique dealer?

Q. Whose debut novel, entitled *Mr MacGregor*, is appropriately about the new presenter of a struggling gardening programme?

66 STARTER

Q. Used to make the first known coins in the western world, which material can occur naturally or be produced by alloying gold with varying amounts of silver?

BONUS QUESTIONS

Three questions on women in the Bible:

Q. What is unusual about all biblical references to Noah's wife?

Q. In St John's Gospel, chapter 11 verses 23-24, who says of her brother, 'I know that he will rise again at the resurrection on the last day'?

Q. Who was the sister of Moses and Aaron who enjoyed an authority among the people and led the celebrations after the successful exodus?

67 STARTER

Q. Which actor, a contemporary of Shakespeare, and later the son-in-law of John Donne, founded Dulwich College in 1619?

BONUS QUESTIONS

Q. Which German physicist in the early 1800s made the first observations of the dark absorption lines in the sun's continuous spectrum, which are now named after him?

Q. The pair of Fraunhofer lines occuring in the yellow region of the sun's spectrum and known as the D-lines are characteristic of which element?

Q. Which Swedish physicist measured the wavelengths of about 1,000 Fraunhofer lines in 1868 and expressed them in units of ten to the minus ten metres, a unit that was subsequently named after him?

68 STARTER

Q. Sometimes known as 'meditation in motion', what is the name of the series of Chinese exercises comprising ritualized flowing movements, intended to attune the body to metaphysical life forces?

BONUS QUESTIONS

Three questions on wading birds:

Q. According to popular belief, the wading bird called the knot was so named because of an association with which king of England?

Q. Which wading bird gets its name because of its habit of lifting pebbles in search of food?

Q. Which wading birds get their name from the neck feathers which male birds fluff out to intimidate each other?

69 STARTER

Q. Which substance was introduced into Europe in the thirteenth century, although it had been in use in China for several centuries; its usual composition being 75 per cent potassium nitrate, 10 per cent sulphur and 15 per cent charcoal?

BONUS QUESTIONS

Q. Elizabeth Filkin, a former adjudicator of Customs and Excise, succeeded Sir Gordon Downey in which post in February 1999?

Q. For which position did John Silkin unsuccessfully stand for election in 1981, being defeated by Dennis Healey?

Q. Nina Milkina is a soloist on which instrument, particularly noted for her interpretations of the works of Mozart?

70 STARTER

Q. In astronomy, what are Monet, Raphael and Goya, which can all be found about 58 million kilometres from the sun?

BONUS QUESTIONS

Q. Which gold medallist at the 1964 Olympics in Tokyo had two sons who at one time played for Manchester City Football Club?

Q. What was the surname of the husband and wife who both won medals for Britain in the 1968 Olympics?

Q. Under what name did Mrs Jon Bigg win a gold medal for Great Britain in the 1992 Olympics?

71 STARTER

Q. Commonly prescribed as a tranquillizer and muscle relaxant, Valium is a proprietary name for which drug?

BONUS QUESTIONS

Three questions on the name 'Fraser':

Q. In 1747 Simon Fraser, Lord Lovat, became the last peer to be beheaded. Which cause had he supported, which led to his execution?

Q. Fraser Island, off the coast of Queensland, is considered to be the largest island in the world to have soil consisting entirely of what substance?

Q. Which major city in British Columbia lies between an arm of the Straits of Georgia and the Fraser River delta?

72 STARTER

Q. Which soft, mild French cheese with a distinctive orange rind has a name meaning 'haven of safety', derived from the Trappist abbey where it was originally made?

BONUS QUESTIONS

Q. Which form of electromagnetic radiation ranges in wavelength from about 400 nanometres to 10 nanometres, between that of visible light and X-rays?

Q. Ultraviolet rays in the spectrum were discovered in 1802 by which German physicist during his work at Jena?

Q. Vitamin D may be produced by the action of ultraviolet radiation upon which sterol present in the skin?

73 STARTER

Q. Which word of Nahuatl origin means 'men of the north', and refers to the people and civilization dominant in Mexico before the Spanish conquest of the sixteenth century?

BONUS QUESTIONS

Three questions on zodiac constellations:

Q. Which large southern constellation, lying near Scorpius and partly in the Milky Way, includes the Omega, Trifid and Lagoon Nebulae?

Q. The two brightest stars in the Zodiac constellation of Gemini – Alpha Geminorum and Beta Geminorum – are more familiarly known by which names?

Q. Regulus, at the base of a pattern of stars called the Sickle, is a triple star in which constellation?

74 STARTER

Q. Which event was celebrated in Leni Riffenstahl's 1935 film *Triumph Of The Will*?

BONUS QUESTIONS

Q. Of what is oology the science or study?

Q. Who, in the most usual version of the Greek myth, laid the eggs from which hatched Helen Of Troy, Clytemnestra, Castor and Polydeuces?

Q. Which English sporting term is thought to derive from the French for 'the egg'

75 STARTER

Q. La Rance power station near St. Malo was opened in the 1960s and was the first in the world to be powered by which natural power source?

BONUS QUESTIONS

Q. Which state is the most northerly of the New England states?

Q. The Maine Coon and the Rag Doll are American breeds of which domestic animal?

Q. Which football league club played its first home game at Maine Road against Sheffield United in August 1923?

76 STARTER

Q. In the Christian calendar, on which date does the festival of the annunciation take place?

BONUS QUESTIONS

Q. Founded in 1942, what is the name of the official overseas radio broadcasting network of the United States Information Agency?

Q. Which actress stars in the film *Little Voice*, about a shy girl with an uncanny ability to mimic famous singers?

Q. Rosina sings the aria 'Una Voce Poco Fa' in which opera by Rossini?

77 STARTER

Q. Complete the quotation, attirubted to Margot Asquith: '...if Kitchener was not a great man, he was at least a great ...'.

BONUS QUESTIONS

Three questions on bridges:

Q. The 1814 Craigellachie Bridge over the River Spay is the oldest surviving metal bridge in Scotland by which engineer?

Q. Designed by Robert Stephenson and completed in 1850, what is the name of the railway bridge over the Menai Straits, which was the first to employ a hollow tubular construction?

Q. Better known for another construction, whose major bridges include the 1877 Pia Maria Bridge over the Douro river and the Garabit viaduct over the Truyère river in the south of France?

78 STARTER

Q. Called in Arabic 'abu al-hawl', or 'father of terror', which giant sculpture portraying the face of King Khafre with the body of a lion, was unveiled, after a lengthy refurbishment, at Giza in Egypt in May 1998?

BONUS QUESTIONS

Q. Which English town has a street named after it in Moscow, because of its association with the founding of the Co-operative Movement?

Q. Which romantic poet inherited his great-uncle's title in 1798, to become the 6th Baron of Rochdale?

Q. Which England football star's father, Terry, played 87 first team games for Rochdale between 1977 and 1979?

79 STARTER

Q. What started with Singapore in 1940, before Zanzibar in 1941, and Morocco in 1942?

BONUS QUESTIONS

Three questions on inflation:

Q. Correctly known as the 'all items retail prices index', and compiled from a basket of goods and services, what term is used for the overall rate of inflation?

Q. Sometimes called the underlying rate of inflation, the RPIX excludes what payments from calculations of the inflation rate?

Q. The HICP is used in the EU to measure inflation and may be introduced in Britain; what do these initials stand for?

80 STARTER

Q. What name is given to the technique of inlaying iron or steel with gold and silver?

BONUS QUESTIONS

Three questions on fountains:

Q. In Greek mythology, the Hippocrene Fountain on Mount Helicon was said to have been created by an imprint of the hooves of which horse?

Q. Which first century Greek scientist and mathematician describes in his book *Pneumatica* his so-called 'fountain', as well as coin-operated machines, a fire engine and the 'aeolipile', a fore-runner of the jet engine?

Q. Which fountain in Rome is generally considered the masterpiece of eighteenth century sculptor, Niccolo Salvi?

81 STARTER

Q. Who was the Director General of MI5 between 1956 and 1965, during which time he faced repeated official enquiries into the service, and according to Peter Wright's book *Spycatcher* in 1987, may have been a Soviet agent?

BONUS QUESTIONS

Q. In the stories by P.G. Wodehouse, Jeeves particularly advocated which protein food as being good for the brain?

Q. Who, in his poem 'How To Get On In Society', wrote, 'phone for the fish knives, Norman/as cook is a little unnerved: you kiddies have crumpled the serviettes/and I must have things daintily served'?

Q. Which novelist, a foundling born in 1959, was adopted by Pentecostal evangelists, raised in Accrington, and had her first lesbian affair at the age of 16 with a fish filleter?

82 STARTER

Q. Which capital city is on the island of Luzon?

BONUS QUESTIONS

Three questions on Doctor Johnson:

Q. What did Johnson describe as 'the triumph of hope over experience'?

Q. What was described by Johnson as being 'like a dog's walking on his hind legs. It is not done well; but you are surprised to find it done at all'?

Q. Whose letters did Johnson describe with the words: 'they teach the morals of a whore, and the manners of a dancing master'?

83 STARTER

Q. Generally known as 'no win, no fee' deals, what is the correct term for an arrangement whereby lawyers only charge fees if they are successful in litigation?

BONUS QUESTIONS

Three questions on speech:

Q. Which German word, meaning play or game, has been used colloquially in English to mean talk intended to persuade or advertise?

Q. Which word, meaning to talk quickly and trivially, originally referred to the short vocal sounds of birds and animals?

Q. Ultimately derived from 'paternoster', what word is used for the stylized language of salesmen, conjurers or comedians?

84 STARTER

Q. A waltz entitled 'Le Sphinx', by the French composer Francois Popy, has made money for his descendants because it featured in which film, released in Britain in 1998?

BONUS QUESTIONS

Three questions on the names for Elements 101 to 109, finally agreed upon by the International Union of Pure and Applied Chemistry in 1997:

Q. Element 105 has been named dubnium after Dubna, a city in which country with a large nuclear research facility?

Q. Element 106 is named after which American nuclear chemist whose discoveries include plutonium, making it at that time the only element to have been named after a living person?

Q. Element 109 is named after which Austrian-born physicist who, with Otto Hahn and Fritz Strassmann, won the 1966 Enrico Fermi award for their work which led to the discovery of the fission of uranium?

85 STARTER

Q. Who, in 1792, was the author of the play *L'Autre Tartufe Ou La Mère Coupable*, the third in a trilogy with *Le Barbier de Seville* and *Le Mariage de Figaro*?

BONUS QUESTIONS

Three questions on towns which have become cities:

Q. Which town became a city to commemorate the investiture of Prince Charles as Prince of Wales in 1969?

Q. Which Northern Irish town became a city in 1995, because of its ecclesiastical heritage?

Q. Which Welsh village became Britain's smallest city in the same year, and for the same reason?

86 STARTER

Q. 'All I know is that I am not a Marxist.' To whom did Frederick Engels attribute these words, in a letter of 1890 to Conrad Schmidt?

BONUS QUESTIONS

Q. In mathematics, what name is given to a hypothetical point where two parallel lines join at infinity?

Q. Which philosopher, who lived from 1685 to 1753, is considered to have been the first to expound the concept of philosophical idealism?

Q. In the 1999 film version of Oscar Wilde's *An Ideal Husband*, which actor plays Lord Goring?

87 STARTER

Q. Equivalent to the British abbreviation PLC, what do the letters SA stand for when they appear after the name of a French, Belgian or Luxembourg company?

BONUS QUESTIONS

Three questions on the novels of Ian McEwan:

Q. Which of Ian McEwan's novels was considered by some to be a surprising winner of the 1998 Booker Prize over Beryl Bainbridge's *Master Georgie*?

Q. Which of Ian McEwan's novels opens with a description of a ballooning accident, and contains an account of obsessive behaviour classified as 'De Clerambault's Syndrome'?

Q. Which novel by Ian McEwan is set in Berlin in 1955, and concerns a British Post Office technician involved in electronic surveillance?

88 STARTER

Q. What name is given to a coastal body of shallow water, characterized by a connection with the sea which is restricted by islands or an atoll?

BONUS QUESTIONS

Q. Which singer's recording of 'Wicked Game' featured in the David Lynch film *Wild At Heart*?

Q. *Wicked Speed* is the autobiography of which veteran DJ and broadcaster?

Q. *The Wicked Lady*, released in 1945, starred which British actress in the title role?

89 STARTER

Q. What name is given to the process whereby a hygroscopic solid absorbs water from the atmosphere to such an extent that a concentrated solution of the solid eventually forms?

BONUS QUESTIONS

3 questions on classical music:

Q. Which composer was born in lower Austria in 1732 and produced over 100 symphonies, many of which have nicknames, such as *The Philosopher, The Passion* and *The Imperial*, with groups of symphonies nicknamed *The Paris* or *The London* symphonies?

Q. Who composed *Crown Imperial* for the coronation of George VI in 1937?

Q. *The crown of India* is an imperial masque written to celebrate the Delhi Durbar of 1912, with music by which English composer?

90 STARTER

Q. In October 1997, who adopted what the papers called 'the beekeeper look' and also donned navy blue socks in order to visit Pakistan's Faisal Mosque in Islamabad?

BONUS QUESTIONS

Q. Referred to as 'the zealot' in the gospel of Luke, which of Christ's twelve disciples is called 'the Cananaean' in both Matthew and Mark?

Q. Simon, the bystander compelled to carry the cross on the way to Calvary, hailed from which Greek city in North Africa where great numbers of Jews had been settled during New Testament times?

Q. Named only in the gospel of John, Simon was the father of which apostle, keeper of the disciples' money-bag?

91 STARTER

Q. Prevalent amongst athletes, what common term is used for medial tibial syndrome, characterized by pain in the lower leg, often due to muscular swelling resulting in inadequate blood supply to the muscle?

BONUS QUESTIONS

Q. The Little Bighorn Battlefield Museum, marking the scene of Custer's defeat in 1876, is sited in which state of the USA?

Q. Born in 1949, the French designer Claude Montana is best known for which 'look' in coats and jackets introduced during the late 1970s?

Q. *Montana* is a vigorous variety of which climbing hardy perennial plant, sometimes known as old man's beard or traveller's joy?

92 STARTER

Q. Leading north-west off the Firth of Clyde near Dunoon, which inlet became the subject of controversy in 1961 when US nuclear submarines began to use it as a base, continuing to do so until 1992?

BONUS QUESTIONS

Q. Documenting the rise of Jim Hacker from Minister of Administrative Affairs to Premier, the TV comedy series originally titled *Yes, Minister* was created by Jonathan Lynn and which other writer, knighted by Margaret Thatcher?

Q. Once the youngest MP in the house, Tory politician Alan B'stard sat as the member for which North Yorkshire consituency?

Q. In Andrew Davies' television dramatization of the Michael Dobbs novel *House of Cards*, which Machiavellian government Chief Whip contrived his own advancement to party leader and Prime Minister?

93 STARTER

Q. Developed for Columbus Day in 1892 and first published in *The Youth's Companion*, a North American weekly magazine, what form of words originally referred to 'my flag', altered over 30 years later to 'the flag of the United States of America'?

BONUS QUESTIONS

Three questions on DIY:

Q. What name is given specifically to the material used to fill the narrow gaps left after ceramic tiles have been fixed to a surface?

Q. Paints that are solvent-based and dry to a sheen rather than a high gloss are referred to by what technical term?

Q. By what name are rigid sheets of resin-impregnated paper known? They usually have a decorative finish and are applied to surfaces such as worktops.

94 STARTER

Q. Diseases such as cholera, diphtheria and tetanus are embraced by which adjective because if diagnosed, or even suspected, it is a legal requirement they be reported to Public Health Authorities?

BONUS QUESTIONS

Three questions on music:

Q. Which form of musical counterpoint involves a *dux*, or antecedent, being the first voice to enter with the melody and also a *comes*, or consequent, being the imitating voice?

Q. The earliest known piece of music that is a canon from start to finish is the setting for which thirteenth-century anonymous English verse?

Q. *The Goldberg Variations*, a set of thirty variations on a theme of which each third variation is a canon, is the work of which composer, born in 1685?

95 STARTER

Q. Which word, from the Greek for 'potsherd', arose from the ancient custom of voting to banish anyone who was a danger to the state, with citizens writing on a piece of broken pottery the name of the person to be banished?

BONUS QUESTIONS

Q. In Chinese philosophy which term, meaning 'breath' or 'force', refers to the ethereal substance of which everything is composed, techniques having been developed to alter and control its movement within the body to achieve longevity and spiritual power?

Q. In February 1999, 'Chi' was the middle name chosen for the child of Melanie Brown, otherwise known as 'Scary Spice'. What was the child's first name?

Q. Which cricket club announced in March 1999 that its identity for the new national league one-day competition would be the name of Phoenix, accompanied by an appropriate flame-orange outfit?

96 STARTER

Q. What part of the eye is operated on in the procedure known as keratoplasty?

BONUS QUESTIONS

Three questions on academic titles:

Q. In North American universities, what title is given to a person of the academic rank immediately below a full professor?

Q. A professor holding a university chair founded by a monarch or filled by crown appointment is known by what title?

Q. What word refers to a retired professor who is allowed to retain the title as an honour?

97 STARTER

Q. Which historic expedition was instigated by a proclamation of Pope Urban II at the Council of Clermont in 1095?

BONUS QUESTIONS

Three questions on flags:

Q. What term is often used as an alternative to 'ground' to describe the background colour of a flag?

Q. Which word denotes the free end of a flag, furthest from the staff, and can also mean the flag's full horizontal length?

Q. A rope used to hoist and lower a flag is known by what name?

98 STARTER

Q. Left in sketch form at his death in 1934, which English composer's third symphony was constructed by Anthony Payne and performed for the first time by the BBC Symphony Orchestra in February 1998?

BONUS QUESTIONS

Three questions on uprisings:

Q. The former priest John Ball was executed in 1381 for his part in which popular movement, originating in the south-eastern counties?

Q. Later applied to similar risings, which name was first given to the peasant revolution in north-eastern France, which ended in the massacre of the insurgents at Meux and Claremont-en-Beauvaisis in June 1358?

Q. Originally a resistance to the invading Japanese, and later a movement of tenant farmers against landowners, the Huk Rebellion of the 1940s occurred in which newly independent republic?

99 STARTER

Q. What can be found in St Matthew's Gospel, chapter six verses 9 to 13, and in a slightly abbreviated form in Luke, chapter eleven, verses 2 to 4?

BONUS QUESTIONS

Three questions on names:

Q. At the end of which film is the title character revealed to be named Laura, although she has never been called this by her mother?

Q. In the final episode of *Blackadder Goes Forth*, which character, played by Tim McInnerny, is revealed to have the first name Kevin?

Q. In a novel by Colin Dexter, Morse's first name was revealed to be 'Endeavour', because of his father's admiration for which explorer?

100 STARTER

Q. Under the 22nd Amendment to the United States constitution, what, theoretically, is the maximum number of years one person could serve as president?

BONUS QUESTIONS

Three questions on the homes of writers:

Q. Which English essayist and critic became a close associate of William Wordsworth in 1807 and two years later rented his former home, Dove Cottage at Grasmere, which remained his base until 1833?

Q. Coole Park in Dublin was the home of Lady Augusta Gregory, the patron and lifelong friend of which writer who used the estate as a setting for several poems and in 1917 bought Thoor Ballylee, a derelict Norman stone tower near Coole Park, restoring it as a summer home?

Q. Twentieth century English composer Elizabeth Poston lived for most of her life in Rook's Nest House in Stevenage, famous as the childhood home of which novelist and short story writer, who died in 1970 at the age of 91?

101 STARTER

Q. Who was the mythological daughter of Aesculapius, the Greek god of healing, whose name has entered the English language to mean any universal cure or solution?

BONUS QUESTIONS

Q. How and why was a volcano inaccurately described in the title of a 1968 film?

Q. Alfred Hitchcock's 1959 film *North by Northwest* has a climax set on which national monument?

Q. Which character in Shakespeare claims, 'I am but mad north-north-west'?

102 STARTER

Q. In terms of area, which is the largest country through which the Tropic of Capricorn passes?

BONUS QUESTIONS

Three questions on muscles:

Q. What is the name of the triangular muscle attached to the collarbone and shoulder blade above, and to the humerus below, the action of which raises the arm from the side?

Q. The four rectus muscles, the superior, inferior, medial and lateral, are part of which organ of the human body?

Q. What is the name for the longest muscle in the human body, positioned in the front of the thigh?

103 STARTER

Q. Which cathedral in Cambridgeshire is surmounted by an octagonal tower, known as the lantern tower, erected in the fourteenth century to replace the original Norman tower which had collapsed?

BONUS QUESTIONS

In which month did each of the following three sets of events take place:

Q. Henry V's defeat of the French at Agincourt in 1415, the stockmarket crash of 1929 and Anwar Sadat's assassination in 1981?

Q. The Glencoe massacre in 1692, Queen Elizabeth II's accession in 1952 and the adoption of decimal currency in the UK in 1971?

Q. Lady Jane Grey was deposed as Queen of England in 1553, Thomas Cranmer was born in 1489, and Neil Armstrong walked on the moon in 1969?

104 STARTER

Q. Much used in the food industry, what three words are represented by the letters TVP?

BONUS QUESTIONS

Identify each of the following Shakespeare plays from their final lines:

Q. 'Give me your hands, if we be friends / and robin shall restore amends.'

Q. 'See justice done on Aaron, that damn'd moor, / by whom our heavy haps had their beginning: / then, afterwards, to order well the state, / that like events may ne'er it ruinate.'

Q. 'As you from crimes would pardon'd be, / let your indulgence set me free.'

105 STARTER

Q. Salt's Mill in the nineteenth-century model village of Saltaire in Yorkshire is now a museum and gallery displaying the works of which locally born artist?

BONUS QUESTIONS

Q. Which French composer was born in 1866 and is particularly remembered for his piano pieces, which include 'Gymnopedies' of 1888?

Q. In the novel by Charles Dickens, which jilted bride kept the trappings of her wedding reception on display at Satis House?

Q. The motto of which Premiership football club is 'nil satis nisi optimum', loosely meaning 'nothing but the best is good enough'?

106 STARTER

Q. The word 'barcarole' derives from the Italian for boat, and refers to the traditional song of which group of working men?

BONUS QUESTIONS

Q. Alma, the daughter of artist Emil Schindler, married which Austrian composer in 1902?

Q. In 1911, Alma Mahler had an affair with which Austrian Expressionist painter and writer, who left the relationship by joining the Austrian army on the outbreak of war?

Q. In 1915, Alma Mahler married which German architect, divorcing him in 1918?

107 STARTER

Q. Which father and son both served as Lord Chancellor this century; the father from 1928 to 1929 and his son from 1970 to 1974 and from 1979 to 1987?

BONUS QUESTIONS

Three questions on types of novels:

Q. Its literal French meaning being 'novel with a key', which term is used for a novel in which real people appear under fictional names, but are still recognizable?

Q. Literally meaning 'river novel', which French term is used for a sequence of novels linked by recurrent characters, such as Trollope's 'Barsetshire' novels?

Q. Sometimes called a 'condition of England novel', which French term is used for novels such as *Hard Times*, intended to promulgate an idea or a cause?

108 STARTER

Q. Durango, Sinaloa and Sonara are all states of which Central American country?

BONUS QUESTIONS

Q. The law of octaves – formalizing the observation that every eighth element of the periodic table has similar properties – was proposed in 1844 by which British chemist?

Q. Element 101 is named after which Russian chemist who devised the periodic classification in 1869, predicting the existence of several undiscovered elements?

Q. Killed at Gallipoli, which British physicist resolved discrepancies in the Medeleyev system when he derived the atomic numbers from the frequency of vibration of X-rays emitted by each element, concluding the atomic number to be equal to the charge on the nucleus?

109 STARTER

Q. Which word was used in the Middle Ages to describe someone outside the feudal and customary bounds of English society; later used to describe a foreign national living here, it is now more widely used for an intelligent life form from another planet?

BONUS QUESTIONS

Three questions on publishing:

Q. Which periodical was issued twice-weekly from 20 March 1750 to 14 march 1753, written almost exclusively by Samuel Johnson?

Q. Begun in 1817 as the *Edinburgh Monthly Magazine*, which periodical was established as a Tory rival to the whiggish *Edinburgh Review*?

Q. Which publisher and magazine proprietor who founded *Titbits* in 1881 formed a brief partnership with W.T. Stead before setting up the *Strand Magazine* in 1892?

110 STARTER

Q. Which practice was defined as a felony by an Act of Parliament of 1542, the last English trial for the offence being held in 1712, before the act was repealed in 1736?

BONUS QUESTIONS

Q. In Greek mythology, which prophet – capable of assuming any form he chose in order to evade questioning – served as the warden of Poseidon's sea beasts?

Q. Said to represent Ramsay MacDonald, the evasive Proteus is a character from which play by George Bernard Shaw?

Q. Proteus, discovered in 1989, is the second largest satellite of which planet?

111 STARTER

Q. Who worked under Henry Bradley on the *New English Dictionary*, was Professor of Anglo-Saxon at Oxford from 1925 and Merton Professor of English Language and Literature from 1945, and is now best remembered for a series of fantasy stories?

BONUS QUESTIONS

Q. The hundreds of Stoke, Desborough and Burnham which together represent the Notional Office of Profit Under The Crown – the Chiltern Hundreds – are parts of which county?

Q. Chequers, the Buckinghamshire country house and official country residence of the Prime Minister, was presented to the nation in 1921 by which Conservative politician?

Q. The notorious Hellfire Club, founded by Francis Dashwood, met at which ruined thirteenth century Cistercian monastery near Marlow in Buckinghamshire?

112 STARTER

Q. In March 1998, a very rare poster advertising which film of 1933 was sold at auction for almost £29,000?

BONUS QUESTIONS

Three questions on school fiction:

Q. Which eponymous hero of school fiction was the creation of Anthony Buckeridge, and was a pupil of Linbury Court school?

Q. In the stories by Enid Blyton, which school did the close friends Darrell Rivers and Sally Hope attend?

Q. The girls' school fiction of Angela Brazil was a particular enthusiasm of which writer and broadcaster, who had himself been a schoolmaster at Oundle?

113 STARTER

Q. Which French song called 'Comme d'Habitude' with English lyrics by Paul Anka, has provided British chart hits for Dorothy Squires, the Sex Pistols and Elvis Presley?

BONUS QUESTIONS

Three questions on Jacobean playwrights:

Q. Which playwright is best known for his collaboration with John Fletcher, although recent analysis seems to show that *The Knight Of The Burning Pestle* was his alone?

Q. Who is best remembered for the satirical comedy *A New Way To Pay Old Debts*, although he also collaborated with Fletcher after the withdrawal of Beaumont?

Q. Which dramatist collaborated with Thomas Dekker and others in *The Witch Of Edmonton* and other plays, but is possibly best remembered for *Tis Pity She's A Whore*, which he wrote alone?

114 STARTER

Q. Which American author wrote, in a novel of 1851: 'a whaleship was my Yale College and my Harvard'?

BONUS QUESTIONS

Q. From the Greek meaning 'well' and 'standing', what geological term describes a worldwide change in sea-level caused by advancing or receding polar ice caps?

Q. Bartolommeo Eustachio, a sixteenth-century Italian anatomist, gave his name to the tube he discovered that connects the middle ear to what?

Q. In which novel of 1878 does Eustacia Vye drown herself after becoming partially, but unknowingly, responsible for her mother-in-law's death?

115 STARTER

Q. Acetate and viscose are the two types of which artificial fibre, made from wood cellulose?

BONUS QUESTIONS

Three questions on twentieth century poetry:

Q. The hyacinth girl, Madame Sosostris, Albert and Lil, and Mister Eugenides are all referred to in which poem of 1922?

Q. In which of T.S. Eliot's poems is the evening 'spread out against the sky / like a patient etherised upon a table'?

Q. Which significant day in the Christian calendar gives the title for Eliot's sequence of six poems, published in 1930?

116 STARTER

Q. Commonly used as a unit of distance in astronomy, how is an astronomical unit defined?

BONUS QUESTIONS

Q. Standing more than nine hundred feet in height, the highest of which American city's hills are the twin peaks, Mount Davidson and Mount Sutro?

Q. Which of San Francisco's hills became particularly associated with the wealthy when, from the 1870s, many extravagant mansions began to be built there?

Q. Which of San Francisco's many ethnic communities was removed at a stroke by the infamous 'executive order 9066' of 1942, which ordered them to be removed to 'relocation centres'?

117 STARTER

Q. What title was originally held by a Roman emperor's representative in a province, or the commander of a legion, but is now held by a diplomatic representative of the Pope?

BONUS QUESTIONS

Three questions on the Louvre in Paris:

Q. Which monarch's collection of works of art formed the basis of the Louvre collection; he was also responsible for the present building, on which work commenced in the 1540s?

Q. The Louvre ceased to be a royal residence in 1682 on the completion of which new palace?

Q. Which American architect, in the 1980s, designed the controversial steel and glass pyramids in front of the Louvre, and also the former Richelieu wing, opened in 1993?

118 STARTER

Q. In which European country is Chernobyl, scene of the 1986 nuclear power station disaster?

BONUS QUESTIONS

Three questions on deaths:

Q. Which Florentine artist and scientist moved to France in the latter years of his life and, according to legend, died in the arms of King Francis I in 1519?

Q. Queen Victoria is reputed to have died in the arms of which of her grandsons, also a head of state?

Q. Which screen canine died at the age of 16 in 1932 in the arms of the screen sex-symbol Jean Harlow, and his trainer captain Lee Duncan?

119 STARTER

Q. Measuring 173 feet by 101 feet, and with a spire 152 feet high, which religious organization opened its largest edifice in Britain in 1998, near Chorley in Lancashire?

BONUS QUESTIONS

Three questions linked by a name:

Q. Whose Arthurian stories were printed by Caxton under the title of the final book *Le Morte D'Arthur*?

Q. Born in Norway in 1892, sportswoman Molla Bjurstedt Mallory settled in the USA in 1914, and won which sport's championship eight times between 1915 and 1926?

Q. What was the name of George Mallory's partner, who accompanied him on his ill-fated attempt to reach the summit of Everest on 8 June 1924?

120 STARTER

Q. 'Give a little whistle' is the title of a song performed by which character in the 1940 Disney animated film *Pinocchio*?

BONUS QUESTIONS

Three questions on twentieth-century furniture designers:

Q. Which French designer, who came to prominence when he designed President Mitterand's apartment in the Elysée Palace, has designed 'Doctor Glob', 'Von Vogelsang' and 'Louis 20' chairs?

Q. Which Danish designer created the 'ant' chair for Fritz Hansen in 1951, and later the 'swan' and 'egg' chairs for the same manufacturer?

Q. What nationality was the architect and furniture designer Alvar Aalto, born in 1898 and particularly remembered for his chairs of moulded plywood?

SECOND ROUND

1 STARTER

Q. Which writer of detective fiction also writes novels under *nom-de-plume* Barbara Vine?

BONUS QUESTIONS

Three questions on units of measurement:

Q. Used in measuring the height of horses, how many inches are there in a hand?

Q. Which ancient unit of measurement, equal to nine inches, was originally the distance between the ends of the thumb and little finger when the hand is stretched out?

Q. What name was given to the unit of measurement of 66 feet, defined by a jointed measuring-line of linked metal rods?

2 STARTER

Q. One of the finest examples in the world, which archaeological discovery was made in Altimira in northern Spain in 1879?

BONUS QUESTIONS

Three questions on radio broadcasting:

Q. Which is the only one of the BBC national radio services to broadcast on the long waveband?

Q. Radio 4 broadcasts between the frequencies 92.4 to 96.1 FM, and 198 kilohertz between the hours of 5.30 am and 1.00 am; which service occupies these frequencies overnight?

Q. By what name was Radio 4 known before the major reshuffle of 1967, which saw the introduction of Radio 1?

3 STARTER

Q. Which Russian word, meaning destruction or devastation, is now applied to any organized massacre, particularly of an ethnic or religious minority?

BONUS QUESTIONS

Three questions linked by a name:

Q. Which disease, caused by progressive atrophy of the cortex of the adrenal glands, is named after a nineteenth century English physician?

Q. Which periodical, first published in London on 1 March 1711 by the essayists Sir Richard Steele and Joseph Addison, succeeded *The Tatler* which Addison had launched some two years earlier?

Q. James Addison Baker the third, having successfully managed George Bush's presidential campaign in 1988, later held which post in his administration from 1989 to 1992?

4 STARTER

Q. With about one per cent by volume, which is the third most abundant gas in the earth's atmosphere?

BONUS QUESTIONS

Q. Which jazz trumpeter, composer and leader of the Lincoln Center Jazz Orchestra, includes in his discography Haydn, Hummel and Leopold Mozart trumpet concerti with Raymond Leppard?

Q. The fading actress Lily Winton features in the short story 'Glory In The Daytime' by which American writer, poet and critic, born in 1893?

Q. Andrew of Wyntoun's *Orygynale Cronykil* is the original source for Shakespeare's account of Macbeth's meeting with whom?

5 STARTER

Q. First levied on air travellers in 1994 with rates of £5 or £10 per person, what is represented by the initials APD?

BONUS QUESTIONS

Q. Based on the theory, advanced in the 1980s, that serious crime would not flourish if the authorities cracked down on minor offences, what two-word term is used for the type of tough policing methods adopted in New York city by Mayor Rudolph Giuliani?

Q. The so-called 'year zero jinx' is the fact that only one US president elected since 1840 in a year ending in '0' has left the White House alive; which post-World War II president was the first to have broken the jinx?

Q. Which singer and songwriter was described as 'a good poet' by the poet laureate Andrew Motion, who included his 'Love Minus Zero/No Limits' as one of his choices on *Desert Island Discs*?

6 STARTER

Q. In February 1998 Rosemary Coventry, a chemistry undergraduate at Trinity College Oxford, found herself in trouble with her university when it was discovered that she had been intending to represent Cambridge; at what?

BONUS QUESTIONS

Three questions on European history:

Q. Which playwright became president of Czechoslovakia in December 1989 after the fall of communism, and president of the Czech Republic in January 1993?

Q. Vaclav III, who was assassinated in 1306, was the last king of which dynasty, which had ruled Bohemia and its associated lands for almost four centuries?

Q. The tenth century Duke Vaclav of Bohemia, who was converted to Christianity by his grandmother Saint Ludmila, and stabbed to death in 929 by his pagan younger brother Boleslav, is better known in the west as whom?

7 STARTER

Q. With a population of about three million, what is Pakistan's second largest city, the principal city of the Punjab?

BONUS QUESTIONS

Three questions on telegrams:

Q. The publication of which telegram, sent on 13 July 1870 in an edited version, reporting an encounter between King Wilhelm I of Prussia and the French ambassador, precipitated the Franco-Prussian war?

Q. The Kruger telegram, from Kaiser Wilhelm the Second to President Kruger of the South African Republic, which aroused the first wave of anti-German feeling in Britain before World War I, congratulated him on repelling which 'raid', an attack on the Transvaal from the British-controlled cape colony?

Q. The Zimmermann telegram, which became one of the prinicipal factors leading to the US declaration of war against Germany in 1917, proposed an alliance between Germany and which country, part of the agreement being that that country should recover territory lost to the United States?

8 STARTER

Q. What name is given to the scum separated from pure metal in the smelting process? The word is in general use where it is applied to any refuse, or anything regarded as worthless.

BONUS QUESTIONS

Three questions on international politics:

Q. Which future head of the US National Security Council and Secretary of State became established as a leading authority on US strategic policy with the publication in 1957 of the book *Nuclear Weapons and Foreign Policy*?

Q. Kissinger was joint winner of the 1973 Nobel Prize for peace; what was the name of the North Vietnamese negotiator who was the co-recipient of the prize but who refused it?

Q. Which two-word phrase is applied to the technique, associated with Kissinger after the 1973 Arab-Israeli war, in which an intermediary in an international dispute repeatedly travels between the countries in question in an effort to broker a solution?

9 STARTER

Q. Which order of mendicant friars took its name from the Middle Eastern mountain where the order was established in the twelfth century?

BONUS QUESTIONS

Q. Who was born Philip Schleswig-Holstein-Sonderburg-Glücksburg, on a kitchen table in a holiday retreat called 'Mon Repos'?

Q. Which fictional character, in the first television series to feature him, was styled 'Duke of Edinburgh'?

Q. The trout stream Blackadder Water is a tributary of Whiteadder Water, which itself flows into which major river near its mouth on the Scottish border?

10 STARTER

Q. Which object was made in London but is now regarded as one of the USA's national treasures, and bears an inscription from the Book of Leviticus, 'proclaim liberty throughout the land unto all inhabitants thereof'?

BONUS QUESTIONS

Q. Which play was Chekhov's last, and concerns the attempts of Madame Lyubov Ranevskaya and her family to save their estate, with the feature that gives the play its title, from bankruptcy?

Q. The episcopal clergyman and itinerant publisher's agent, Mason Locke Weems, inserted the apocryphal story of the chopping down of a cherry tree into the fifth edition of his biography of whom?

Q. Which poisonous substance can be obtained from the stone of a wild cherry?

11 STARTER

Q. Threatened by a recent hydro-electric scheme, on which of the world's major rivers is the spectacular natural phenomenon known as 'the three gorges'?

BONUS QUESTIONS

Three questions on scientists who have been played in films:

Q. Which nineteenth century chemist and microbiologist was played by Paul Muni in a 1936 film biography?

Q. In the 1994 film *IQ*, Walter Matthau played which scientist during his time at Princeton University?

Q Which musical member of a family noted for comedy played Isaac Newton in the 1957 film *The Story of Mankind*?

12 STARTER

Q. In 1998 who, at the age of 18 years and two months, became the youngest player to represent England at soccer this century when he played against Chile at Wembley?

BONUS QUESTIONS

Q. A dish served with a sauce of mushrooms, shallots, tomatoes and white wine is described on a French menu as 'chasseur'; what does this mean?

Q. The 'Huntsmen's Chorus' comes from which opera by Weber, about a marksman with magic bullets?

Q. Which biblical figure was the brother of Jacob, and is described in Genesis as 'a cunning hunter, a man of the field'?

13 STARTER

Q. Which African language, a member of the Bantu sub-group of languages, has about 30 million speakers, and is widely spoken in Zaire and Uganda, but more extensively used in Kenya and Tanzania where it is one of the official languages of those countries?

BONUS QUESTIONS

Three questions on Venus and Adonis:

Q. The poem 'Venus and Adonis' in 1593 is regarded as being probably the first published work by whom?

Q. Which Venetian painter's depiction of *Venus and Adonis*, completed around 1554, is usually displayed at the Prado in Madrid?

Q. Which organist and composer, who died in 1708, is remembered for his church music and for *Venus and Adonis*, regarded as the first true English opera?

14 STARTER

Q. What was the basic unit of the French monetary system before the introduction of the franc?

BONUS QUESTIONS

Three questions on opera:

Q. What, in English, is the full title of Wagner's four opera Ring cycle?

Q. At which opera house was the Ring cycle first performed in 1876?

Q. What, in German, is the title of the last opera in the cycle?

15 STARTER

Q. According to Greek mythology, the seven daughters of Atlas and Pleione are represented by the open cluster of stars known as the Pleiades, found in which constellation?

BONUS QUESTIONS

Identify the following novels from their subtitles:

Q. *The Parish Boy's Progress* by Charles Dickens, first published in book form in 1838?

Q. *A Pure Woman Faithfully Presented* by Thomas Hardy, first published in 1891?

Q. *A Study of Provincial Life* by George Eliot, first published in 1871 and 1872?

16 STARTER

Q. Who was the Swedish diplomat whose actions saved thousands of Hungarian Jews during World War II? In 1945 he was arrested by the Red Army and imprisoned in Lubyanka, where it is said he was executed in 1947.

BONUS QUESTIONS

Three questions on Indian cooking:

Q. What name is given to certain forms of Indian food, and comes from the distinctive clay oven in which they are cooked after being marinated in yoghurt and spices?

Q. What term is used for spiced cubes of chicken or other meat, usually cooked on a skewer in a tandoor oven or on charcoal?

Q. At the 1999 cricket world cup final, a Pakistan supporter carried a placard saying, 'Inzamam ate all the parathas'; what is a paratha?

17 STARTER

Q. Of which European country is Prince Phillipe the heir to the throne?

BONUS QUESTIONS

Three questions on tennis:

Q. In tennis, what name is given to a stroke made by returning the ball before it bounces?

Q. In John Betjeman's poem 'Pot Pourri from a Surrey Garden', what was the name of the 'mountainous sports girl, whizzing them over the net, full of the strength of five'?

Q. Brat's 1982 single 'Chalk Dust – the Umpire Strikes Back', features an impression of which Wimbledon champion?

18 STARTER

Q. Which cartoon strip heroine is skilled at unarmed combat and is a master of disguise, has the loyal ex-con Willie Garvin as a sidekick, and was created by Peter O'Donnell for the *Evening Standard* in 1963?

BONUS QUESTION

Three questions on laws relating to addition and multiplication:

Q. The fact that 'a' multiplied by the product of 'b' and 'c' is equal to the product of 'a' and 'b' multiplied by 'c', is an example of which law of mathematics?

Q. The fact that 'a' multiplied by the sum of 'b', 'c' and 'd' is equal to 'a' times 'b' plus 'a' times 'c' plus 'a' times 'd', exemplifies which law?

Q. The fact that 'a' times 'b' is equal to 'b' times 'a', and 'a' plus 'b' is equal to 'b' plus 'a', is an example of which law?

19 STARTER

Q. Sir Walter Scott's novel *Kenilworth* gives a fictionalized account of the controversial death of Amy Robsart, the wife of which aristocrat, who was a favourite of Queen Elizabeth I?

BONUS QUESTIONS

Three questions on tram accidents:

Q. Which Catalan architect died of his injuries after being struck by a tram in Barcelona in 1926?

Q. Which nineteenth century poet and critic, son of a celebrated schoolmaster, died of a heart attack in Liverpool in 1888 after running for a tram?

Q. Which novel by Evelyn Waugh was first published in 1928 and includes the schoolmaster Captain Grimes, who allows his pupils to think his wooden leg is a war wound, when in fact it was caused by his falling under a tram in Stoke-on-Trent whilst drunk?

20 STARTER

Q. Douglas Engelbart, working at the Stanford Research Institute in the mid 1960s, developed which input device used in computing?

BONUS QUESTIONS

Three questions linked by a word:

Q. What name is given to the incombustible residue of fused ash, found at the bottom of furnaces and coke-fired boilers?

Q. If a boat or ship is described as 'clinker-built', how would the planks of wood be arranged?

Q. *The Expedition of Humphry Clinker* was the last novel by which eighteenth century Scottish writer?

21 STARTER

Q. In Judaism, what name is given to that part of the Talmudic literature which is not concerned with religious law, but devoted to folklore and the legends of heroes?

BONUS QUESTIONS

Q. Of which island in the Mediterranean is Palermo the capital?

Q. Which Italian composer's opera *Les Vêpres Siciliennes*, or *The Sicilian Vespers*, was commissioned for the Great Exhibition of Paris in 1855?

Q. Which composer, born in Catania, Sicily, in 1801, is best remembered for the operas *Norma* set in ancient Gaul, and *I Puritani*, ultimately derived from Scott's *Old Mortality*?

22 STARTER

Q. Subtitled 'the flowers of progress', which comic opera by Gilbert and Sullivan was first performed in London in 1893, and presents an idealized society run on the lines of a British liability company?

BONUS QUESTIONS

Three questions on non-nutritive sweetening agents:

Q. Which sweetening agent, widely used in the diet of diabetics, was discovered in 1879 by the chemists Ira Remsen and Constantin Fahlberg, and is also known as orthosulphobenzimide?

Q. Which sweetening agents, discovered by Michael Sveda in 1937 and banned in many countries because of their supposed production of carcinogens in the gastro-intestinal tract, are salts of cyclohexysulphamic acid?

Q. Which sweetener, marketed as Nutrasweet or Canderal, was discovered in 1965 and has the alternative name aspartylphenylalanine?

23 STARTER

Q. What word derives ultimately from the word for 'scissors' used by the the Tupi people of the Amazon valley, and refers to a freshwater fish of the genus *Serrasalmus*, noted for its sharp teeth and predatory behaviour?

BONUS QUESTIONS

Three questions on the London underground:

Q. The deepest section of the underground, at 221 feet, is at Hollybush hill, near Hampstead; on which tube line?

Q. Which Buckinghamshire town, at some 27 miles west of London on the Metropolitan Line, is the most distant station from Central London?

Q. The longest single journey possible is the 34.1 miles from West Ruislip to Epping, on which line?

24 STARTER

Q. Tunisia, South Africa, Cameroon, Morocco and which other African nation qualified for football's 1998 world cup finals in France?

BONUS QUESTIONS

Three questions on writers who have also been teachers:

Q. Which writer spent four years as a pupil teacher in Nottingham, speaking later of, 'the savage teaching of collier lads'?

Q. Which former grammar-school teacher served in the late 1950s as an education officer in the colonial service, during which time he published what became known as *The Malayan Trilogy*, the first of which was *Time for a Tiger* in 1956?

Q. Which writer of horror stories had a teaching career which included a stint at the Hampden Academy in Maine?

25 STARTER

Q. 'They went and told the sexton and the sexton toll'd the bell' and 'a cannon-ball took off his legs, so he laid down his arms' are lines from 'Faithless Nellie Gray', a poem by which nineteenth century English writer, poet and humourist?

BONUS QUESTIONS

Three questions on things buried:

Q. Which Pre-Raphaelite artist and poet buried a number of his poems with his wife, Elizabeth Siddal, but later had a change of heart and exhumed them?

Q. Which Hungarian-born actor, best known for his horror roles, was buried in 1956 with the cape he wore in the role of Dracula?

Q. A gold whistle, a memento of a line from the film *To Have and Have Not*, was placed with the ashes of which film actor by his wife after his death in 1957, a memory of their first film together?

26 STARTER

Q. BASIC, the computer-programming language using familiar English words and designed for beginners, is so named because it is an acronym of which words?

BONUS QUESTIONS

Three questions on an American state:

Q. John Steinbeck's novel *The Grapes of Wrath* concerns farmers attempting to move to California from which 'dustbowl' state?

Q. Which country singer was born in 1937 into a family of dustbowl Oklahomans, and wrote 'Okie From Muskogee' in 1969, a novelty song which became controversial for its apparent attack on hippies?

Q. In the 1955 film version of Rogers and Hammerstein's musical *Oklahoma!*, which actor plays the villainous farm-hand Jud Fry?

27 STARTER

Q. In dyeing, what purpose is served by a mordant?

BONUS QUESTIONS

Q. Which resort and village in Devon was named after a novel published by Charles Kingsley in 1855?

Q. Which poet and playwright wrote *Eastward Hoe* with Chapman and Marston, and voluntarily joined them when they were imprisoned after a passage in the play, derogatory to the Scots, caused offence at court?

Q. 'Southward Ho' is the name given to the twelfth hole on which golf course, used for the Open Championship in 1999 for the first time since 1975?

28 STARTER

Q. Proposing graded and increased income tax and supertax, the so called 'People's Budget', rejected by the House of Lords in 1909, was introduced by which chancellor of the exchequer?

BONUS QUESTIONS

Three questions on Surrey cricketers:

Q. Which batsman, who began his first-class career for Surrey in 1905, became the first professional English cricketer to be knighted?

Q. Which spin bowler, who was voted BBC sports personality of the year in 1956, left Surrey in 1959, joining Essex for a brief spell in 1962?

Q. Which batsman, who captained Cambridge university at soccer, though not at cricket, also played for minor county Berkshire before joining Surrey in 1953, going on to captain the county and England?

29 STARTER

Q. From the Greek for 'stretched around', what name is given to the protective, fluid-secreting tissue covering the viscera and lining the abdominal cavity and digestive organs of humans?

BONUS QUESTIONS

Three questions on genealogies:

Q. Which term, denoting a genealogy as set forth in a chart orther form, is derived from an old French term for 'crane's foot', a sign resembling a crane's foot having been used to indicate lines of descent?

Q. In chart pedigrees, an equals sign denotes marriage, but what does a crinkled line between partners indicate?

Q. What form of record was first kept in England in 1538, and has helped many people trace their family tree?

30 STARTER

Q. In Classical architecture, and particularly a feature of Greek temples, what term is used for a low triangular structure, crowning the face of a building and surmounting a portico of columns?

BONUS QUESTIONS

Q. Mohammed Sarwar became Britain's first Moslem MP when he won which seat at the 1997 General Election?

Q. The fictional Govan resident 'Rab C. Nesbitt' is played on television by which actor?

Q. Which football manager, who took his first managerial post at East Stirling in July 1974, was born in Govan on 31 December 1941?

31 STARTER

Q. Which word derives ultimately from a Greek term meaning a boy's guide, and refers to a strict or pedantic teacher?

BONUS QUESTIONS

Three questions on the events of 1888:

Q. Mary Ann Nichols, who was murdered in the early hours of 7 August 1888, is generally regarded as having been the first victim of whom?

Q. Organized by Annie Besant, a strike by women workers took place in July 1888 in Bow, East London, in a factory making what?

Q. A one-time rival for the *Evening Standard* and the *Evening News*, which London evening paper went on sale for the first time on 17 January 1888?

32 STARTER

Q. Levied on coastal districts of England from the Middle Ages, which tax was imposed by Charles I upon the whole country without the consent of Parliament and was opposed in particular by John Hampden who, with others, refused to pay it?

BONUS QUESTIONS

Three questions on cricket, relating to the first test against New Zealand in July 1999:

Q. Prior to Nasser Hussain in the first Test against New Zealand in July 1999, which fast bowler, in the 1982 Lords Test against India, was the last England captain to win his first Test in charge?

Q. When Alex Tudor scored 99 not out in the second innings of that same match, he beat the record score by an England night watchman. Which fast bowler's score of 98, at Sydney in his final match for England in 1933, had set the record?

Q. Which Nottinghamshire player, at the age of twenty in that same Test, became the youngest-ever wicket keeper to play for England?

33 STARTER

Q. According to Edward Lear's poem published in 1877, who lost his toes while fishing for his Aunt Jobiska's runcible cat in the Bristol Channel?

BONUS QUESTIONS

Three questions on Middle Eastern capital cities:

Q. Which Middle Eastern capital was the largest port on the eastern Mediterranean coast and a major banking centre, until civil war broke out in 1975?

Q. Which Middle Eastern capital is considered to be the oldest continuously inhabited city in the world?

Q. Which Middle Eastern capital was founded by Al-Mansur, Caliph of the Abbasid Dynasty in about 762 AD, and features in many of the stories in *The Thousand And One Nights*?

34 STARTER

Q. The twentieth-century American psychologist B.F. Skinner devised a box, named after him, for use in the observation of which aspect of animal behaviour?

BONUS QUESTIONS

Q. According to an old Sicilian proverb, God first made the world, and then he made which straits to separate men from madmen?

Q. What two names are given to the rocks and whirlpools in the Straits of Messina, personified in Greek mythology as female monsters?

Q. In which of Shakespeare's comedies does Beatrice, niece of the Governor of Messina, fall in love with Benedick, a young lord of Padua?

35 STARTER

Q. Formerly widely observed in Britain by processions around parish boundaries, the rogation days of the Christian calendar precede which feast day?

BONUS QUESTIONS

Q. Which five-letter word, beginning with 'L', derives from the Latin for wan or yellowish, but is now used to mean rather the opposite?

Q. Originally meaning discoloured as by a bruise, which five-letter word beginning with 'L' is now used colloquially to mean 'very angry'?

Q. Originally meaning 'lively', which five-letter word beginning with 'V' is now frequently used to mean a very bright colour?

36 STARTER

Q. Working with UN Representative Cyrus Vance, which former British Foreign Secretary replaced Lord Carrington as the European Community's negotiator at the Bosnia-Herzogovena peace talks in 1992?

BONUS QUESTIONS

Three questions on parks in pop music:

Q. Which park gave the Small Faces a top three hit in 1967?

Q. Which park provided hits for Richard Harris and later for Donna Summer?

Q. 'Parklife', the 1994 single by the band Blur, featured a vocal contribution from which actor, who starred in the 1979 film *Quadrophenia*?

37 STARTER

Q. The gemstone form of the hard, glassy, greenish mineral olivine is known by which name?

BONUS QUESTIONS

Q. What name was given to the American submarine-launched ballistic missile which was developed during the late 1950s, and formed the mainstay of Britain's nuclear deterrent during the 1970s and 1980s?

Q. In which constellation is the pole star, Polaris?

Q. In 1871, the American explorer, Charles Francis Hall, set sail from New York aboard the naval steamer 'Polaris' on a US government-sponsored expedition attempting to reach where?

38 STARTER

Q. Snozzcumbers, 'the most disgustuous food in all the world,' are the staple diet of which character created by Roald Dahl?

BONUS QUESTIONS

Three questions on Kent:

Q. Which river distinguishes a Kentish man from a man of Kent?

Q. Said to have originated in reference to meetings held in Kent in 1828 and 1829 in opposition to the Catholic Emancipation Bill, 'Kentish fire' is a prolonged and ordered volley of what?

Q. 'Kentish rag' is a hard, compact type of which rock?

39 STARTER

Q. What is the full name of the United States government organization which assesses and collects federal taxes, and is known by the initials IRS?

BONUS QUESTIONS

Three questions on revolutionaries:

Q. Who, in 1955, whilst in exile in Mexico, formed a revolutionary group called 'The 26th of July Movement' in memory of an attack on an army barracks he had led two years earlier?

Q. Which fellow revolutionary did Castro first meet whilst in Mexico?

Q. On 17 April 1961, over twelve hundred Cuban exiles landed in the Bahia de Chochinos, with the aim of ousting the communist regime of Fidel Castro. How is this landing area known in English?

40 STARTER

Q. Which English judge and legal reformer wrote *The Pattern of Law Reform* in 1967, campaigned in the 1970s for a Bill of Rights, and became best known for his report into the Brixton riots of 1981?

BONUS QUESTIONS

Q. Which SI unit may be expressed in terms of an ampere second per volt?

Q. The constant of electricity, the Faraday, which is used in electrolysis and has the value 96,485 coulombs, is equal to the charge on the electron, 'E', times which fundamental constant?

Q. Faraday's Law of Induction states that the EMF induced in a circuit is equal to the rate of change of what through the circuit?

41 STARTER

Q. Dating from around the seventh century, the Maronites of Lebanon, Southern Europe and the Americas represent a sect of which religion?

BONUS QUESTIONS

Three questions on art history:

Q. One of the earliest known works of which Florentine sculptor, born around 1386, is a marble David, originally intended for the cathedral in Florence , although he is better known for his bronze David, the first large-scale free-standing statue of the Renaissance?

Q. Whose giant marble statue of David, which had originally been attempted but abandoned by other sculptors, was completed in 1504 and can be found in the Accademia, Florence?

Q. Which Neapolitan sculptor and architect completed a statue of David in 1624 which is in the Borghese Gallery in Rome, although his most obvious contribution to that city are his fountains?

42 STARTER

Q. Conventionally expressed in Roman numerals, what name is given to the number conveying the valency of a chemical element?

BONUS QUESTIONS

Q. The ancient Indian war game, Chaturanga, is generally reckoned to be the forerunner of which modern-day game?

Q. One of the most famous collections of chessmen is the 78 walrus ivory pieces found on the Isle of Lewis in 1831; which people are believed to have made these chess pieces?

Q. Said to have been designed and registered by Nathaniel Cook in 1849, modern-day chess sets are named after which chess player, considered the best in the world at the time, who endorsed Cook's design?

43 STARTER

Q. Which theologian is this? Born probably in Britain around 354 AD, he was cleared of heresy by a synod in Jerusalem in 415 although he was later condemned by the Pope; he taught the doctrine of free will and the possibility of salvation for all?

BONUS QUESTIONS

Three questions on jazz:

With which register of the saxophone are the following jazz musicians most associated?

Q. Charlie Parker?

Q. Sidney Bechet?

Q. Gerry Mulligan?

44 STARTER

Q. Which organic acid is present in vegetable tissues and fruit juices in the form of salts of potassium and magnesium, and is used in the manufacture of carbonated drinks and baking powder?

BONUS QUESTIONS

Q. Which English surname originally meant 'a dealer of candles'?

Q. Although more famous for creating the private detective Philip Marlowe, Raymond Chandler also co-wrote which 1951 film, directed by Alfred Hitchcock?

Q. The 'chandler wobble' leads to a variation of what on the Earth's surface?

45 STARTER

Q. From the French for 'quibble', what term in the game of bridge describes a hand containing no trumps?

BONUS QUESTIONS

Three questions on famous sailing ships:

Q. The *Marigalante* was the original name of which famous ship?

Q. On what date of 1492 did the *Santa Maria* run aground off Haiti?

Q. What were the names of her sister ships which, though less than half her size, returned safely to Spain?

46 STARTER

Q. According to the title of a long-running BBC television series, which three-word phrase referred to the characters Bob Ferris and Terry Collier?

BONUS QUESTIONS

Q. What name was given to an early type of printing head in a computer printer or typewriter, which consisted of a small disc made up of many spokes, each carrying a character in relief?

Q. In a film of 1968, which fictional computer sang 'Daisy, Daisy' as its thinking apparatus was disconnected?

Q. What is the alternative name for the plant Michaelmas daisy?

47 STARTER

Q. Which title, along with *Titus Groan* and *Gormenghast*, completes the trilogy of novels written by Mervyn Peake?

Q. Which lane in London's East End runs from Bethnal Green Road down through Spitalfields, and has been a traditional home for immigrants since the Huguenots arrived in the seventeenth century?

Q. Which Roman emperor's love of architectural splendour was encapsulated in his boast that he had 'found Rome brick, and left it marble'?

Q. Which art gallery in 1972 acquired the work entitled *Equivalent Eight* by Carl Andre, a work sometimes referred to as 'a pile of bricks'?

48 STARTER

Q. Colombey-Les-Deux-Eglises, a village in north-eastern France, was the home of which French statesman who retired there twice, first in 1953 and again in 1969?

BONUS QUESTIONS

Three questions on hundreds:

Q. What is the title of the hymn which is usually sung to the tune 'Old Hundredth', and is a metrical version of Psalm One Hundred?

Q. Which Yorkshire and England opening batsman scored his 100th first class century in a match at Headingley in 1977, and was the first to do so in a Test match?

Q. 'The city of one hundred spires' is a poetic description often applied to which European capital city on the River Vltava?

49 STARTER

Q. The opera house known as the Gran Teatre Del Liceu, a monument marking the spot where Columbus stepped ashore after discovering America, and museums dedicated to the works of Joan Miro and Pablo Picasso are sited in which European city?

BONUS QUESTIONS

Three questions on child prodigies:

Q. Which Russian dominated the chess world from the mid-1970s until the mid-1980s, was rated a first category player at the age of nine, and became World Champion in 1975?

Q. Which British philosopher and economist had, by the age of eight, read Aesop's *Fables* and Xenophon's *Anabasis* in the original Greek, and also the whole of Herodotus?

Q. Which Israeli pianist and conductor made his debut in Buenos Aires at the age of seven in 1950 and, after studying in Paris, made his solo concert debut in London in 1956?

50 STARTER

Q. First used in 1957, when it measured 7 feet by 18 feet although it is now down to a mere 9 inches by 18 inches, by what acronym is the computer which generates winning premium bond numbers known?

BONUS QUESTIONS

Three questions on different types of beer:

Q. In the brewing industry, what do the letters IPA stand for?

Q. Introduced by Labatt's in 1993, what name is given to beer whose temperature is lowered during the brewing process until ice crystals form, which are then removed, supposedly eliminating impurities?

Q. Which town, now in the Czech Republic, has given its name to bottom or cold fermented golden lager, first brewed by Joseph Groll, although it was too late to limit the name to beers actually brewed in the town?

51 STARTER

Q. Pantone Red 186 is the official colour of the logo of British varieties of which fruit, a staple of Mediterranean cookery, which originated in South America?

BONUS QUESTIONS

Three questions on post-war inventions:

Q. Which type of lawn mower was invented by the Swede, Karl Dahlman, based on an earlier invention by Sir Christopher Cockerell?

Q. What was patented by the Hoffman La Roche Chemical and Pharmaceutical Company in 1970, making its first appearance the following year in the windows that reveal the numbers on pocket calculators and digital watches?

Q. In 1971, Owens-Brockway, an American glass container company, introduced the 'clik-lok', which was to prevent children opening what?

52 STARTER

Q. Which London underground station first opened in 1907 as part of the Charing Cross, Edgware and Hampstead Railway, and was in 1998 reopened after modernisation by the cast of Radio 4's *I'm Sorry, I Haven't A Clue*, who play a game named after it?

BONUS QUESTIONS

Q. Which breed of hunting dog has a long, silky coat, and was brought to Europe in the late nineteenth century by British soldiers who had been fighting on the borders of India?

Q. In 1853, which British explorer and orientalist disguised himself as an Afghan pilgrim to make the pilgrimage to Medina and Mecca, becoming one of the first Europeans to enter the cities?

Q. Which strategically important pass connects Afghanistan and Pakistan through the Sefid Koh mountain range?

53 STARTER

Q. Zootoxins, or animal poisons, can be divided into three main categories; crinotoxins are released into the environment, and oral poisons are poisonous when eaten; which is the third catogory, which are injected into the victim?

BONUS QUESTIONS

Q. Otherwise known as tailor's chalk, what name is given to the type of talc used by tailors to mark cloth?

Q. Used in the manufacture of French polish, what is the common name for the resin made from the secretions of the insect *laccifer lacca*?

Q. A French knot is used in which handicraft?

54 STARTER

Q. What term is used for the range of frequencies within which the performance of an electronic device does not differ from its maximum value by a specified amount?

BONUS QUESTIONS

Three questions on Woody Allen films:

Q. In *Everyone Says I Love You*, Woody Allen as 'Joe' attempts to woo 'Von', played by Julia Roberts, in which European city?

Q. Which English actress played Woody Allen's character's wife in *Mighty Aphrodite*, in which Mira Sorvino won an Academy Award for best supporting actress?

Q. The film documentary *Wild Man Blues* features Woody Allen playing which musical instrument?

55 STARTER

Q. To the nearest whole number, what is the value of absolute zero on the Fahrenheit temperature scale?

BONUS QUESTIONS

Q. Which nursery-rhyme character features in the alternative name for a nursery rhyme, popularly used in America?

Q. Which French composer, born in 1875, wrote the piano work for four hands entitled 'Ma Mere L'Oye', or 'Mother Goose', which was later orchestrated and made into a ballet?

Q. Quote: 'I don't believe in God because I don't believe in Mother Goose.' Which Ohio-born lawyer used these words in 1925, at the time of his defence of John T. Scopes, who was being tried for the teaching of Darwinism in Tennessee?

56 STARTER

Q. After making her maiden speech in the House of Commons in 1969, which 21-year-old was called 'Fidel Castro in a mini skirt' by an Ulster Unionist MP?

BONUS QUESTIONS

Three questions on mountain ranges:

Q. The Greater Caucasus mountain range forms the boundary between Russia and two states which gained independence when the Soviet Union broke up; one is Azerbaijan, which is the other?

Q. The High Tatras form the boundary between Poland and which country, which became an independent state on 1 January 1993 having split from its neighbour?

Q. The Karawanken, a mountain range of the eastern Alps, extend along the border of Austria and which country, which declared its independence from Yugoslavia on 25 June 1991?

57 STARTER

Q. What single word is used for the finely-grained, clayey, metamorphic rock which cleaves readily into thin slabs with great tensile strength, its principal colours being black or grey and its principal uses including blackboards and roof tiles?

BONUS QUESTIONS

Q. At which location could you see Michelangelo's depictions of the brazen serpent, the punishment of Haman, and David slaying Goliath?

Q. The Sistine Chapel is so named because it was built by Pope Sixtus IV. Which Pope was Sixtus' nephew, and commissioned Michelangelo to decorate it?

Q. Normally open to the public, why was the Sistine Chapel closed in August and October of 1978?

58 STARTER

Q. A radio wave which travels directly from the transmitter to the receiver is known as a ground wave. Also known as an ionospheric wave, what term means a wave which travels from transmitting aeriel to receiving aeriel by reflection from the ionosphere?

BONUS QUESTIONS

Q. What is the common name for the wingless insects of the order Thysanura, of the class Hexapoda, which are covered in small scales, are capable of very fast movement, and are common household pests, feeding on starchy materials such as wallpaper and books?

Q. What type of material would be treated in a silver bath?

Q. Which fellow-poet was Robert Browning castigating in his 1845 poem 'The Lost Leader', when he wrote: 'just for a handful of silver he left us,/just for a riband to stick in his coat'?

59 STARTER

Q. In the 13th edition of the *Encyclopaedia Britannica*, the article on conjuring was written by which escapologist and illusionist?

BONUS QUESTIONS

Q. Who was the Scottish-born American released from Beirut in November 1991, along with Terry Waite ?

Q. A month after Tom Sutherland's release, which journalist became the last and longest-held of the American hostages in Lebanon to be freed?

Q. Published in 1993, what is the title of John McCarthy and Jill Morrell's autobiography ?

60 STARTER

Q. Andorra's independence is traditionally credited to which emperor, who liberated the region from the Muslims in AD 803 and whose son, Louis I, or the Pious, granted the inhabitants a charter of liberties?

BONUS QUESTIONS

Three questions on environmentally harmful substances:
In each case, what do the initials stand for?

Q. CFCs?

Q. PCBs?

Q. HCB?

61 STARTER

Q. Which Hebrew term meaning 'gathering' is used for the modern Israeli Parliament?

BONUS QUESTIONS

Three questions on corruption:

Q. Who, in his 1903 essay *Democracy*, wrote 'democracy substitutes election by the incompetent many, for appointment by the corrupt few'?

Q. Which American wrote in 1800: 'if the principle were to prevail of a common law, that is, a single government, being in force in the United States... it would become the most corrupt government on the earth'?

Q. Which American president died in office when it looked likely that he would be impeached for corruption over the so-called 'teapot dome scandal'?

62 STARTER

Q. In Greek mythology, what was the name of the King of Elis whose ox-stalls housed 3,000 animals and had not been cleaned for 30 years until Heracles, as one of his labours, diverted the River Alpheus through them?

BONUS QUESTIONS

Three questions on hands:

Q. Which German artist and engraver, born in 1471, produced many detailed anatomical studies, his drawings and engravings of praying hands being perhaps the best known examples?

Q. Which creatures were created by Edward Lear, and had blue hands, despite the fact that their heads were green?

Q. 'Che Gelida Manina', or 'Your Tiny Hand Is Frozen', is one of the best known tenor arias in opera. Which character sings it?

63 STARTER

Q. Usually symbolized by the letter 'Z', what term is used for the quantity that determines the amplitude of the current for a given voltage in an alternating current circuit?

BONUS QUESTIONS

Q. Which English architect, born in 1573, did much to establish Palladianism as the dominant style of English architecture, and created The Queen's House in Greenwich, which was completed in 1635?

Q. The author of several books on management, and the presenter of two television series in which he applied his expertise to failing enterprises, of which multinational company was Sir John Harvey Jones the chairman between 1982 and 1987?

Q. Staged annually each April, which major sporting event was won by Hugh Jones in 1982, and by Steve Jones in 1985?

64 STARTER

Q. Also used in the production of the liqueur chartreuse, the green stalk of which aromatic plant can be candied and used as a cake decoration?

BONUS QUESTIONS

Three questions on bulls:

Q. Which musical instrument is sometimes referred to as a 'bull fiddle' in the USA?

Q. In John Arbuthnott's allegorical work *The History of John Bull*, John Bull represented Britain, France was represented by Lewis Baboon.

Which country was represented by Bull's friend, Nicholas Frog?

Q. Tatanka Yotaka, otherwise known as 'Sitting Bull', became in 1867 the leader of which Native American people?

65 STARTER

Q. Which Swiss city gave its name to an international agreement, first drafted in 1864, concerning the status and treatment of captured and wounded military personnel in wartime?

BONUS QUESTIONS

Three questions on fictional detectives:

Q. Which amateur detective solved the mystery of the murders in the Rue Morgue?

Q. Which wealthy, laconic detective first appeared in the story 'Fer-de-Lance' in 1934?

Q. Which detective made his debut in the 1939 novel *The Big Sleep*?

66 STARTER

Q. The 50th anniversary of the founding of which state was celebrated on 30 April 1998?

BONUS QUESTIONS

Q. What were first classified by Karl Landsteiner at the Vienna Pathological Institute in 1900?

Q. At the Battle of Blood River in 1838, the Voortrekkers fought with which African people?

Q. What event led to the instigation of Judge Jeffreys' 'Bloody Assizes'?

67 STARTER

Q. Of which of his own works, about the soul's judgment and salvation, did Edward Elgar say 'this is the best of me'?

BONUS QUESTIONS

Three questions on transport in films:

Q. Which silent screen comedian was the star of the 1927 classic *The General*, in which he played the driver of a locomotive of that name?

Q. What was the name of the eponymous vessel which was the setting for Humphrey Bogart's only Oscar-winning performance?

Q. In the Orson Welles film, Citizen Kane's last word was 'rosebud'. What form of transport was rosebud?

68 STARTER

Q. The daughter of a commodore, she is prone to migraines and is unable to make saliva. Having been described as being 'like the sun, only without the warmth', she is often referred to during editions of *Frazier*, but never actually appears. Who is she?

BONUS QUESTIONS

Three questions on particle physics:

Q. In physics, what name is given to a collision between two particles in which the total kinetic energy of the particles is conserved?

Q. A particle of mass 'M' and velocity 'V' collides elastically head-on with a particle at rest, also of mass 'M'; what fraction of the moving particle's kinetic energy is transferred to the stationary particle?

Q. If the collision were completely inelastic, the two particles would stick together after the collision and move off with a new velocity 'U' in the same direction as 'V'; what fraction of 'V' is the magnitude of the velocity 'U'?

69 STARTER

Q. Celebrated in 1998 on 13 April, Baisakhi Mela is the new year festival of which religion?

BONUS QUESTIONS

Three questions on regents and protectors:

Q. During the minority of which English king did William Marshall, Earl of Pembroke, act as regent until his death in 1219, when he was succeeded by Hubert de Burgh?

Q. John of Lancaster, Duke of Bedford, was Regent of France and Protector of England during the minority of which king, who was also his nephew?

Q. During whose minority did Edward Seymour, Earl of Hertford, become protector of the realm in 1547?

70 STARTER

Q. Which snooker player knocked Stephen Hendry out of the 1998 World Championships in the first round, having lost to him in four finals between 1990 and 1994?

BONUS QUESTIONS

Three questions on natural phenomena:

Q. Which natural phenomenon is located at approximately 43 degrees north, 79 degrees west, is about two thirds of a mile wide, and 169 feet high at its highest point?

Q. Which rock formation rises to a height of just under 1400 feet at 36 degrees north and 5 degrees west?

Q. Which natural phenomenon is located at approximately 25 degrees south and 131 degrees east, is 1100 feet high, two miles long and a mile and a half wide.

71 STARTER

Q. What term is used for the process of heating and gradually cooling glass and metals in order to produce toughening or tempering?

BONUS QUESTIONS

Q. Which character, with enormous physical power, was drawn by Clarence Beck, and first appeared in the pages of *Whiz* comics in 1940; the name was later applied to the Manchester United and England Footballer Bryan Robson?

Q. The Walt Whitman poem 'O Captain! My Captain!' was an elegy on the death of which American president in 1865?

Q. In the novel by Jules Verne, which submarine was commanded by Captain Nemo?

72 STARTER

Q. What name is given to the process, carried out under elevated temperature but below the melting point of the metal, by which metal particles are compressed into a coherent solid body?

BONUS QUESTIONS

Three questions on sevens:

Q. Whose orchestral work, *Reel of Seven Fishermen*, received its European premier in 1999, the composer taking his inspiration from the Orkneys, his home for over 30 years?

Q. Which English writer, reformer and critic was the author of *The Seven Lamps of Architecture*, published in 1849?

Q. Who directed the 1957 allegorical film *The Seventh Seal*?

73 STARTER

Q. Born Adrian Thaws in Bristol, which vocalist and multi-instrumentalist first tasted chart success in 1989 as a member of the 'Fresh 4' Collective?

BONUS QUESTIONS

Three questions on decisive battles in nineteenth century wars:

Q. The 1866 Battle of Konniggrätz was the decisive engagement of which war?

Q. The capitulation of Marshal Bazaine's force at Metz in 1870 was the last critical action of which war?

Q. Selma in 1865 was the scene of the last major engagement of which war?

74 STARTER

Q. She made her first appearance as a young girl in the novel *L'Assommoir*, but how is prostitute Anna Coupeau known in the title of the succeeding novel by Emile Zola?

BONUS QUESTIONS

Q. In what capacity was Will Somers employed at the court of Henry VIII, and Muckle John employed by Charles I, the latter being probably the last man to hold the office?

Q. Which chess piece is known in France as 'le fou' or 'the fool'?

Q. Born in 1943, which actor and director's earliest work in the theatre was with the Bishop's Company Repertory Players? Later in his career he also became a noted playwright, his works including *Fool for Love* and *A Lie of the Mind*?

75 STARTER

Q. Who is being described? The son of an architect, he was born in Pergamun in what is now Turkey in a 129 AD. He was doctor to a succession of Roman emperors and his influence lived on in medical theory and practice dominating Europe until the Renaissance.

BONUS QUESTIONS

Three questions on theatrical history:

Q. The theatrical dynasty founded by Roger Kemble in the eighteenth century included many of his 12 children; Sarah, the eldest, achieved fame as an actress under which married name?

Q. Which actor and producer, also co-manager of the Drury Lane Theatre, offered Sarah Siddons an engagement in 1774 after his agents had seen her playing Rosalind in a barn in Worcestershire, whilst pregnant?

Q. Perhaps the best known portrait of Sarah Siddons is 'Mrs Siddons as the tragic muse'; who was the artist?

76 STARTER

Q. Which nineteenth-century Irish writer is particularly remembered for his stories of the supernatural, his notable works including *The House By The Churchyard* in 1861 and the collection *In A Glass Darkly* in 1872?

BONUS QUESTIONS

Three questions on arboriculture:

Q. Usually employed on fruit trees, what name is given to the type of cultivation in which a supported tree is trained to form a vertical main stem, with pairs of branches stretching horizontally to form fruit-bearing tiers?

Q. Practised in ancient and ornamental woodlands, what is the name of the technique whereby a tree is cut about two metres from the ground, stimulating the development of lateral branches?

Q. Practised for centuries in British woodlands, what is the name of the technique of allowing shoots to grow from the base of a felled tree, providing a continuous supply of timber for fencing and fuel?

77 STARTER

Q. Born in 1845, which French composer's 'Pavanne' was selected to feature in the opening sequence of the BBC's coverage of the 1998 World Cup?

BONUS QUESTIONS

Three questions on trademarks and trade names:

Q. In February 1999, the patents office refused a second application for an image to be recognized as a trademark, an application for the same image having been refused in July 1998. Of whom, or what, was the image?

Q. The German inventor Johann Maelzel took out many patents, including the mechanical trumpeter and the mechanical orchestra, but is best remembered for his device patented in 1816 and based on the pendulum, which received a seal of approval when Beethoven started using one the following year. What was it?

Q. Which famous trade name was devised by Herbert Grime in 1890, comprising the opening letters of the two latin words meaning 'strength of man'?

78 STARTER

Q. Which monotheistic religion refers to god by the plural of the word 'Eloah'?

BONUS QUESTIONS

Q. Which British physician first identified acute and chronic nephritis in the nineteenth century, the condition being known by his name for many years?

Q. Gavin Maxwell's book *Ring of Bright Water* is an account of the author's relationship with which semi-tame mammals?

Q. The aria 'Let The Bright Seraphim' was first performed in 1743 when the oratorio *Samson* was staged in London. Who was the composer?

79 STARTER

Q. What term is used for a parasite whose host is itself a parasite on another species?

BONUS QUESTIONS

Q. Which European capital city is this? Built on the site of a tenth century village, it became the seat of the country's royal family in the fifteenth century, and noted for its manufacture of porcelain in the eighteenth. It fell to German forces on 9 April 1940, remaining in their hands until their surrender on 8 May 1945?

Q. Who is the author of the play *Copenhagen*, which concerns a meeting between Neils Bohr, his wife and the German physicist Werner Heisenberg?

Q. Which British military commander rode a chestnut stallion named 'Copenhagen', commemorating his part in the Copenhagen expedition of 1807?

80 STARTER

Q. Which four-letter word is correctly used for highly decomposed organic matter in which the original plant material is unrecognizable, a well-known proverb implying that there's money in it?

BONUS QUESTIONS

Three questions on monarchs who died unpleasant deaths:

Q. Which monarch's death in 1135 was said to have been of severe food poisoning after devouring lampreys, against the advice of his physicians? His demise is often described as being due to 'a surfeit of lampreys'?

Q. Which Scottish monarch died of leprosy in 1329 after ruling for 23 years?

Q. Which English king died in 1553 at the age of aged 15, after – quote: 'eruptions came out over his skin, his hair fell off, and then his nails, and afterwards the joints of his toes and fingers', these symptoms having been suggested to indicate congenital syphilis, his father's legacy to his children?

81 STARTER

Q. 238 is the atomic mass number of the most abundant isotope of which element, which has the atomic number 92 and the chemical symbol U?

BONUS QUESTIONS

Three questions on word origins:

Q. The American coin worth ten cents is a known as a dime. From which language does the word 'dime' derive?

Q. Which five-letter word entered the English language early in the twentieth century via Australia, and is thought to be a corruption of the French for white wine?

Q. Which five-letter slang term is thought to derive from the French meaning 'to dodge' or 'slink away', and generally means to evade work or duty?

82 STARTER

Q. In Turin, Torino are the usually less successful rivals to which other football club?

BONUS QUESTIONS

Three questions on colours:

Q. In which work, published in 1590, is the 'redcrosse knight of holiness' a personification of the Anglican Church?

Q. Although the appropriate insignia are red, a member of the Roman Catholic clergy said to be 'raised to the purple' would have achieved what position?

Q. Now used generally to mean a highly privileged start in life, what is the strict meaning of the term 'born in the purple', or 'porphyrogenitus'?

83 STARTER

Q. What do you do in bed if you suffer from bruxism?

BONUS QUESTIONS

Which sports or pastimes gave rise to the following phrases:

Q. To come up to scratch?

Q. Back to square one?

Q. To win hands down?

84 STARTER

Q. What word derives from the Latin words for 'flax' and 'oil', and means a material consisting of a canvas backing coated with a preparation of linseed oil and powdered cork, often used as a floor covering?

BONUS QUESTIONS

Of which plays by Shakespeare are these the last words:

Q. 'a great while ago the world begun,/with hey, ho, the wind and the rain,/but that's all one, our play is done,/and we'll strive to please you every day'

Q. 'the oldest hath borne most; we that are young/shall never see so much nor live so long'

Q. 'I'll make a voyage to the holy land,/to wash this blood off from my guilty hand./march sadly after; grace my mournings here/in weeping after this untimely bier!'

85 STARTER

Q. What, in 1934, connected the Coliseum, the Louvre Museum, a symphony by Strauss, a Shakespeare sonnet and Mickey Mouse?

BONUS QUESTIONS

Q. Now used figuratively to describe any oppressive tribunal, which court, situated in the Palace of Westminster, earned a reputation for harsh and summary punishments, and was abolished by the Long Parliament of 1641?

Q. Which Dominican friar was appointed grand inquisitor by Queen Isabella in 1483?

Q. In Orwell's novel *1984*, in which room did O'Brien conduct his final interrogation of Winston Smith?

86 STARTER

Q. What is the length of the hypoteneuse of a right-angled triangle, the lengths of whose other two sides are, respectively, 15 units and 36 units?

BONUS QUESTIONS

Three questions on bridges:

Q. Which golf course would you be playing if you crossed the 'valley of fear' by the Swilcan Bridge?

Q. Who, according to Livy, defended the Sublican Bridge over the Tiber against the entire invading Etruscan army?

Q. The industrial towns of Runcorn and Widnes are linked by a road bridge over which river?

87 STARTER

Q. Which alcoholic drink is referred to in Russian as 'pivo'?

BONUS QUESTIONS

Three questions on poetic walks and walkers:
In each case, identify the poet who wrote the lines:

Q. Firstly, from a poem published in 1798: 'like one that on a lonesome road/doth walk in fear and dread,/and having once turned round walks on,/and turns no more his head'?

Q. Who wrote these lines, from a poem of 1815: 'she walks in beauty like the night/of cloudless climes and starry skies;/and all that's best in dark and bright/meet in her aspect and her eyes'?

Q. Who wrote these lines, from a poem of 1824: 'swiftly walk over the western wave,/spirit of the night!/out of the misty eastern cave,/where, all the long and lone daylight/thou wovest dreams of joy and fear'?

88 STARTER

Q. What single word refers in art to a painting or sculpture depicting the Virgin Mary holding the dead body of Christ in her arms or on her lap?

BONUS QUESTIONS

Q. Which adjective, applied specifically to Germanic peoples, and more generally to Scandinavians and Anglo-Saxons, derives from the name of a people who inhabited part of northern Europe around 2000 ago?

Q. Which country of northern Europe derives its name from the tribes of the lower Rhine, a fusion of Celtic and Germanic stock?

Q. Which country's name is derived from the name given to Viking raiders of the ninth century by the Byzantines, and is suggested to have come from the colour of the invaders' hair?

89 STARTER

Q. Which organ of the body converts ammonia into the much less toxic urea?

BONUS QUESTIONS

Can you identify the eponymous operatic characters from these descriptions:

Q. First, a famous singer and the lover of an artist, in an opera by Puccini first performed in Rome in 1900?

Q. A druidic priestess living at the time of the Roman conquest of Gaul, in an opera by Bellini which premiered in 1831?

Q. From a Verdi opera first performed in 1851, the humpbacked jester of the Duke of Mantua?

90 STARTER

Q. Which town in Belgium has given its name to a coarse woollen cloth with a thick nap, and also to a hooded overcoat made of this material?

BONUS QUESTIONS

Three questions on politicians who were sportsmen:

Q. In the US mid-term elections of 1998, Jesse Ventura of the Reform Party was elected Governor of Minnesota, having formerly been a professional sportsman. What was his sport?

Q. Which politician competed for Great Britain at the 1964 Olympics, and captained the UK athletics team in 1965 and 1966, before entering Parliament?

Q. Which conservative MP, having made his name as an athlete, lost the seat for Falmouth and Cambourne in the 1997 General Election?

91 STARTER

Q. What other name is given to the edible cruciferous annual plant known by the Italian word 'arugula'?

BONUS QUESTIONS

Q. In the title of the novel by Henry Rider Haggard, how was Ayesha known?

Q. Who became the first French solo artist to top the UK singles chart, with the song 'She' in 1974?

Q. Elvis Costello's version of 'She' was featured in which 1999 film, starring Hugh Grant and Julia Roberts?

92 STARTER

Q. Which comedian was formerly a psychiatric nurse and early in her career performed under the name 'the sea monster'?

BONUS QUESTIONS

Q. Which mansion in Gloucestershire was purchased by the Queen as a wedding present for Princess Anne?

Q. Which economist, whose best-known work, *Principles of Political Economy and Taxation*, was published in 1817, died at Gatcombe Park in 1823 at the age of 51?

Q. Which writer's *Wealth of Nations* first attracted Ricardo to the study of economics?

93 STARTER

Q. Originating on American radio in the 1930s with 15-minute daytime episodes and inherited by television in the early 1950s, what term is used for a particular genre of serial programmes and comes from the product made by many of the early sponsors?

BONUS QUESTIONS

Q. Which political leader described the writer George Bernard Shaw as 'a good man fallen among Fabians', according to a conversation recorded by the journalist and novelist Arthur Ransome?

Q. Whose body was placed alongside Lenin's in the Lenin mausoleum in Red Square, Moscow, but removed in 1960?

Q. The *Lenin*, launched in 1959, was the world's first nuclear powered surface ship; for what specific purpose was it built?

94 STARTER

Q. Under what name did the former Yaron Cohen achieve fame in 1998?

BONUS QUESTIONS

Three questions about films aimed at a teenage audience, but based on classic works:

Q. The film *Ten Things I Hate About You* is based on which of Shakespeare's comedies?

Q. The 1995 film *Clueless*, starring Alicia Silverstone, was based on which of Jane Austen's novels?

Q. The film *Cruel Intentions* is a teenage version of which classic French novel by De Laclos?

95 STARTER

Q. In which English city are the Graves Art Gallery, the Abbeydale Industrial Hamlet, Meadowhall Shopping Centre and the Crucible Theatre?

BONUS QUESTIONS

Q. From which malign Scandinavian monster did Harry Potter and his friend Ron rescue Hermione in the school cloakrooms at Hogwarts, in *Harry Potter and the Philosopher's Stone*?

Q. Which composer, born in 1843, wrote 'The March of the Trolls'?

Q. In the song made famous by Frank Crumitt, who were prevented from crossing the bridge by a large troll until the largest of them butted it into the next county?

96 STARTER

Q. Which king was the father of Frederick Augustus, the Duke of York who is remembered in a nursery rhyme for marching ten thousand men up and down a hill?

BONUS QUESTIONS

Q. Which avant-garde French composer was associated with the Surrealists, and was known as the 'man in the velvet suit' from the large number of grey velvet suits he habitually wore?

Q. The hero of which nineteenth-century novel by Frances Hodgson Burnett was noted for his velvet knickerbocker suit and for wearing his hair in long golden ringlets, setting a fashion for boys for a generation?

Q. Which influential French fashion designer popularized velvet knickerbockers for women in 1967?

97 STARTER

Q. Widely used in radar, and having either rectangular or circular cross-sections, what term is used for the hollow metal conductors through which microwaves may be propagated?

BONUS QUESTIONS

Three questions on Jaguar cars:

Q. Which future Labour MP and government minister became chief executive of Jaguar in 1973, but resigned in 1975 when the government-sponsored Ryder Report questioned the company's independence?

Q. Which Labour politician has been nicknamed 'Two Jags', because of his fondness for the car?

Q. Which television detective drove a red 1960 Mark 2 Jaguar, with the registration 243 RPA?

98 STARTER

Q. The wreck of the *SS Politician* in the Western Isles in 1941, and the efforts of the islanders to save its cargo before the wreck broke up, provided Compton Mackenzie with the plot of which of his novels, later a successful film?

BONUS QUESTIONS

Q. Black, thorny and stony are types of which invertebrate marine organism, including the so-called red or precious, which are used in jewellery?

Q. *Coral Island* by R.M. Ballantyne, first published in 1858, inspired William Golding to write which book?

Q. The words 'full fathom five thy father lies' are sung by which spirit, in Shakespeare's play *The Tempest*?

99 STARTER

Q. Which American honorary society for distinguished scholars takes its name from the initial letters, in Greek, of the motto 'philosophy is the guide to life'?

BONUS QUESTIONS

Three questions on sport and South America:

Q. Which city is the site of the only Test cricket ground in South America?

Q. Which is the largest of the South American countries never to have qualified for the final stages of the football World Cup?

Q. When Jefferson Perez won the twenty kilometre walk at Atlanta, which country joined Argentina and Brazil as the only South American countries whose athletes have won track and field Olympic gold medals?

100 STARTER

Q. Which biblical king has a name which means literally 'we will rebel', is described in Genesis as 'a mighty hunter before the Lord', and gave his name to the ninth of Elgar's *Enigma Variations*?

BONUS QUESTIONS

Three questions on parliamentary elections:

Q. In 1985, the deposit a candidate must put up to stand at a parliamentary election was increased from £150 to how much?

Q. At the same time, the condition of forfeiture was reduced from 12½ per cent to how many per cent?

Q. Before going on to bigger things, who, along with T. L. Keen of the 'Campaign for a More Prosperous Britain', lost a by-election at Beaconsfield in 1982?

101 STARTER

Q. Which American journalist and broadcaster was born in St Joseph, Missouri in 1916, wrote eye-witness reports of the war in Europe in the 1940s, and was considered a national institution when, from 1962 and 1981, he anchored the CBS evening news?

BONUS QUESTIONS

Q. Lysergic acid, an active constituent of LSD, is found in which fungus, that develops particularly on rye?

Q. The pure lager yeast culture was first isolated at which Copenhagen brewery, whose name is used in its classification?

Q. Which short novel of 1949 was released in a film version in the same year, and concerns the last days in the life of a racketeer dealing in sub-standard penicillin in post-war Vienna?

102 STARTER

Q. In Paris, what stands at the meeting point of the Avenue Foch, Avenue de la Grande Armée, Boulevard Haussmann, and the Avenue des Champs Élysées?

BONUS QUESTIONS

Three questions linked by a surname:

Q. Which American general was Supreme Allied Commander, Europe, of the NATO forces during the war in Kosovo?

Q. General Mark Clark led the liberation by the American 5th Army of which capital city on 4 June 1944?

Q. Who, with Lieutenant William Clark, led the first overland return crossing of the American north-west in their expedition of 1804 to 1806?

103 STARTER

Q. The Mississippi community originally called Gum Pond, but later renamed after the local tupelo trees, was in 1935 the birthplace of which singer?

BONUS QUESTIONS

Three questions on paintings:

Q. A painting of 1623 by Rembrandt depicts Doctor Nicholaes Tulp's lesson in which subject?

Q. Which English portrait painter's 1756 picture of Dr Samuel Johnson is usually displayed in the National Portrait Gallery, London?

Q. Whose portrait of Doctor Paul-Ferdinand Gachet was sold at auction by Christie's in 1990 for 82½ million dollars?

104 STARTER

Q. Which large oceanic fish which often swims in huge schools numbering up to 50,000, and has species called Yellowfin, Albacore, Bigeye and Bluefin?

BONUS QUESTIONS

Three questions on an ethnic group:

Q. The Treaty of Sèvres of 1920, which was never ratified, made provision for an independent homeland for which people who inhabit parts of Turkey, Iraq and Iran?

Q. Which twelfth century warrior leader, who died in Damascus in 1193, is arguably the Kurd best known to the western world?

Q. Which Liberal-Democratic peer and MEP has given constant support to Iraqi Kurds in their fight for democracy against the Iraqi government?

105 STARTER

Q. The inverse of the Hubble Constant, which has the dimensions of time, gives a measure of the age of what?

BONUS QUESTIONS

Q. Named after President Woodrow who effectively gained the country its independence in 1918, Wilsonova is a thoroughfare in which European capital city?

Q. The Czech spa town of Mariánské Lázne was known by which German name in its heyday last century?

Q. Famous for its brewery, the Czech town of Ceske Budejovice is known internationally by which German name?

106 STARTER

Q. Which island is known to the Indonesians as 'Kalimantan', though that state covers only about three-quarters of its area, the rest of the island including Sarawak, Sabah and the Sultanate of Brunei?

BONUS QUESTIONS

Three questions on radio broadcasting:

Q. UK domestic radio services are broadcast across three wavebands; which waveband extends in frequency from 87.5 megahertz to 108 megahertz?

Q. Which type of radio is allocated the frequencies 217.5 megahertz to 230 megahertz in the UK?

Q. Some radios are still calibrated in wavelengths rather than frequency; which number must be divided by the frequency in megahertz to obtain the wavelength in metres?

107 STARTER

Q. In 1998, the publishers of the *New Oxford Dictionary of English* controversially acknowledged which slang expression, which it defined as a term signifying approval of the physical appearance of a member of the opposite sex?

BONUS QUESTIONS

Q. Who, in June 1999, became the first Briton to be appointed principal conductor of the Berlin Philharmonic Orchestra?

Q. Which of the war poets wrote of 'the stuttering rifle's rapid rattle' in his poem of 1917 entitled 'Anthem for Doomed Youth'?

Q. Who said at the Royal Variety performance in November 1963: 'those in the cheaper seats clap. The rest of you rattle your jewellery'?

108 STARTER

Q. Which textile has a French name meaning 'shaggy', and is made in the pile weave of silk, cotton or synthetic fibres, giving a soft, downy surface with a smooth back?

BONUS QUESTIONS

Q. Who, in the election results announced in May 1999, finally succeeded Binyamin Netenyahu as Prime Minister of Israel?

Q. Married to a famous novelist in 1930, which British archaeologist's excavations include the ancient site at Tall Birak in Syria?

Q. Who, according to certain traditions, was taken to heaven on a winged horse called Buraq?

109 STARTER

Q. Which country's kings were, from the eleventh century onwards, consecrated in the cathedral town of Viborg, whose name means 'sacred hill' and was the largest town in Jutland?

BONUS QUESTIONS

Q. Which pressure group was established in 1935 with the aims of encouraging people to enjoy the countryside, and ensuring that public access to it was protected?

Q. In 1932, the 'freedom to roam' movement, a so-called 'mass trespass' by thousands of walkers, took place on which stretch of upland in the Peak District?

Q. Who, as Minister of State for the Environment, promised in March 1999 to introduce a statutory 'Right to Roam' Bill, covering over four million acres of open countryside?

110 STARTER

Q. Who has, for many years, held the same job as safety officer at the Springfield nuclear power plant?

BONUS QUESTIONS

Three questions on literary heroines:

Q. Anna Tellwright is the eponymous heroine of which 1902 novel by Arnold Bennett?

Q. What is the surname of the orphan Anne, the eponymous heroine of Anne Of Green Gables?

Q. Whose historical novel of 1829, *Anne of Geierstein*, was written three years before the author's death, and was the first published under his own name?

111 STARTER

Q. Which word is the German term meaning a coat of chain-mail, and was particularly used during the Second World War referring to heavily armoured military forces?

BONUS QUESTIONS

Q. Which body was established in 1970 with 574 members divided between the House of Bishops, the House of Clergy and the House of Laity, and has the power to frame statute law known as 'a measure' on any matter concerning the Church of England?

Q. Shakespeare's play *Measure for Measure* is set in which city?

Q. Who was eventually awarded a prize of £20,000 for his invention of the chronometer, which was able to measure longitude accurately for the first time?

112 STARTER

Q. In April 1998, who was the only woman included with Peter Cook, Les Dawson, Eric Morecambe and Tommy Cooper on a set of postage stamps commemorating comedians, the publicity for the issue including her line, 'George, don't do that...'?

BONUS QUESTIONS

Three questions on battles in the war of the Spanish succession:

Q. After his victory at Blenheim in 1704, the Duke of Marlborough, in an attempt to establish himself among the fortresses of Flanders, confronted French forces on which site, which was to be the site of a great battle in the following century?

Q. In which city was the fortress of Montjuich, alongside what later became the site of a stadium for the Olympic Games, where the allies proclaimed Charles III to be King of Spain?

Q. The village of Malplaquet, scene of the last major battle of the war, is 16 kilometers south of which town, the site of the first battle between the British and the Germans in 1914?

113 STARTER

Q. Which playwright is said to have kept a pet scorpion in a beer glass on his desk whilst writing his first major drama *Brand*, during which time he was working at the Norwegian Theatre in Bergen?

BONUS QUESTIONS

Three questions on islands with animal names:

Q. Which native animal gives its name to the third largest island off the coast of mainland Australia?

Q. Which island separates the Horseshoe Falls, or Canadian section of the Niagara Falls, from the American section?

Q. Mount Alvernia, on Cat Island, is the highest point of which Commonwealth country, consisting of about 700 islands extending from the coast of Florida almost to Haiti?

114 STARTER

Q. 'I owe much, I possess nothing. I give the rest to the poor' are some of the last words attributed to which French writer of bawdy satire who died in 1553 in poverty, despite the success of his works which included *Gargantua* and *Pantagruel*?

BONUS QUESTIONS

Three questions on business terms:

Q. Which two-word term usually refers to specific financial inducements used to tie valued senior employees to a particular firm?

Q. What two-word term is used for a payment of compensation, often tax-free, made by a company to a senior employee whose contract is prematurely terminated, often as the result of a merger or take-over?

Q. What term is used for a clause in the employment contract of a senior executive that provides benefits if he or she is sacked or leaves after a change of ownership or takeover?

115 STARTER

Q. The Shugiin, or House of Representatives, and the Sangiin, or House of Councillors, are the two legislative chambers of which modern constitutional monarchy?

BONUS QUESTIONS

Q. When applied to the Internet, what do the initials FTP stand for?

Q. What was the name of the fraudulent document, said to be a report of meetings held at Basel in 1897, which served as a pretext and rationale for anti-semitism in the early twentieth century?

Q. The term protocol sentence, as used in the philosophy of logical positivism, is particularly associated with which German-born American philosopher whose first major work, *The Logical Structure of the World*, was published in German in 1928?

116 STARTER

Q. Characterized by swellings beneath the jaws and transmittable to humans, 'The Glanders' is a malignant disease affecting which animals?

BONUS QUESTIONS

Three questions on Stanley Kubrick films:

Q. Who starred as 'Private Joker' in Kubrick's 1987 film *Full Metal Jacket*?

Q. Which epic, starring Kirk Douglas, was the only film that Kubrick made in a major Hollywood studio?

Q. The music to which costume drama of 1975 includes Irish folk group the Chieftains and Schubert's Trio in E minor?

117 STARTER

Q. Deriving from the Latin for 'things to be done', which Spanish word refers to an estate or plantation with a dwelling-house?

BONUS QUESTIONS

Q. What term was used in the building industry for the sub-contracting of labour to self-employed men to evade tax and National Insurance payments?

Q. Who coined the term 'the lumpen proletariat'?

Q. Tony Lumpkin, an idle frequenter of the Three Jolly Pigeons, is a character in which eighteenth century comedy by Oliver Goldsmith?

118 STARTER

Q. Thought to be a reference to a tattoo which marked members of a nomadic clan, which biblical figure was, according to Genesis, 'marked' by God after the murder of his brother?

BONUS QUESTIONS

Three questions on famous polio sufferers:

Q. Which Scottish writer developed his love of Border tales and ballads while convalescing from polio in the company of his grandfather at Sandyknowe?

Q. Which former royal spouse caught polio as a child, but went on to cox the victorious 1951 Cambridge boat race crew?

Q. Which future president of the USA was elected Governor of New York state in 1929, in spite of the polio which had disabled him eight years earlier?

119 STARTER

Q. What was the Viking name for that part of North America, thought by some to have been Northern Newfoundland, visited by Leif Eriksson around the end of the tenth century?

BONUS QUESTIONS

Used in computer circuitry, identify the following two input logic gates:

Q. Output low only if both inputs are low, otherwise output high?

Q. Output low only if both inputs are high, otherwise output high?

Q. Output high if two inputs are different, otherwise output low?

120 STARTER

Q. Wiltshire, Gloucestershire, Warwickshire, Buckinghamshire and Berkshire all border which other English county?

BONUS QUESTIONS

Q. Often called poteen in Ireland, what term is used in the United States for illicitly distilled whiskey?

Q. Born in 1896, which actor won the 1975 Academy Award for 'best supporting actor' for his appearance in *The Sunshine Boys*?

Q. The song 'Good Morning Starshine' featured in which musical, which opened on Broadway in 1968?

QUARTER-FINAL

1 STARTER

Q. Originally applied to a male drinking session at the end of a meal in ancient Greece, which word has come to mean a collection of essays by various writers on one subject, or a conference at which academic experts discuss a particular topic?

BONUS QUESTIONS

Q. Which actress made her London stage debut in 1927, and won a Best Supporting Actress Oscar for her role in the 1984 film *A Passage To India*, and a BAFTA award for the television series *The Jewel In The Crown*?

Q. Who made the UK singles charts in 1957 with the song 'Peggy Sue'?

Q. Measuring 10 by 14 inches, a 'peggy' is a size of which object, used in house construction?

2 STARTER

Q. Under the constitution of the Republic of Ireland, the Deputy Prime Minister who acts for the Taoiseach during absence or incapacity is known by which title?

BONUS QUESTIONS

Three questions on chemistry:

Q. Which element occurs naturally in two stable isotopes: 10, comprising 19.8 per cent, and 11, comprising 80.2 per cent? It was first isolated in 1808 by Joseph Gay-Lussac and Baron Louis Thenard, and independently by Sir Humphrey Davy, by heating its oxide with potassium metal?

Q. Because of its high capture cross-section, the rarer isotope boron-10 and some of its compounds have been used as biological shields against which type of radiation?

Q. Boron oxide, B_2O_3, is mixed with silica to make a heat-resistant form of what?

3 STARTER

Q. Which Spanish word derives from the Latin term meaning the sixth hour, and refers to an afternoon period of sleep or relaxation?

BONUS QUESTIONS

Three questions on early nineteenth century American politics:

Q. A major influence on the planning and ratification of the US constitution, and later secretary of state under Thomas Jefferson, who in 1809 became the country's fourth president?

Q. On 2 November 1810, Madison proclaimed 'non-intercourse' with which country, following that country's interference with American shipping?

Q. Which form of corrupt electoral practice takes its name from the man who was Madison's vice-president from 1813 to 1814?

4 STARTER

Q. Sometimes called an abney level, the hand instrument used in surveying to measure angles of slope is more commonly known by what name?

BONUS QUESTIONS

Three questions on unlikely actors who played popes:

Q. Which actor, who married six times and whose wives included the actresses Kay Kendall and Rachel Roberts, played Pope Julius II in the 1965 film *The Agony And The Ecstasy*?

Q. Which rock drummer played the pope in Ken Russell's film *Lisztomania*?

Q. Which actor played Father Albinizi, who becomes pope due to a computer error in the 1991 film *The Pope Must Die*?

5 STARTER

Q. Used as a German naval base in both world wars, which North Sea island is part of the North Frisian group and was ceded by Britain to Germany in 1890 in exchange for Zanzibar?

BONUS QUESTIONS

Three questions on the writings of Emile Zola:

Q. Which novel of 1867 is considered Zola's first important work, and is a psychological study of murder and passion?

Q. Which of Zola's novels was published in 1885, and was an indictment of the working conditions of miners?

Q. What name was given to the letter Zola wrote to the Paris newspaper *L'Aurore* in 1898, in support of the artillery officer Alfred Dreyfus?

6 STARTER

Q. *Zabriskie Point*, *La Notte* and *Blow-Up* were all directed and co-written by which Italian film-maker?

BONUS QUESTIONS

Q. Who, in Roman religion, was the personfication of the dawn and the counterpart of the Greek Goddess, Eos?

Q. Also known as the 'southern lights' what is the equivalent of the aurora borealis in the southern hemisphere?

Q. A blank shot fired from the cruiser *Aurora* in 1917 was the signal for the start of the assault on the Winter Palace in which city?

7 STARTER

Q. *A Treatise On Money* in 1930, and *General Theory Of Employment, Interest And Money* in 1936, were the works of which economist?

BONUS QUESTIONS

Three questions on drums:

Q. Which traditional Irish one-sided drum made from goatskin has a name meaning 'thunder'?

Q. What is the name of the stage performance which first came to prominence during the 1994 Eurovision Song Contest, which uses drums evolved from the bodhran?

Q. Named after a village on Lough Neagh, the outsize bass drum known as the lambeg drum is an essential feature of which controversial events?

8 STARTER

Q. Now a World Heritage Site, Ichkeul is a national park in which North African country?

BONUS QUESTIONS

Q. What term of Greek origin is used for the localized death of animal soft tissue, caused by the prolonged interruption of the blood supply that may result from injury or infection?

Q. Also called *thromboangiitis obliterans*, which disease, affecting the peripheral arteries, occurs chiefly in men and is one of the causes of gangrene?

Q. Which French novelist who, despite his name, was not an aristocrat, died of gangrene in 1850 aged 51?

9 STARTER

Q. Chiefly a mixture of methane and other hydrocarbons, and explosive when mixed in certain proportions with air, combustable coal gas is commonly known by what name?

BONUS QUESTIONS

Three questions on the history of soft drinks:

Q. Which English scientist, better remembered as one of the discoverers of oxygen, has been called the 'father of the soft drinks industry' because of his experiments on gas obtained from the fermenting vats of a brewery?

Q. Which Geneva jeweller, having read the papers of Priestley, started manufacturing highly carbonated artificial mineral waters in the late eighteenth century, later starting a business in London?

Q. Which drink was invented in 1886 by John Pemberton, a pharmacist in Atlanta?

10 STARTER

Q. Which English novelist had the unusual middle name Klapka, although he generally used only its initial letter, and is particularly remembered for a humorous novel of 1889 recounting a rowing holiday on the Thames?

BONUS QUESTIONS

Q. The first stone of which fortress was laid on 22 April 1370 on the orders of Charles V of France, to protect his wall around Paris from the English, although it was first used in its more familiar role by Cardinal de Richelieu?

Q. After 1946, which prison in Berlin housed Nazi war criminals sentenced by the Allies?

Q. Which Moscow prison was originally the home of an insurance company but was taken over by 'Cheka' in the 1920s and became its headquarters and those of its successors, the NKVD and the KGB? It became notorious for the political assassinations which took place in its basement.

11 STARTER

Q. *Ad majorem dei gloriam* is the Latin motto adopted by which religious order, originally dedicated to missionary work but now more clearly distinguished as educators and scholars?

BONUS QUESTIONS

Q. Which under-secretary for defence, the heir of the Fifth Earl of Durham, resigned his position in 1973 after compromising photographs of him with a call girl called Norma Levy were offered to the press?

Q. The television presenter Lucinda Lambton, the daughter of Lord Lambton, married which former editor of the *Sunday Telegraph* and doyen of the right wing in 1991?

Q. According to a north-east folk song, what did a young member of the Lambton family catch whilst fishing on a Sunday, despite warnings that to do so was unlucky? His catch turned into a ferocious beast after he threw it into a well.

12 STARTER

Q. Which extinct elephantine mammal has a name derived from the breast-like cusps forming the grinding surfaces of its molars?

BONUS QUESTIONS

Three questions on films:

Q. In which science-fiction film of 1997 do six people, including a policeman called Quentin and a young mathematician called Leaven, find themselves one morning locked in an endless maze of chambers, most of which hold different unpleasant surprises?

Q. In which 1998 film, starring Dustin Hoffman and Sharon Stone, is a spaceship found submerged in the Pacific Ocean. Carbon dating reveals it to be 400 years old, although a computer keyboard is found which says made in USA 2048?

Q. In which 1998 film does Maximillian Cohen, a mathematical genius on the edge of insanity, build a super-computer which provides something that can be understood as a key for understanding all existence?

13 STARTER

Q. *The Prodigal Son, Romeo and Juliet* and *Cinderella* are ballets with music by which twentieth-century Russian composer?

BONUS QUESTIONS

Q. Which precious metal was discovered in the alluvial deposits of the Rio Pinto in Colombia and transported to Europe, the name given to it by the Spaniards reflecting its resemblance to silver?

Q. Which metal is often added to platinum to give a harder, stronger alloy, the prototype international standard kilogram having been made from this alloy?

Q. Platinum metals are used in which devices on cars, designed to reduce pollution?

14 STARTER

Q. In 1924, the Town of Simbirsk in western Russia was renamed Ulyanovsk in honour of which political figure, who was born there in 1870?

BONUS QUESTIONS

Three questions on popular misquotations:

Q. Which familiar four-word phrase indicates Sherlock Holmes' superior powers of deduction, although it is not found in any book by Sir Arthur Conan Doyle?

Q. Which familiar misquotation arose from a speech Harold Wilson gave to the Labour Party conference in 1963, describing Britain's forward-looking industrial practices?

Q. Which phrase is attributed to former chancellor Norman Lamont, although he did *not* use that form of words in his upbeat assessment of Britain's improving economic outlook, in a speech to the Conservative Party conference in 1991?

15 STARTER

Q. James Kirkup's poem 'The love that dares to speak its name' became the subject of a prosecution for blasphemous libel following its appearance in 1976 in which publication?

BONUS QUESTIONS

Q. In which American state is Mount Waialeale, often called the wettest spot on earth with an average annual rainfall of over 400 inches per annum?

Q. Captain James Cook, who is credited with the European discovery in 1778 of the Hawaiian Islands, gave which name to them?

Q. Travelling directly due east from Hawaii, on which country of the American mainland would you make landfall?

16 STARTER

Q. Caused by an infection carried by lice, which disease is characterized by relapsing fever, headaches, a pink rash and pains in the back and limbs, and was common amongst troops in World War I?

BONUS QUESTIONS

Three questions on nineteenth century French socialists:

Q. Which social theorist who died in Paris in 1837 advocated a society based on communal associations of producers called phalanges, one of the best known co-operatives based on his ideas being at Brook Farm, Massachussets, which lasted from 1841 to 1846?

Q. Étienne Cabet established a settlement at Nauvoo, Illinois, in the late 1840s which he called Icaria; which religious sect had lived at Nauvoo from 1839–1846?

Q. Louis-Auguste Blanqui was a revolutionary martyr figure of French socialism; what name was given to the uprising which broke out the day after his arrest on 17 March 1871?

17 STARTER

Q. The conjecture that there are no numbers 'x', 'y' and 'z', such that 'x' to the 'n' plus 'y' to the 'n' equals 'z' to the 'n', if 'n' is a positive integer greater than two, is usually known by what name?

BONUS QUESTIONS

Three questions on Olney in Buckinghamshire:

Q. What type of race is thought to have taken place for the first time in the village of Olney in Buckinghamshire, around 1445?

Q. Which of the Olney hymns, written in the village in the 1770s, provided the Royal Scots Dragoon Guards with a number one hit in April 1972?

Q. Which poet, translator and letter-writer lived in Orchard House, Olney, where he collaborated with the curate John Newton on a number of hymns including 'Amazing Grace'?

18 STARTER

Q. In law, which two-word Latin phrase is used to refer to 'the sum or aggregate of ingredients which make a given fact a breach of a given law'?

BONUS QUESTIONS

Q. A reptile has what sort of tongue if it is described as fissilingual?

Q. Which of Shakespeare's monarchs described unaccomodated man as, 'a poor bare, forked animal'?

Q. 'Lady Forkbender' was a character appearing in a spoof diary written by Richard Ingrams and John Wells. Whose diary was it supposed to be?

19 STARTER

Q. In Russian, Welsh and Greek respectively, what precisely are 'vosem', 'devyat' and 'desyat'; 'wyth', 'naw' and 'deg'; and 'okto', 'ennea' and 'deka'?

BONUS QUESTIONS

Three questions on a nineteenth-century radical group:

Q. What name was given to the groups of early nineteenth-century handicraftsmen, who broke up the textile machines that were replacing them?

Q. Which of the Romantic poets wrote 'A song for the Luddites', which was not published until 1830, six years after his death?

Q. Whose second published novel, *Shirley*, is set in Yorkshire at the time of the Luddite riots?

20 STARTER

Q. Which musical landmark is being described? Its first clients, in 1931, were Sir Edward Elgar and the London Symphony Orchestra. Pink Floyd became the band most associated with it after the break-up of the Beatles, who recorded an album there in 1969?

BONUS QUESTIONS

Q. Derived ultimately from the Greek for 'skin' or 'leather', what name is given to any small sac within the body found between tendon and bone, skin and bone or muscle and muscle, whose function is to facilitate movement without friction between these surfaces?

Q. Bursa was the first capital of which empire, created by Turkish tribes in Anatolia, which lasted from the decline of the Byzantine Empire until the establishment of Turkey as a republic in 1922?

Q. Classified as *Capsella bursa-pastoris*, what popular name is given to a common weed of the cabbage famly, and derives from its fruit's resemblance to an old-fashioned leather bag?

21 STARTER

Q. The Leferve Gallery in London's New Bond Street was, in 1945, the venue for an exhibition which included *Three Studies for Figures at the Base of a Crucifixion*, by which artist?

BONUS QUESTIONS

Three questions on language:

Q. Which word, derived from the Greek word for 'common', is used for a compromise language made up, usually, of several dialects of the same language but often heavily reliant on one dominant dialect?

Q. Which form of Greek, deriving from the Hellenistic Koine, was declared the official language of Greece in 1976?

Q. Which 'purist' variety of modern Greek was, until 1976, the official written form of Greek?

22 STARTER

Q. Which country's flag inspired that of Malaysia, although the latter has a star and crescent in its blue canton and 14 horizontal stripes rather than 13?

BONUS QUESTIONS

Three questions on Pythagorean triples:
What is the length of the hypoteneuse of a right-angled triangle, whose two shorter sides are as follows:

Q. 8 units and 15 units?

Q. 7 units and 24 units?

Q. 20 units and 21 units?

23 STARTER

Q. Which English businessman, in a speech to the Institute of Directors in April 1991, compared his own company's products unfavourably to a Marks and Spencer's prawn sandwich?

BONUS QUESTIONS

3 questions on German dogs:

Q. Which powerfully-built standard breed of dog with a wiry coat, shaggy whiskers and bushy eyebrows originated in Germany during the 15th century when it was used to kill rats, and takes its name from the German for 'snout'?

Q. Taking its name from the area of Germany in which it originated in the 1800s, which hunting dog usually has short smooth fur, a grey coat and nose and amber eyes?

Q. Developed in south Germany and descended from the camp dogs that followed Roman armies, which muscular breed has short black hair with tan markings on the head, chest and legs ?

24 STARTER

Q. Which colloquial term refers to the clustering of politicians around a speaker during a televised debate to make him or her appear well-supported, the term deriving from the name of a small fried cake?

BONUS QUESTION

Three questions on Russian and Soviet biologists:

Q. Literally meaning 'big eaters' in Greek, what name did the nineteenth century Russian biologist Elie Metchnikoff give to scavanger cells which are able to break down foreign particles in the body, and stimulate specific immune responses?

Q. What is the name of the ecological principle established by the Soviet biologist G.F. Gause and the American naturalist J. Grinnel, which states that two or more resource-limited species, having identical patterns of resource use, cannot co-exist in a stable environment?

Q. The Soviet biologist Ilya Ivanov, in his programme to develop new breeds of domestic animals more adaptable to the harsh Russian winters, is generally reckoned to be the first person to have used which technique?

25 STARTER

Q. What is the decimal equivalent of the fraction 9/25?

BONUS QUESTIONS

Identify the following British places from these unflattering descriptions in various tourist guides:

Q. First, which northern town is, quote: 'unrivalled worldwide as a taste-less dispenser of uninhibited fun'?

Q. Which Warwickshire town is described thus in *The Rough Guide*'?: 'this ordinary little place is nowadays all but smothered by package tourist hype and tea shoppe quaintness, representing the worst of England-land heritage marketing.'

Q. More terse words from *The Rough Guide*: which Sussex venue is, quote, 'on one level a repellent spectacle, its awns thronged with gentry and corporate bigwigs ingesting champagne and smoked salmon.'

26 STARTER

Q. In her book *Are You Sitting Comfortably?*, Julie Burchill described which 1950s children's television character as 'an effete prancing ... doll plas-tered in rouge and swathed in satin rompers – a great male role model'?

BONUS QUESTIONS

Three questions on a species of tree:

Q. The wood of which tree, with the Latin name *Fraxinus excelsior*, has been used to make handles for tools, oars and hockey sticks?

Q. In pre-Christian times, which people believed that the first man had been created from a piece of ash wood, and that a giant ash tree united heaven and hell?

Q. Glucoside fraxin, sometimes used as a tonic, is found in which part of the ash?

27 STARTER

Q. In order to score a maximum 147 break in snooker, how many consecu-tive pots have to be made?

BONUS QUESTION

Three questions on parliamentary posts:

Q. The treasurer of Her Majesty's household, the controller of her Majesty's Household and vice chamberlain of Her Majesty's household are posts held by which government members, responsible for party discipline?

Q. In the House of Lords, male whips are known as Lords-in-Waiting; by what name are their female counterparts known?

Q. What title is held by the deputy speaker of the House of Commons?

28 STARTER

Q. When converted into decimal currency, how much is 25 guineas?

BONUS QUESTIONS

Q. What is the English term for the Japanese ceremony of *cha-do*, which is rooted in Zen Buddhism and founded upon the adoration of the beautiful in the routine of daily life?

Q. *Tea with Mussolini* is an account of which film director's childhood in wartime Tuscany?

Q. Hybrid teas are the most popular class of which garden flowers?

29 STARTER

Q. Inspired by twelfth century Norse chessmen in the British Museum, which fictional character was created by Peter Firmin, and has a name which means 'small barrel'?

BONUS QUESTIONS

Three questions on men proclaimed prematurely dead:

Q. Born in 1835, which American writer was quoted in 1897 as saying, 'the report of my death was an exaggeration'?

Q. Which former Fairport Convention violinist read his obituary in the *Daily Telegraph* while recovering in hospital from a chest infection in April 1999?

Q. Which comedian, born in Britain in 1903, was eating his breakfast in June 1998 when his death was announced in Congress?

30 STARTER

Q. 'A total sale equal to one per cent of the current population of the continental United States in the decade in which it was published'. This is a definition of which adjective, often applied to popular books?

BONUS QUESTIONS

Three questions on economics and economists:

Q. Which members of the Fabian Society, along with R.B. Haldane, founded the 'London School of Economics and Political Science' in 1895?

Q. Who is the author of *The Third Way: The Renewal of Social Democracy*, who was appointed director of the LSE in 1997?

Q. Which of the Rolling Stones was a student at the LSE, although he left without taking his degree?

31 STARTER

Q. In Greek mythology, the goddesses Clotho, Lachesis and Atropos determined the birth, life and death of men and women, and were collectively known as whom?

BONUS QUESTIONS

Three questions on celebrity supporters of football clubs:

Q. Which American pop star revealed himself to be a Fulham supporter when he appeared at the ground with Mohammed al Fayed on Easter Saturday 1999, when 'his' team played Wigan Athletic?

Q. Which former Russian leader is said to have been a supporter of Wigan Athletic ever since he visited the town in 1969?

Q. Who, while promoting her biography by Andrew Morton in Britain, changed her allegiance from Newcastle United to Manchester United in the space of two days?

32 STARTER

Q. Which word can mean all of the following: the adjustment of the eye to a change in distance, a loan of money, a compromise, or living quarters?

BONUS QUESTIONS

Three questions on philosophical terms:

Q. What word derives from the Latin terms for 'alone' and 'self', and refers to the view that self-existence is the only certainty?

Q. What term derives from the Greek for 'to appear' or 'to show', and refers to the doctrine that physical objects can be reduced to sensory experiences?

Q. What loose term is used for the reaction, led by Kierkegaard, against the abstract rationalism of Hegel's philosophy?

33 STARTER

Q. Which term is derived from the words 'electricity' and 'magnet', and is used for a permanently electrified substance or body that has opposite charges at its extremities?

BONUS QUESTIONS

Three questions on the novels of Charles Dickens:

Q. Which eponymous Dickens hero goes to America to seek his fortune as an architect to the fraudulent 'Eden Land Corporation'?

Q. Who is found at the end of *David Copperfield* to be prospering as a much-respected colonial magistrate in Australia, finally relieved of his debt?

Q. In which novel does one of the title characters send his employee Walter Gay to the West Indies, because he disapproves of his daughter Florence's relationship with him?

34 STARTER

Q. Which is the largest taxonomic grouping used in the classification of organisms, with traditionally only two being used, all organisms being divided into plants or animals?

BONUS QUESTIONS

Q. All developed during the eighteenth and nineteenth centuries, what were 'Mersey flats', 'dukers' and 'Tom puddings'?

Q. What was the specific purpose of a canal boat called a 'lighter'?

Q. A 'dumb barge' is a barge without what?

35 STARTER

Q. The Portuguese for 'wine with garlic' is thought to be the derivation of the name of which very hot curry?

BONUS QUESTIONS

Three questions on the sky in poetry:

Q. Who wrote, in a letter to Maria Gisborne in 1820: 'we watched the ocean and the sky together,/under the roof of blue Italian weather'?

Q. Who wrote, in a collection first published in 1899: 'when shall the stars be blown about the sky, like the sparks be blown out of a smithy and die'?

Q. From which work of 1898 do the following lines come: 'I never saw a man who looked/with such a wistful eye/upon that little tent of blue/which prisoners call the sky'?

36 STARTER

Q. Which Middle Eastern capital city was known as Rabbah in biblical times, as Philadelphia to the ancient Greeks, and is now the capital of the Hashemite kingdom of Jordan?

BONUS QUESTIONS

Three questions on claimants to European thrones:

Q. The middle-aged South African businessman Leka Zogu, whose father was dethroned by Italian fascists in 1939, claimed to be the legitimate king of which country when he visited its capital in 1997?

Q. The Madrid business consultant Simeon Corburgotski claims to be the legitimate king of which country, having been deposed as Simeon II after a ballot by communists in 1946, which he claims was rigged?

Q. The London insurance broker Alexander Karadjordjevic claims the throne of which country, after his father fled the country in 1941 after the Nazi occupation and sought sanctuary at Claridge's?

37 STARTER

Q. The seventeeth-century antiquarian John Aubrey discovered a circle of 56 shallow holes, now named after him, at which site in Wiltshire?

BONUS QUESTIONS

Q. Which baseball star died in March 1999 at the age of 84, having been known as 'The Yankee Clipper' or 'Joltin' Joe'?

Q. Which Paul Simon song contains the line, 'Joltin' Joe has left and gone away'?

Q. Which Nobel prize-winning novelist wrote the lines: 'I would like to take the great Joe DiMaggio fishing. They say his father was a fisherman. Maybe he is as poor as we are and would understand'?

38 STARTER

Q. Which Russian city is this? Founded as a military outpost in 1860 and given a name meaning 'rule the east', it became the main Russian naval base on the pacific. Located on the coast of the Sea of Japan, it is the eastern terminus of the Trans-Siberian railway?

BONUS QUESTIONS

Three questions on modern art:

Q. Noted for his wrapped works, which sculptor was born in Bulgaria in June 1935 with the surname Javachev?

Q. One of Christo's first wrapped pieces was a portrait of which French actress, who starred in *And God Created Woman* in 1956?

Q. Christo's *Valley Curtain* of 1972 involved draping a woven nylon curtain across rifle valley in which American state?

39 STARTER

Q. Published in 1942, the report of which civil servant declared war on the five giants that threatened society; want, ignorance, disease, squalor and idleness?

BONUS QUESTIONS

Q. Which film of 1962 was directed by Bryan Forbes, starred Hayley Mills, and was based on a novel by her mother?

Q. Which poet wrote the lines, in 1788, 'tho' father and mother should baith gae mad,/o whistle, and I'll come to you, my lad'?

Q. Gomera, where the locals communicate from hilltop to hilltop in a whistling language, is one of which group of islands?

40 STARTER

Q. Which procedure would have been performed by a phlebotomist, often with the intention of lowering a fever or curing a headache?

BONUS QUESTIONS

Q. In August 1995, which British colony did what no other British colony has done in the twentieth century, when it voted against independence?

Q. Which former home secretary under Margaret Thatcher was governor of Bermuda from 1992 to 1997?

Q. Appointed Governor of Bermuda in 1943, what sporting distinction was achieved by David George Brownlow Cecil, Lord Burghley, in 1928?

41 STARTER

Q. 'Unlawful homicide with malice aforethought' is a general legal definition of which crime?

BONUS QUESTIONS

Three questions on the mathematics of Father Christmas' trip around the World delivering presents on Christmas Eve:

Q. According to UNICEF, there are about 2,100 million children in the world; assuming 2.5 children per household, how many stops must Santa make on Christmas Eve?

Q. Assuming all the homes are uniformly distributed across the planet's land masses which cover an area of about 52.5 million square miles, what is the distance between households?

Q. Assuming Santa starts at the international date line and travels against the Earth's rotation, giving him 48 hours to deliver the presents, to the nearest million miles per hour, at what speed must Santa travel?

42 STARTER

Q. In the plays of Shakespeare, what name is shared by the woman in love with Demetrius in *A Midsummer Night's Dream*, and the heroine of *All's Well That Ends Well*?

BONUS QUESTIONS

Three questions on politics:

Q. Which 12-year-old boy sold his collection of toy soldiers in 1973, and began devoting his attention to politics?

Q. Which seat did William Hague win at a by-election in February 1989, partly as a result of the SLD and Liberals both fielding candidates?

Q. To which post was William Hague appointed by John Major in 1995, to make him the youngest cabinet minister since Harold Wilson?

43 STARTER

Q. Which folk instrument of Austria and Southern Germany consists of between 30 to 45 strings over a sounding box, is played with a plectrum, and had perhaps its most celebrated usage in the theme to Carol Reed's *The Third Man*?

BONUS QUESTIONS

Q. In which Central American country did the constitution, promulgated in 1949, forbid the establishment or maintenance of an army?

Q. What was the name of the Costa Rican president awarded the Nobel Peace Prize in 1987 for his efforts to end the bloody struggles in Central America?

Q. Costa Rica is bounded by Nicaragua on the north, the Caribbean on the east and the Pacific to the south and west; with which country does it share its south-eastern border?

44 STARTER

Q. Which element is the heaviest of the group VII A, or halogen elements, and has 'At' as its chemical symbol?

BONUS QUESTIONS

Q. The title 'Infanta de Castile', referring to Eleanor of Castile who, at the age of ten in 1254 became the wife of the future King Edward I, is believed by some to be the origin of the name of which area of London?

Q. Which cabinet minister, after the volcanic damage in Montserrat prompted claims for compensation, said, quote: 'it'll be golden elephants next'?

Q. The Order of Knighthood 'the Order of the Elephant', is said to have been instituted in 1462 by Christian I, King of which European country?

45 STARTER

Q. Which fish is most properly the principal ingredient of the Scandanavian dish gravadlax?

BONUS QUESTIONS

Q. Which playwright became the guardian of the sons of his friend Sylvia Llewellyn-Davies after her death, and based his best-known play on stories he had first told them during walks in Kensington gardens?

Q. Which architect designed sets for Barrie's *Quality Street* and was involved in the design for *Peter Pan*, although it was credited to William Nicholson?

Q. The 'Peter Pan Cup' is competed for by swimmers in a 100-yard race in which stretch of water on Christmas Day?

46 STARTER

Q. Born Rodolpho d'Antonguolla in 1895, which actor's credits include *The Four Horsemen of the Apocalypse* and *Blood and Sand* in 1921, and *The Sheik* in 1922, his death in 1926 initiating a personality cult based on his reputation as a screen lover?

BONUS QUESTIONS

Three questions linked by a name:

Q. Which former Head of English at Gordano school in Bristol was appointed her Majesty's Chief Inspector of Schools at Ofsted in 1994, resigning in the year 2000?

Q. The three-mile-long Woodhead Tunnel which, when it was opened in 1845, was the longest in Britain, was on the now closed railway line between Manchester and which city?

Q. In January 1938, the British government appointed a commission under Sir John Woodhead to reconsider an earlier plan suggested by the Peel Commission for the partition of which of the world's troublespots?

47 STARTER

Q. Deriving from the Greek for 'middle', what name is given to the geological era which broadly coincides with the so-called 'age of dinosaurs', and extends over the Cretaceous, Jurassic and Triassic periods?

BONUS QUESTIONS

Q. Which Abbot of Malmesbury, and later Bishop of Sherbourne, lived from about 639 to 709, and is believed to be the author of a translation of the psalter into Anglo-Saxon?

Q. In which county are the headlands of Durlston Head and St Aldhelm's Head?

Q. St Aldhelm's church hall, in a fictional town supposedly near Eastbourne, featured prominently in which television series, first screened in 1968?

48 STARTER

Q. Which outmoded form of pension provision emerged in the seventeeth century, and consisted of an annuity shared by subscribers, the shares increasing as the subscribers died off, until the sole survivor got all the proceeds?

BONUS QUESTIONS

Three questions on the names of cities:

Q. Which African former capital city has a name which means 'house, or haven, of peace'?

Q. The shortened name of which South American seat of national government means 'the peace'?

Q. Which disputed capital city has a name thought to mean 'house of peace', or 'possession of peace'?

49 STARTER

Q. Born in 1926, which children's author is best known for a character who celebrated his fortieth birthday in 1998; he has said that he would have found the famous piercing stare of his ursine creation useful when coping with the Jesuits who educated him?

BONUS QUESTIONS

What do the following abbreviations stand for in the field of nuclear reactors?

Q. The 'mag' in the abbreviation magnox?

Q. PWR?

Q. The 'can' in the abbreviation 'candu'?

50 STARTER

Q. 'Kids are not sweet and innocent – they are mean and vindictive and they don't have any social graces. That's what makes them funny;' a quote from Matt Stone, co-creator of which animated series featuring Stan, Kyle, Cartman and Kenny?

BONUS QUESTIONS

Q. Which African country's name is derived from the Arabic for 'country of the blacks'?

Q. The Battle of Sedan in 1870 was the decisive battle in which war?

Q. In the 1998 Football World Cup final, Zinedine Zidane scored two of France's goals. Which player scored the third?

51 STARTER

Q. Born Amy Lyon in 1765, at 16 she became the mistress of Charles Greville MP, later becoming mistress to his uncle in return for the latter paying the former's gambling debts. In 1793, she met the man with whom her name is usually linked. Who was she?

BONUS QUESTIONS

Q. The Fields Medal, founded by a Canadian who died in 1932, is awarded every four years to someone under 40 in which academic field?

Q. The Fields Medal is made of solid gold and depicts the head of which famous Greek mathematician and inventor, who was killed by a Roman soldier in Syracuse in 212 BC?

Q. Scripted by its stars Matt Damon and Ben Affleck, and telling the story of a young layabout from Boston who is also a genius at mathematics, which film helped publicise the Fields Medal?

52 STARTER

Q. Which celebrated food product consists of a sun dried Bummalo fish, deep fried before serving, the supply of which is gradually dying out in this country due to EU legislation of 1997 banning the import of fish products from India?

BONUS QUESTIONS

Three questions on particle waves:

Q. Which French nobleman was the first to suggest that the dual wave-particle nature accepted for light might be extended to particles?

Q. The amplitude of a particle wave, or de Broglie wave, is conventially denoted by which Greek letter?

Q. What is the physical significance of the square modulus of the amplitude of a particle wave, mod psi squared?

53 STARTER

Q. 'The great crowd will feel proud,/seeing Barlow and Bates with the urn, the urn,/and the rest coming home with the urn'. These lines refer to which sporting trophy, which, it was revealed in 1998, may not contain what it is popularly supposed to?

BONUS QUESTIONS

Q. The Cullin Hills rise in the south of which Scottish island?

Q. With words by Harold Boulton set to a traditional sea shanty, 'The Skye Boat Song' commemorates whose escape from Benbecula to Skye, after Culloden?

Q. Like the Skye Terrier, which small black and tan dog was originally bred on the island to drive vermin out of rocky terrain?

54 STARTER

Q. In 1998, DNA analysis of remains found near the old Lehrter Railway Station in 1972, appear to prove that which high-ranking Nazi committed suicide in 1945, although conspiracy theorists remain sceptical?

BONUS QUESTIONS

Three questions on millennium monarchs:

Q. Otto III, crowned in 999, was ruler of which empire at the time of the first millennium?

Q. Basil II, known as 'Bulgaroctonus', or 'slayer of the Bulgars' was ruler of which empire at the time of the first millennium?

Q. Who was on the throne of England at the time of the last millenium?

55 STARTER

Q. In an atom or molecule, what is the value of the orbital angulas momentum or sub-shell quantum number of an electron in an s-orbital?

BONUS QUESTIONS

Q. Pristina is the capital of which autonomous region within the Republic of Serbia?

Q. Which people make up about 90 per cent of Kosovo's population?

Q. Which forces won a decisive victory over a Hungarian-Walachian coalition led by the Hungarian commander, Janos Hunyadi, at the battle of Kosovo in October 1448?

56 STARTER

Q. Which popular table-top game is thought to have been named after the inventor discovered he was unable to patent the word 'hobby' as a game title, and chose instead the taxonomic name of the small British falcon called the hobby?

BONUS QUESTIONS

Three questions on fish:

Q. Fish fall into three distinct classes; the agnatha are commonly known as jawless fish, the osteichthyes, are commonly known as bony fish, and as what are the other class, the chondrichthyes, commonly known?

Q. What general term is used for over two hundred species of chondrichthyes, characterized by placoid scales and numerous teeth arranged in rows?

Q. Placoid scales, from the Greek term for a flat plate, are common to sharks and to over three hundred species of which cartilaginous broad flat fish of the order Batoidei?

57 STARTER

Q. By what collective name are Blatt, Appleton, Appleton and Lewis known?

BONUS QUESTIONS

Q. The edible fruit of certain varieties of *Cucurbita pepo* are known in the USA as squash and by what other name?

Q. Which building on the south coast of England did William Hazlitt describe as being 'like a collection of stone pumpkins and pepper-boxes'?

Q. Who originally formed the group 'Smashing Pumpkins' in 1987 as a duo with bassist, D'Arcy, augmented by a drum machine?

58 STARTER

Q. Which imaginary creations live in a valley to the south of 'Daddy Jones kingdom', on the Gulf of Finland? They are small, white, hibernating creatures with large snouts, short tails and smooth hairless skin, and they communicate by whistling.

BONUS QUESTIONS

Q. What, in the Islamic religion, is the 'azan'?

Q. The muezzin's call to prayer begins with the words 'allahu akbar'; what does this mean?

Q. How many times a day does the muezzin make his call to prayer?

59 STARTER

Q. Who was killed on 25 August 1941, when his Sunderland flying boat crashed *en route* from Invergordon to Iceland, thus becoming the first son of a monarch to be killed on active service for five centuries?

BONUS QUESTIONS

Q. In political circles, what derogatory term is given to the circuit of fund-raising dinners, and refers to what is said to be the staple meat of such functions?

Q. Which French king is reputed to have said: 'I want there to be no peasant in my kingdom so poor that he is unable to have a chicken in his pot every Sunday'?

Q. Baba Yaga, a witch who lives in a house on chicken-legs and flies about in a mortar, using a pestle as an oar, is a character in the folklore of which country?

60 STARTER

Q. In the context of music, if his 4th is tragic, his 6th is little and his 9th is great, what is the problem with Schubert's 8th?

BONUS QUESTIONS

Q. Who was dubbed 'cap the knife' when serving as a cost-cutting, tax-reducing director of finance to Governor Ronald Reagan of California, and 'cap the ladle' when handing out billions to military projects when serving as Reagan's defence secretary?

Q. Steven Weinberg, Abdus Salam and Sheldon Glashow shared the 1979 Nobel Prize for physics for establishing the link between electromagnetic and which type of fundamental interaction?

Q. Which British mathematician in 1908 discovered independently of German physician Wilhelm Weinberg, the law jointly named after them which describes the genetic equilibrium within a population?

61 STARTER

Q. Originally called 'Le Manège Enchanté', featuring an English dog called Pollux who spoke French badly, what is the English title of the 400 eight-minute films by Serge Danot, rescripted by Eric Thompson, and later voiced by Nigel Planer?

BONUS QUESTIONS

Three questions about headlines:

Q. In a possibly apocryphal example of 'finding the local angle to a story', which event of April 1912 had the sub-headline in a Yorkshire paper 'Heckmondwyke man aboard'?

Q. A headline to celebrate the hundredth anniversary of which political anthem in 1989 ran 'Good tune, shame about the words'?

Q. What completes this headline in a popular tabloid after England, under Graham Taylor, lost a European soccer championship qualifying match to Sweden in June 1992. 'Swedes 2 ...'?

62 STARTER

Q. Now a generic term for all publishers of popular sheet music, what name was given to West 28th Street between Broadway and Sixth Avenue in Manhattan, where many fledgling music publishers had their offices?

BONUS QUESTIONS

Of which planets are the following the largest satellites:

Q. Titan?

Q. Titania?

Q. Triton?

63 STARTER

Q. In what context, in May 1998, did Arsenal beat Croydon at the New Den?

BONUS QUESTIONS

Q. Which Christian sect, originating in Asia Minor and Syria, takes its name from a Bishop of Constantinople whose views on the nature and person of Christ led to the calling of the Council of Ephesus in AD 431?

Q. According to the *Iliad* and the *Odyssey*, Nestor, reputedly the oldest of the Greek warriors, was king of where?

Q. What is the alternative name for the modern Greek town of Pilos by which the naval battle of 1827, at which Greek independence from the Turks was established, is known?

64 STARTER

Q. The trial of Madeleine Smith in 1857, on charges of poisoning her lover, is a celebrated example of a Scottish court awarding which verdict, establishing neither guilt nor innocence and criticised by some as 'not guilty, but don't do it again'?

BONUS QUESTIONS

Three questions on first symphonies:

Q. Which German composer's first symphony, first performed in 1841 under fellow composer Felix Mendelssohn, is known as the 'Spring Symphony'?

Q. Which Austrian composer's first symphony, originally subtitled 'Titan', was first performed in Budapest in 1889, its original five movements being reduced to four in 1896?

Q. Which Russian composer's first symphony, first performed in Petrograd in 1918 under his own conducting, is known as the 'Classical Symphony', being deliberately written in the style of Haydn?

65 STARTER

Q. Nitric acid has the chemical formula HNO_3, but which acid has the chemical formula HNO_2?

BONUS QUESTIONS

Q. Which of Ibsen's plays concerns the widow, Helen Alving, whose son Oswald suffers from a congenital disease, and uses venereal disease as a symbol of inherited and collective guilt?

Q. Which philosopher, in his book *The Concept of the Mind*, uses the phrase 'ghost in the machine' to describe the Cartesian tradition that the human body is somehow inhabited and operated by the non-physical spirit?

Q. Which group released the album *Ghost In The Machine*, which reached number two in the charts in October 1981?

66 STARTER

Q. The Alan Burgess book *The Small Woman* was filmed in 1958, starring Ingrid Bergmann, and was an account of the life of which missionary, who trekked for 27 days across war-torn China to save 100 children during the Sino-Japanese war?

BONUS QUESTIONS

Q. Which century saw the event that precipitated the final separation between the eastern Christian churches, led by Patriarch Michael Cerularius, and the western church, led by Pope Leo IX?

Q. In the Eastern Orthodox Church, the ecumenical patriarch of which city holds the titular or honorary primacy?

Q. Which church in Istanbul, built by the Emperor Justinian in the sixth century, was the centre of religious life in the Eastern Orthodox world?

67 STARTER

Q. In May 1998, a record was set at auction for a work by the artist Andy Warhol, when a buyer paid £10.5 million for a portrait of which film star and twentieth-century icon?

BONUS QUESTIONS

Q. What is the name of the structure in a green-plant cell within which photosynthesis takes place?

Q. Orthochlorobenzylidenemalononitrile, widely used as tear gas, is more commonly known by what name?

Q. Belonging to the genus *Chlorophytum*, what is the common name for the houseplant which has long, grassy, green and white striped leaves?

68 STARTER

Q. Which endangered primate, with species called red-bellied, broad-nosed, gentle and ring-tailed, is almost completely confined to diminishing forest areas of Madagascar?

BONUS QUESTIONS

Three questions on John Osborne plays:

Q. What is the name of the music hall comedian, played by Laurence Olivier in both the stage and film versions of Osborne's *The Entertainer*?

Q. Albert Finney has appeared on stage in the title role of which play by Osborne about a Protestant reformer?

Q. In which of Osborne's plays, first performed in 1964, did Nicol Williamson create the role of the alcoholic solicitor Bill Maitland?

69 STARTER

Q. 'I hate music' is a cycle of songs by which American composer, who also wrote a musical about the problems of housekeeping called *1600 Pennsylvania Avenue*, and the film score for *On The Waterfront*?

BONUS QUESTIONS

Q. Which board game is thought to have been introduced into Britain by the Vikings, was known as the royal game, and was the favourite of kings such as Richard I, Ivan the Terrible and Peter the Great, who carried special campaign boards made of soft leather?

Q. Which board game is renowned among philosophers as one of Hume's methods of recovery from philosophical melancholy and scepticism?

Q. In the 1998 World Cup edition of Monopoly, Brazil, predictably, is equivalent to Mayfair, and Switzerland, who did not qualify, is Whitechapel; which European country, who did qualify, was slighted by occupying the Old Kent Road site, the cheapest on the board?

70 STARTER

Q. Called the Minerva of the North for her wit and learning, which European monarch was taught philosophy by René Descartes, and was crowned queen in 1644, abdicating ten years later after her secret conversion to Roman Catholicism?

BONUS QUESTIONS

Q. By what name do we know the peninsula formed by a loop in the Thames, which is now the site of the London Docklands development?

Q. Which island group in the Atlantic derives its name from the large wild dogs which, according to Pliny, were found there?

Q. Which Hebridean island gives its name to the breed of terrier which originated on the island as a hunting dog?

71 STARTER

Q. Dolphin bent knee, barracuda back pike somersault, walkover front and ballet leg double are all figures in which aquatic activity, which became an Olympic competition sport in 1984?

BONUS QUESTIONS

Q. In which future state of the United States did both Americans and Mexicans become disgruntled with Mexican rule after General Lopez de Santa Anna became president, declaring an independent republic in 1836?

Q. In which future American state did the 'Bear Flag' revolt take place in 1846, American settlers rebelling against Mexican authorities and declaring an independent republic?

Q. After the Mexican-American war of 1846 to 1848, the territory known as New Mexico was ceded to the United States, and eventually became two states of the union; one was New Mexico, which was the other?

72 STARTER

Q. In gambling, how many separate bets make up a 'yankee', covering four horses in all possible combinations of doubles, trebles and an accumulator?

BONUS QUESTIONS

Q. Which affectionate diminutive of a word for a 'little child' has come to be used in the twentieth century as a slang term for a type of young woman, especially those in whom a superficial attractiveness outweighs intelligence?

Q. 'Tetty' was the name given to Elizabeth Porter by which writer, many years her junior, whom she married in 1735?

Q. Titty, John, Susan and Roger are the central characters in which children's novel, published in 1930 and set in the Lake District?

73 STARTER

Q. Which two-word phrase, now meaning any period of great success, enjoyment or activity, originally applied to an occasion when troops were taken on outdoor exercises or manoeuvres?

BONUS QUESTIONS

Q. What term is used for a person who can attend a court hearing as the friend and adviser of either party, but may not address the court, the term arising from the parties involved in a case heard in the Court of Appeal in 1970?

Q. In which Lennon and McCartney song did Father McKenzie write 'the words of a sermon that no one will hear'?

Q. What name was given to the device invented by the political scientist and broadcaster Robert McKenzie, to illustrate the shifting fortunes of the major parties during the announcement of election results?

74 STARTER

Q. Which hill in County Meath in the Irish Republic was the site of the residence of the high kings of Ireland until around the beginning of the sixth century?

BONUS QUESTIONS

Three questions on fictional doctors:

Q. In which of Shakespeare's plays is the French physician doctor Caius a suitor for the hand of Anne Page?

Q. *Doctor Thorne*, first published in 1858, is the third in which series of novels by Anthony Trollope?

Q. In which novel by George Eliot does the ambitious Doctor Tertius Lydgate make a disastrous marriage with the beautiful Rosamund Vincy?

75 STARTER

Q. Also known as animal starch, which polysaccharide is the major store of carbohydrate energy in animal cells?

BONUS QUESTIONS

Q. What name is given to the metal bar or framework, originally fitted to the front of vehicles to protect them against collisions with animals, but which is now likely to be a fashion accessory?

Q. The Oxford, nicknamed the 'bullnose', which first appeared in 1913 and was built at Cowley, was the first car from which company, whose founder later became Lord Nuffield?

Q. Which American statesman said of himself in 1900, shortly before he became president: 'I am as strong as a bull moose and you can use me to the limit', thus giving rise to 'bull moose' as a popular name for the progressive party?

76 STARTER

Q. Which 12-a-side field game, native to the Scottish highlands, uses a leather-covered cork ball, and a club the head of which must pass through a ring two and a half inches in diameter?

BONUS QUESTIONS

Q. In the Bible who is assisted by Nicodemus in wrapping the body of Jesus according to Jewish burial customs?

Q. Joseph Barsabbas was a candidate for which biblical vacancy?

Q. Joseph, son of Jacob, was so hated by his siblings that they plotted to kill him; which brother urged the others not to take his life but to throw him into a pit instead?

77 STARTER

Q. Amongst the titled prime ministers of the nineteenth century, which was the highest-ranked of the following five names: Liverpool, Derby,

Salisbury, Aberdeen and Rosebery, four of them being earls and one a marquess?

BONUS QUESTIONS

Three question on the 1999 Queen's Birthday Honours:

Q. Which former 5,000-metres world record holder was granted the OBE for his work in salvaging British athletics from the wreckage of the British Athletics Federation, which went into liquidation in 1997?

Q. Which playwright was awarded a CBE for services to literature, whose work has included adaptations of Somerset Maugham's *The Moon and Sixpence* for the screen?

Q. Deborah Bull was made a CBE for services to which field of the arts?

78 STARTER

Q. Winter Daydreams, Little Russian, Polish and Pathetique are four of the six symphonies by which composer, who died in mysterious circumstances in 1893?

BONUS QUESTIONS

Q. Alecto, Megaira and Tisiphone were spirits of vengeance in Greek mythology known collectively as the Erinyes or Eumenides; what name were they given in Roman legend?

Q. *Eumenides*, *Agamemnon* and *Choephoroe* comprise which trilogy by Aeschylus that tells of the fate of Agamemnon's son who is pursued by the furie?

Q. Which American-born writer turned to Aeschylus' play *Eumenides* for the basis of his 1939 drama *The Family Reunion*?

79 STARTER

Q. Whose likeness, along with those of Generals Robert E. Lee and Thomas 'Stonewall' Jackson, is included on the giant Confederate memorial at Stone Mountain in Georgia, because he was president of the Confederacy throughout the civil war?

BONUS QUESTIONS

Three questions on systems of writing:

Q. What name, derived in part from the Latin for 'painted', describes a writing system such as hieroglyphics, in which concepts or words are represented in the form of a sketch or diagram?

Q. Syllabaries are writing systems in which each symbol represents a syllable rather than a concept; which is the only major language using this system today?

Q. Thought to be distantly related to Japanese with a similar grammatical structure, which language is written in a phonetic script called onmun, devised in the mid-fifteenth century to replace the Chinese characters previously in use?

80 STARTER

Q. In nautical superstition, fiddler's green is a place of Elysian happiness; what is its antithesis, the sailors' equivalent of hell?

BONUS QUESTIONS

Three questions on drugs:

Q. Quote: 'O mickle is the powerful grace that lies/in herbs, plants and stones and their true qualities/for naught so vile that on earth doth live / but to the earth some special good doth give.' Which of Shakespeare's characters speaks these lines from his retreat in Verona?

Q. Which toxic semi-metallic element is important in the manufacture of conductors, alloys and solders, was formerly used in medicine for the treatment of syphilis, and has the atomic number 33?

Q. Atropine, the drug used medicinally as a muscle relaxant in the treatment of colic and peptic ulcers, is derived from a toxic alkaloid present in which plant?

81 STARTER

Q. What weighs about thirteen and a half tons, and, according to the inscription on its lip, 'was cast by George Mears of Whitechapel for the clock of the Houses of Parliament under the direction of Edmund Beckett Denison QC, in the 21st year of the reign of Queen Victoria'?

BONUS QUESTIONS

Q. In the Old Testament who refused to curse God despite being 'smote with sore boils from the sole of his foot unto his crown'?

Q. Which nineteenth-century English artist painted 'Satan smiting Job with sore boils', a work that hangs in the Tate Britain?

Q. Which double collection of his lyric poetry did William Blake describe as 'showing the two contrary states of the human soul'?

82 STARTER

Q. Which fictional character, during the course of a trial, became so annoyed by the squeaky slate pencil being used by one of the jury, a lizard called Bill, that she snatched it away from him?

BONUS QUESTIONS

Q. What epithet was given to Elizabeth, eldest daughter of James I of England, on account of her husband, Frederick V, having been chosen as King of Bohemia in 1619?

Q. Britain's 'winter of discontent', under James Callaghan's government, began in which year and was marked by high levels of industrial unrest and strike action?

Q. Shakespeare's *Winter's Tale* centres around the jealous tyranny of which King of Sicilia?

83 STARTER

Q. Which footballer, nicknamed 'giraffe', won 35 England caps during his long career with Leeds United, and went on, in 1986, to manage the Republic of Ireland's team?

BONUS QUESTIONS

Q. Habib Bourguiba was the architect of which country's independence, becoming its first president in 1957 and remaining in power for 30 years?

Q. In which African country in 1943 did the nationalist movement take the new title of Independent Party or Hizb Al-Istiqlal?

Q. In 1964 Ghana was officially designated a one-party state with which man as life president of both nation and party, although he was to be overthrown two years later?

84 STARTER

Q. How is Joseph Hobson Jagger described in the title of Fred Gilbert's music-hall song, of which the chorus runs: 'as I walk along the Bois de Boulogne with an independent air you can hear the girls declare, "he must be a millionaire" '?

BONUS QUESTIONS

Three questions about the French revolution:

Q. Which revolutionary political group drew most of its members from the wealthiest sections of society and derived its name from the fact that it rented premises in Paris from the Dominicans?

Q. When his expectations of high office evaporated, journalist and revolutionary Jacques-René Hebert turned against the Jacobins and accused which body, the first strong government in France since the revolution began, of tyranny?

Q. Which one of the nine original members of the Committee of Public Safety, who abandoned the law for politics after the revolution had begun, helped plan the attack on the Tuileries in 1792 and became Minister of Justice shortly afterwards?

85 STARTER

Q. What form of protein secondary structure describes a polypeptide chain's helical structure stabilized by hydrogen bonds between peptide groups?

BONUS QUESTIONS

Three questions about Glasgow bands:

Q. Formed in 1985, which group received the inspiration for their name from the title of a Steely Dan song and had a major breakthrough with the 1988 single 'Real Gone Kid'?

Q. Which band debuted in 1989 with the top ten single 'I Don't Want a Lover' and top five album *Southside*, although it was another three years before their next top 20 single, a cover of Al Green's 'Tired of Being Alone'?

Q. Who is both bass player and lead vocalist with the group Del Amitri?

86 STARTER

Q. Which deity, whose name means literally 'feathered serpent', was the Aztec and Toltec god of the morning and evening star?

BONUS QUESTIONS

Q. The seventeenth century work with the Greek title *Eikon Basilike*, meaning 'image of a king', is a collection of meditations and prayers supposedly written by which English monarch while in captivity ?

Q. *Eikonoklastes*, also published in 1649, defended the regicides against the impact of *Eikon Basilike* and was the work of which English poet?

Q. For what did John Milton argue in his pamphlet *Areopagitica*, provoked by parliament's imposition of a censorship no less strenuous than the king's?

87 STARTER

Q. Who was the only British prime minister ever to be married to a divorcee, their wedding taking place at Wesley's Chapel in London on 13 December 1951?

BONUS QUESTIONS

Q. According to Joseph Stalin, one death is a tragedy but what do one million deaths constitute?

Q. Which Roman poet and satirist of the first century BC wrote, 'we are just statistics, born to consume resources'?

Q. Twentieth-century Scottish man of letters Andrew Lang once described statistics as being used for support rather than illumination, in the same way that a drunken man uses what?

88 STARTER

Q. Which standard medical textbook, with illustrations by H.V. Carter, was written by Henry Gray in 1858?

BONUS QUESTIONS

Q. The first arms of England, consisting of three golden lions walking and looking outwards on a red shield, appeared on the great seal struck for which king?

Q. To emphasize his claim to the French throne, which English King quartered the French arms with the lions of England in his great seal of 1340?

Q. In 1346 who won the insignia of the Prince of Wales, namely three ostrich plumes together with the motto *ich dien*?

89 STARTER

Q. Which novel did Virginia Woolf condemn as 'the scratching of pimples on the body of the bootboy at Claridges', the book's entire action taking place on 16 June 1904, as Stephen Dedalus and Leopold Bloom wander through Dublin?

BONUS QUESTIONS

Three questions on cities in Pakistan:

Q. A former military station controlling the routeways to Kashmir, which industrial city in Punjab province was interim capital of Pakistan in the 1960s during the construction of Islamabad?

Q. Lying between the Ravi and the Sutlej Rivers, which city is a World Heritage Site that includes the royal fort of Akbar and the Shalimar Gardens among its notable features?

Q. Centrally located in the Punjab plain and having air connections with Lahore and Karachi, which city was founded in 1890 and named after Sir Charles Lyall, Lieutenant Governor of the Punjab, until it adopted its present name in 1979?

90 STARTER

Q. Which actor, who appeared in *Scarface*, *Name Of The Rose* and *Bonfire of the Vanities*, won an Oscar in 1985 for his performance as the composer Salieri in *Amadeus*?

BONUS QUESTIONS

Q. What is the alternative name for the sunda double trench, a deep submarine depression in the eastern Indian Ocean which, for about half its length, is divided into two by an underwater ridge south of Sumatra?

Q. Discovered in 1891 at Trinil in Java, the thighbone and part of the skull of Java man were the first known fossils of which species of early man?

Q. Also called Java cotton or ceiba, which lightweight fibre is too brittle for spinning and has been used in water-safety equipment, and also as insulation or stuffing material?

91 STARTER

Q. Which captain of artillery in the Russian army was arrested in 1945 for writing a letter critical of Stalin, and spent eight years in prison and labour camps, later writing a novel, *The First Circle*, based partly on his experience of working in a prison research institute as a mathematician?

BONUS QUESTIONS

Three questions on insects:

Q. In insects, why are the stridulatory organs so called?

Q. Crickets produce a characteristic chirping sound through friction generated by rubbing together which parts of their bodies?

Q. The males of which long-lived insects, found mainly in tropical regions, produce a loud, almost continuous chirping by vibrating membranes in resonating cavities of their abdomens?

92 STARTER

Q. The feast day of which saint and martyr is marked each year with the blessing of two lambs in a church in Rome, their wool going to make the Pallia sent by the Pope to archbishops as tokens of jurisdiction?

BONUS QUESTIONS

Three questions on types of modern fiction:

Q. Which two-word term derives in part from a type of stove, and is applied to novels , usually with a rural setting, which describe the emotional and domestic lives of middle class characters?

Q. What two-word term denotes a romantic novel with an historical setting, the plot of which features the seduction of the heroine?

Q. What three-word term refers to the genre of popular fiction in which characters have an expensive consumer lifestyle and enjoy frequent and varied sexual encounters?

93 STARTER

Q. In which country was civil war averted in 1481 by the Diet of Stans, a treaty between eight rural and urban cantons?

BONUS QUESTIONS

Q. From the Italian for 'repentance', which art term refers to the reappearance in an oil painting of original elements that the artist tried to obliterate by overpainting; one of the most famous examples being a double hat brim in Rembrandt's *Flora*?

Q. *Pentimento*, published in 1973, is one of the volumes of autobiography of which American playwright and screenwriter, whose works include *The Autumn Garden* and *The Little Foxes*?

Q. When Lillian Hellman's marriage to the playwright Arthur Kober ended in divorce in 1932 she had already formed a romantic alliance with which writer of detective fiction, a relationship that continued until his death in 1961?

94 STARTER

Q. To which type of bird was *The Angling* Times referring in December 1996, when it printed the controversial headline 'these birds must be killed', which brought in over 60 thousand letters of support?

BONUS QUESTIONS

Three questions on the Spanish civil war:

Q. The Nationalists are said to have lost the opportunity to conquer Madrid in 1936, largely due to General Franco's diversion to Toledo to relieve supporters besieged in which fortress?

Q. In May 1937, in the face of mounting dissent from communists, socialists and republicans, who stepped down as Spanish prime minister to be replaced by Juan Negrin?

Q. What name was given to the forces of foreign volunteers organized in Paris by the Comintern to fight on the Republican side against Franco?

95 STARTER

Q. According to Vasari's *Lives of the Painters*, which Florentine artist, when asked to send a design to the Pope, drew a perfect freehand circle to show his skill?

BONUS QUESTIONS

Three questions on hymns:

Q. What is the first line of the hymn whose first verse ends, 'our shield and defender, the ancient of days/pavilioned in splendour and girded with praise'?

Q. What, precisely, is the second line of the hymn that begins, 'Now thank we all our God'?

Q. Which hymn's three verses all end with the chorus 'all good gifts around us/are sent from heaven above;/then thank the Lord, O thank the Lord,/for all his love'?

96 STARTER

Q. Which lipid is a major component of animal cell membranes, occurs rarely in plants, and is a precursor of steroid hormones, elevated levels of it in human blood indicating a risk of heart disease?

BONUS QUESTIONS

Three questions on C. S. Lewis:

Q. 1998 saw the centenary of C.S. Lewis's birth; in which city was he born?

Q. Which mountain range, extending for nine miles between Newcastle and Rostrevor in County Down, has been suggested to be the model for Narnia?

Q. Although not the first to be written, which of the 'Narnia' stories is the first in chronological order, its narrative pre-dating that of *The Lion, The Witch and the Wardrobe*?

97 STARTER

Q. Once believed to prevent intoxication, which gemstone derives its name from the Greek word for 'not drunk', is the birthstone for February, and is a purple variety of quartz?

BONUS QUESTIONS

Three questions on arches:

Q. Dating from 312 AD, the arch near the Colisseum at the north of the Via Di Saint Gregoria in Rome is named after which emperor?

Q. Now sited at the north-east corner of Hyde Park, Marble Arch originally stood as the entrance to which building?

Q. The Arc de Triomphe, commemorating the victories of Napoleon, was designed by which French architect?

98 STARTER

Q. The name of which large black urban complex in South Africa, near Johannesburg, is an acronym for 'south-west township'?

BONUS QUESTIONS

Three questions on record labels established by rock stars:

Q. Which former Beatle founded the 'Dark Horse' record label in 1974?

Q. Alanis Morrisette's album *Jagged Little Pill* was a major success for which record label, founded by Madonna?

Q. Who founded the 'Paisley Park' label in his native Minneapolis in 1985?

99 STARTER

Q. Which Athenian comic dramatist was the author of more than one hundred plays, and is thought to have drowned while swimming at Piraeus, having warned that 'whom the gods love, dies young'?

BONUS QUESTIONS

Three questions on 'Johnsons', and their nicknames:

Q. What nickname was given to the basketball player Earvin Johnson, who retired from the sport in 1991?

Q. What nickname was given to the clergyman Hewlett Johnson, ordained in 1905, who became Dean of Manchester in 1924, and Dean of Canterbury in 1931? An untiring champion of communist ideals, he received the Stalin Peace Prize in 1951.

Q. What was the nickname of the American temperance worker and law enforcer William Eugene Johnson, the name deriving from his stealthy night-raids on gambling saloons? He famously lost an eye during scuffles following a lecture on temperance to British students, who were convinced he'd come to take away their beer?

100 STARTER

Q. Bobbins, yorkies, dorks and favours are all forms of currency in a locally based economic system, which has thousands of members in the UK, and which is commonly known by what four letter acronym?

BONUS QUESTIONS

Q. From the Greek for 'a turn', which five-letter word is now used mainly for a figure of speech, but is also used for a musical embellishment in medieval Christian liturgy?

Q. What name is given to the genus of plants belonging to the *Boraginaceae*, because they turn their flowers and leaves towards the sun?

Q. Which vegetable is a member of the sunflower family, and has a name which is thought to derive in part from a corruption of the Italian 'gira-sole', meaning that it, too, turns towards the sun?

101 STARTER

Q. What writing system did the Irish-born inventor, John. R. Gregg, develop in the 1880s, basing his system on the natural movements of the human hand, though a more popular system had already been created by Isaac Pitman in the 1830s?

BONUS QUESTIONS

What does the letter 'p' stand for in the following computer abbreviations?

Q. AGP?

Q. PCI?

Q. PCL?

102 STARTER

Q. The names of the bones in which part of the body can be recalled by the mnemonic 'some lovers try positions that they can't handle', representing the eight bones scaphoid, lunate, triquetrum, pisiform, trapezium, trapezoid, capitate and hamate, which make up the joint?

BONUS QUESTIONS

Three questions on film people who have achieved success in other fields:

Q. Which film actress was born Hedwig Kiesler in Vienna in 1913, and was involved in secret telecommunications work during World War II which led ultimately to the development of today's secure military communications?

Q. Which art collector and connoisseur was the author of *Drawings of Delacroix* in 1962 and *The Michelangelo Bible* in 1965, and was also the co-author with his second wife of a series of cookery books, but is more popularly known for his appearances in horror films?

Q. Which Italian actress retired from the screen in the 1970s to pursue a career as a professional photographer, and directed the documentary film *Portrait of Fidel Castro* in 1975?

103 STARTER

Q. Which river in Northern France was the scene of the major battle of 1916, during which British tanks were deployed for the first time, a battle that became a byword for pointless slaughter?

BONUS QUESTIONS

Q. What name is given to investment funds that make sophisticated financial bets with money from wealthy investors, often using the money to speculate on relative differences in interest rates among securities?

Q. Born in 1897, which writer's career began with the publication of *Child Whispers* in 1922, and later included bulletins of her home life at 'Green Hedges' near Beaconsfield?

Q. The oval-leafed Japanese species of which shrub has largely replaced the native species *Ligustrum vulgare* for use in hedging?

104 STARTER

Q. Theatre owner George Melies's offer for which new invention, in Paris, in 1895, was rejected with the words, '... my invention is not for sale... it can be exploited for a certain time as a scientific curiosity, but it has no commercial value whatsoever'?

BONUS QUESTIONS

Three questions on political movements of the 1990s:

Q. Which political party was founded in March 1992 to promote the ideas of the Maharishi Mahesh Yogi?

Q. Which political and religious movement was founded in Kandahar in the 1990s under the leadership of Mullah Mohammed Omar?

Q. Who founded the controversial One Nation party in Ipswich, a suburb of Brisbane, on 11 April 1997?

105 STARTER

Q. Used for astronomical observation, a large reflector over 12 feet in diameter is situated on Mauna Kea in Hawaii, and is known by the initials UKIRT. The UK stands for United Kingdom; what do the letters IRT stand for?

BONUS QUESTIONS

Q. Which fantasy role-playing game, created by Dave Arneson and Gary Gygex, was first marketed in 1974 and was an evolutionary advance on earlier computer wargames?

Q. In which opera does Leonora disguise herself as a man to try to rescue her husband, Florestan, from the dungeon where he is slowly starving to death?

Q. What is the common name for the genus of lizards that includes the world's largest lizard, the Komodo Dragon, which can reach up to three metres in length?

106 STARTER

Q. What name is given to the receptors in blood vessels that are sensitive to pressure or changes in pressure?

BONUS QUESTIONS

Three questions on magazines of the 1990s:

Q. From 1988 to 1994, Redwood Publishing Ltd was majority owned by which organization, publishing several of its leading magazines including *Gardener's' World*, *Sport* and *Wildlife*?

Q. Apparently aimed at a readership with a high disposable income, which magazine was launched by Tyler Brule and describes itself as being about 'the stuff that surrounds you'?

Q. Which magazine was launched in April 1994 under the editorship of James Brown, and has become synonymous with the phenomenon known as 'the new lad'?

107 STARTER

Q. Which letter is the only descender to be seen when the word 'conflagration' is printed in lower-case type?

BONUS QUESTIONS

Q. Which word comes from a Greek mispronunciation of the name of the river Sindhu, which also gave its name to the Indus Valley civilization which flourished in India between 2500 and 1500 BC?

Q. In Hinduism, what name is given to the concept that every action has a consequence which will come to fruition in a future life?

Q. From the Sanskrit for 'yoking' or 'joining', what name is given to the means or techniques for transforming consciousness and attaining liberation, this control of consciousness being taught by a guru?

108 STARTER

Q. What word, in a mining context, can mean the washing away of surface soil to expose bedrock and a request for silence?

BONUS QUESTIONS

Three questions on philosophers:

Q. Which German word, usually translated as 'dread', was used by the Danish philosopher Kierkegaard in the title of his work of 1844?

Q. Born in 1889, which German philosopher used the same term to describe a sense of unease concerning the structure of one's life, which is usually translated as 'anxiety'?

Q. A broadly similar phenomenon was described by the French term *angoisse*, usually translated as 'anguish', by which French philosopher, playwright and novelist?

109 STARTER

Q. Of which British company was Rolls-Royce a division until its sale in 1998?

BONUS QUESTIONS

Three questions on synthesizers in pop:

Q. 'Son Of My Father', the first chart-topping single to feature a synthesizer, was recorded by which group?

Q. Which tape-driven strings, choir and flute synthesizer was used on 1960s classics such as 'Strawberry Fields Forever' and the Moody Blues' 'Nights In White Satin'?

Q. Which singer-songwriter installed a Fairlight synthesizer and sampler at her home, first using it for her 1985 album *Hounds Of Love*, which entered the charts at number one?

110 STARTER

Q. Which woman scientist, born in Edinburgh, obtained a doctorate in botany from the University of Munich in 1904, taught at Manchester University, and wrote books entitled *Married Love* and *Wise Parenthood*, before opening the first instructional clinic for birth control in London, in 1921?

BONUS QUESTIONS

Q. Which Indian poet, philosopher and Nobel laureate was knighted in 1915 by George V, but renounced his knighthood in 1919 following the Amritsar massacre of 400 Indian demonstrators by British troops?

Q. Keshab Chandra Sen, who was much influenced by Christianity, became the third leader of which movement, founded in 1843 by Rabindranath Tagore's father, Debendranath?

Q. Which economist, noted for his work on poverty and famine, was born in Shantiniketan in 1933, and was awarded the Nobel Prize for economics in 1998?

111 STARTER

Q. The Ming Dynasty, the last native dynasty to rule China, did so for nearly 300 years, until the middle of which century?

BONUS QUESTIONS

Q. Now in Paris, which statue was created in Antioch about 150 BC and was discovered by Admiral Dumont D'Urville in 1820?

Q. In Roman mythology, who was the husband of Venus?

Q. Named in honour of a Portuguese navigator, which space probe in 1990 sent back the first high-resolution radar images of the planet Venus?

112 STARTER

Q. Michael Portillo was one of the most senior Conservatives to lose his seat in the 1997 general election. Which cabinet post did he hold immediately prior to the election?

BONUS QUESTIONS

Three questions on Latin phrases about death:

Q. Describing it as 'the old lie', which of the war poets borrowed from Horace the line: *dulce et decorum est pro patria mori*?

Q. Which Scottish-born novelist wrote a mordant study of old age entitled *Memento Mori*, first published in 1959?

Q. Which seventeenth-century French painter's works include *Et in arcadia ego*, the title meaning in this context 'I, death, am also in arcadia'?

113 STARTER

Q. What was the name of the eighteenth-century movement, involving Goethe and Schiller, that rebelled against literary conventions and sought a return to 'nature'?

BONUS QUESTIONS

Three questions on Americans abroad:

Q. The American writer Gertrude Stein became a leading figure in the artistic and literary circles of which European city, to which she moved in 1903 and where, in the thirties, she wrote *The Autobiography of Alice B. Toklas*?

Q. Which novel by Henry James recounts the efforts made, through personal emissaries, by an American widow to recall her son, Chadwick, from his sojourn in Paris with the beguiling Comtesse de Vionnet?

Q. Who in 1928 was the composer of the tone poem 'An American in Paris'?

114 STARTER

Q. What, in criminal law, is understood by the term *mens rea*?

BONUS QUESTIONS

Three questions on re-located capital cities:

Q. Formerly at Dar es Salaam, the capital of Tanzania was transferred in 1974 to which city?

Q. Following major hurricane damage to the previous capital, Belmopan was established in 1970 as the capital city of which Central American country?

Q. In 1975, Lilongwe replaced Zomba as the capital of which country?

115 STARTER

Q. Which play by Noel Coward takes its title from the opening line of a poem by Shelley, and features the medium Madame Arcati?

BONUS QUESTIONS

Three questions on dates:

Q. In the context of the church calendar, what links the 1 March, 17 March, 23 of April and the 13 November?

Q. Since the fifteenth century, what two-word terms have applied in England, Wales and Northern Ireland to the 25 March, 24 June, 29 September and 25 December?

Q. What is celebrated privately on 21 April, and ceremonially on 12 June?

116 STARTER

Q. In statistics, what is the name of the probability distribution in which the mean equals the variance, and which predicts the random occurrence of events in either space or time?

BONUS QUESTIONS

Three questions on composers' finances:

Q. Having fled from Vienna to escape imprisonment for debt, which composer was saved from ruin in 1864 by the patronage of Louis II of Bavaria?

Q. The work of which Austrian-born composer was financed by the Esterhazy family, with whom he remained intermittently in service from 1761 until 1790?

Q. The financial independence of which French composer, married to the Shakespearean actress Harriet Smithson, was secured temporarily by a gift from Paganini for whom the symphony 'Harold En Italie' was written?

117 STARTER

Q. The inhabitants of which island group in the Outer Hebrides were evacuated in 1930, ending settlement there which had been continuous since prehistoric times; the islands now constitute a World Heritage Site supporting the world's largest population of gannets?

BONUS QUESTIONS

Three questions on Christ's disciples:

Q. Which of the disciples was a fisherman and the brother of John, and was among those chosen by Christ to witness his transfiguration and his agony in the Garden of Gethsemane?

Q. Upon which of his apostles did Christ confer the keys to the Kingdom of Heaven?

Q. In modern times a patron saint of desperate causes, which disciple was also called Thaddaeus or Labbaeus?

118 STARTER

Q. Which English architect, a leading exponent of the Victorian neo-Gothic, designed the Natural History Museum, Manchester Town Hall and the original buildings for both Liverpool and Manchester Universities?

BONUS QUESTIONS

Q. Which cartoon character, created by Mary Tourtel in 1920, lived at Nutwood Cottage?

Q. Set in a fictional European kingdom, *Rupert of Hentzau* is the sequel to which romantic novel by Anthony Hope, first published in 1894?

Q. The Prague-born English royalist commander, Prince Rupert of the Rhine, was the grandson of which monarch?

119 STARTER

Q. Which word describes physical symptoms or disorders caused, or aggravated, by emotional or mental factors?

BONUS QUESTIONS

Three questions on disguises:

Q. In which Shakespearean comedy does a disguise adopted by Viola persuade the sea captain, Antonio, to mistake her for her twin brother, Sebastian?

Q. Lieutenant M.E. Clifton James became a significant figure during World War II when, at Gibraltar immediately prior to the Allied invasion of Normandy in June 1944, he appeared in public disguised as which British officer?

Q. Which American journalist adopted the thin disguise of 'Raoul Duke' for his spree on the Las Vegas strip, recounting his antics in a work first published in book form in 1972?

120 STARTER

Q. In what context have the ancient country skills of 'tickling' and 'groping' been outlawed since 1975?

BONUS QUESTIONS

Q. Popularized in the 1920s, which French word originally meant a professional male dancing partner or escort, and is now used for a man who is kept by an older woman?

Q. Who played the title role of Julian Kay, a male prostitute falsely accused of murdering a client in the 1980 film *American Gigolo*?

Q. Whose career has included a stint writing for the erotic magazine *Forum*, a piece entitled 'The Riviera Gigolo' being one of his contributions, as well as being political editor of *The Mirror* newspaper and, from 1994, press secretary to Tony Blair?

SEMI-FINAL

1 STARTER

Q. Which plant, commonly found in Scotland, Ireland and the North of England, is capable of holding up to 20 times its weight in water and was used on a large scale as a wound dressing in the First World War?

BONUS QUESTIONS

Three questions on the Spanish Civil War:

Q. Who described his departure from Gloucestershire, his walk to London and his months in Spain on the eve of the civil war in 'As I walked out one midsummer morning'?

Q. Who wrote *Homage to Catalonia*, inspired by his experiences of fighting on the Republican side during the Spanish Civil War?

Q. Which novel by Ernest Hemingway, first published in 1940, is set against the background of the Spanish Civil War, in which he actively supported the Republicans?

2 STARTER

Q. Corresponding to the Fates of classical mythology, what collective name is given to the sisters of Norse mythology who lived at the foot of the ash tree Yggdrasil?

BONUS QUESTIONS

Three questions on artistic movements:

Q. The firm of Morris, Marshall, Faulkner and Co, was a business venture that grew out of which nineteenth century artistic movement?

Q. Which artistic style emerged in the early 1920s, was popularized by the international Paris exposition of 1925, and was known in France as 'style moderne'?

Q. Although it had its roots in the nineteenth century, which architectural movement demanded that the form of a building should be determined by practical considerations such as use and material, epitomized by the work of Le Corbusier?

3 STARTER

Q. Which word, now used in English to describe an outstanding success, was originally the name of the ceremonial procession into Rome granted to a victorious general?

BONUS QUESTIONS

Q. Which fairy tale was included in Charles Perrault's seventeenth century collection of stories, translated into English by Robert Samber in 1729, and in 1890 was the basis of a Tchaikovsky ballet choreographed by Petipa?

Q. In which of Shakepeare's plays does the tinker Christopher Sly awaken from a drunken sleep to be told that he is a lord who has gone out of his mind?

Q. Who, according to Henry Newbolt in a poem of 1897, slept 'slung a tween the round shot, listenin' for the drum'?

4 STARTER

Q. Two African countries have over 40 million practising Muslims. One is Egypt, which is the other?

BONUS QUESTIONS

Three questions on clothing and fashion in history:

Q. Worn by followers of the Young Pretender, and later by French revolutionaries, what is a 'cockade'?

Q. Fashionable from the seventeenth to the nineteenth centuries, and still part of some formal dress for members of the legal profession in some European countries, where on the body would a jabot be worn?

Q. Popular at the end of the nineteenth century, particularly with Queen Mary, which woman's name was given to a deep falling lace collar attached to the top of a low-necked dress?

5 STARTER

Q. Which Latin phrase, literally meaning 'from the chair', is used to describe official pronouncements, particularly those made by the Pope?

BONUS QUESTIONS

Which functions of 'x' can be expanded as follows, for all 'x'?

Q. 1 plus 'x' over 1-factorial, plus 'x-squared' over 2-factorial, plus 'x-cubed' over 3-factorial, etc?

Q. 'x' minus 'x cubed' over 3-factorial, plus 'x-to-the-five' over 5-factorial, minus 'x-to-the-seven' over 7-factorial, etc?

Q. 'x' plus 'x cubed' over 3-factorial, plus 'x-to-the five' over 5-factorial, plus 'x-to-the seven' over 7 factorial, etc?

6 STARTER

Q. In 1895, the Portland Club published the first official rules of which game, introduced to its members by Lord Brougham?

BONUS QUESTIONS

Q. Which orchestral brass instrument is known in France as the 'cor d'harmonie', and in German as the 'waldhorn'?

Q. In which American city will you find the French Quarter or 'Vieux Carré'?

Q. Which small African republic at the southern entrance to the Red Sea was once known as French Somaliland?

7 STARTER

Q. UK publishers are legally obliged to send one copy of a new publication to each of the copyright deposit libraries, which are the British Library, The Bodleian, the National Library of Scotland, the National Library of Wales, Trinity College Library in Dublin and which other?

BONUS QUESTIONS

Three questions on breeds of domestic animals:

Q. Which English county has given its name to Britain's smallest breed of draft horse, and a dark-faced breed of sheep bred for its meat?

Q. Which breed of sheep, known for its high quality wool, takes its name from the reclaimed area of south west Kent where it has been extensively grazed since the seventeenth century?

Q. Which breed of hill sheep, now reared on upland areas throughout England and Wales, takes its name from the northern border hills where it was originally bred?

8 STARTER

Q. Which northern French town has been the scene of three major historical events: the capture of Joan of Arc by the Burgundians in 1430, the signing of the armistice ending World War I and, in 1940, the surrender of France to Germany?

BONUS QUESTIONS

Three questions on biblical constructions:

Q. Described in Genesis, Chapter Six, which construction was approximately 450 feet long, 75 feet wide and 45 feet high?

Q. Described in Exodus, which construction was a frame of acacia wood about 45 feet long, draped with four different coverings, the interior comprising two rooms?

Q. Described in the First Book of Kings, whose temple was a construction about 90 feet long, 30 feet wide and 45 feet high, encompassing three distinct areas within?

9 STARTER

Q. Under the provisions of the Antarctic Treaty of 1959 all territorial claims to Antarctic lands were frozen, but which country lays claim to over 40 per cent of the land area?

BONUS QUESTIONS

Three questions on twentieth-century naval warfare:

Q. Which island group gave its name to the decisive naval engagement fought in the Atlantic in December 1914, in which four German cruisers were sunk, with no loss to the British fleet?

Q. After being severely damaged by the Royal Navy cruisers *Exeter*, *Ajax* and *Achilles*, the German pocket battleship *Graf Spee* was scuttled by her own crew on the orders of Hitler. In which river estuary did she go down?

Q. Which Pacific island group gave its name to the huge naval engagement of June 1942, when the US fleet inflicted severe losses on the Japanese fleet?

10 STARTER

Q. Several government departments and the Royal Household have recently given an ecological lead by converting to LPG. What do the initials LPG stand for?

BONUS QUESTIONS

Q. Which colourful name was given to the Mongolians under the leadership of Batu Khan, the grandson of Genghis, who in the thirteenth century swept westward across western Asia and eastern Europe?

Q. Which sixteenth century goldsmith was also a brilliant sculptor, one of his most famous bronzes being 'Perseus with the head of Medusa'?

Q. Which eighteenth century English poet and critic wrote an epitaph on Oliver Goldsmith, which reads in translation: 'To Oliver Goldsmith, a poet, naturalist and historian, who left scarcely any style of writing untouched, and touched none that he did not adorn'?

11 STARTER

Q. Which composer's Symphony Number 5 in D major was written for the tercentenary of the Augsburg confession, and is popularly known as The Reformation Symphony?

BONUS QUESTIONS

Three observations on nations, by nationals:

Q. Which German philosopher wrote in 1888 'The Germans are like women, you can scarcely ever fathom their depths – they haven't any'?

Q. Which Irish author and playwright, born in 1923, wrote 'other people have a nationality. The Irish and Jews have a psychosis'?

Q. Born in 1860, which Scottish dramatist and novelist wrote: 'there are few more impressive sights in the world than a Scotsman on the make'?

12 STARTER

Q. What name derives in part from the Greek for 'to convey', and is given to a substance secreted by animals, which influences the behaviour of other animals of the same species?

BONUS QUESTIONS

Q. What name was given to the flag of the eleven Confederate states of America that broke away from the Union in 1861?

Q. What name is given to the phenomenon caused by the rotation of the galaxy, which causes stars to appear to drift towards two specific points?

Q. Why is the Cornish dish 'stargazy pie' so called?

13 STARTER

Q. Which Russian town, renamed Sverdlovsk between 1924 and 1991, was the site of the execution of the imperial royal family in the summer of 1918?

BONUS QUESTIONS

By which titles are these nineteenth century prime ministers more commonly known:

Q. Henry John Temple succeeded to his father's Irish peerage while still a minor. He served two terms as British prime minister, having also been Secretary at War in Tory administrations, and foreign secretary.

Q. Edward George Geoffrey Smith Stanley succeeded to his father's earldom in 1851. He served three terms as Tory prime minister, none of them longer than 18 months.

Q. William Lamb was one of a number of men to be cuckolded by Lord Byron. He succeeded to his father's title in 1829 and formed two Whig ministries, the first lasting five months and the second lasting six years. He was a close friend and adviser to Queen Victoria during the early years of her reign.

14 STARTER

Q. Which motor manufacturers took their name from the part of Lambeth in London where they began to produce cars in 1903, although they moved to their present location in Luton only two years later?

BONUS QUESTIONS

Q. Which company was founded in 1711 with a monopoly of British trade in Spanish America? In 1720, parliament accepted its offer to take over almost all the national debt in return for large-scale trading concessions.

Q. Which country has been independent since 1990, and was known as South West Africa until 1968?

Q. Who composed the music for the stage show *South Pacific*, which opened in New York in 1949?

15 STARTER

Q. In what context is number 13, death; number 10, the wheel of fortune; number 14, temperance, and number 15, the devil?

BONUS QUESTIONS

Three questions on houses:

Q. A house named 'Gad's Hill' was bought by which writer in the late 1850s, who shortly afterwards separated from his wife because of his relationship with the actress Ellen Ternan?

Q. A house named 'Robin Hill' was built for which fictional solicitor and his wife Irene, making him the eponymous *Man of Property* in the first of a sequence of novels by John Galsworthy, published between 1906 and 1921?

Q. The cottage 'Cloud's Hill', near Bovington in Dorset, was rented by which writer and soldier in the 1920s?

16 STARTER

Q. What is the name of the waterway formed by the confluence of the Tigris and Euphrates Rivers, the final stretch of which forms a border between Iraq and Iran and drains into the Persian Gulf?

BONUS QUESTIONS

Three questions on quotations:

Q. What was described by Mau Tse Tung in a speech of 1938 as 'war without bloodshed'?

Q. What did Harry S. Truman describe as '... a politician who has been dead 10 or 15 years'?

Q. Which Conservative politician wrote in the epilogue to his biography of Joseph Chamberlain: 'all political lives, unless they are cut off in midstream at a happy juncture, end in failure'?

17 STARTER

Q. Which type of pottery, originally used in Japanese tea ceremonies and deriving its name from the Japanese word for 'enjoyment', is made by a rapid firing technique, after which pots are immediately covered with material such as sawdust and then plunged into cold water?

BONUS QUESTIONS

Q. Which letter of the alphabet is used as a symbol in thermodynamics for the quantity of heat entering a system, and in physics as a symbol for electrical charge?

Q. Which word is used to represent the letter Q in international call signs?

Q. What, during World War I, were 'Q-ships'?

18 STARTER

Q. Which saint is this? Born Wynfrid, or Wynfrith, in Devon at the end of the seventh century, he was renamed by Pope Gregory II in 718 before he began his ministry in Bavaria and Thuringia. He was martyred in 754, and is one of Germany's patron saints?

BONUS QUESTIONS

Three questions on classical music:
Which nations are referred to in the titles of these pieces of music:

Q. A collection of dances by Brahms, originally written for two pianos and published in 1869?

Q. Mendelssohn's Fourth Symphony, inspired by a visit to the country?

Q. An orchestral work by Rimsky-Korsakov composed in 1887 and using themes and rhythms of the folk songs of the country?

19 STARTER

Q. What fabric or material is the product of sericulture?

BONUS QUESTIONS

Three questions on hypnosis and hypnotism:

Q. Which German physician propounded the theory of 'animal magnetism' in 1775, attributing therapeutic value to his hypnotic techniques?

Q. In one of Morey Bernstein's most celebrated cases of hypnotic regression, an American housewife claimed in 1952 to have recalled details of a past life in nineteenth century Ireland. What, did she claim, was her name in this past life?

Q. Which Welsh researcher's name is associated with the tape recordings he made in the 1960s, in which his hypnotized subjects also recalled details of past lives, some of the details apparently being corroborated by subsequent archaeological discoveries?

20 STARTER

Q. The name of which popular garden flower means, literally, 'many flowers'?

BONUS QUESTIONS

Three questions on trials and courts:

Q. Nothing to do with the legal process, who or what emerged from the Rainhill Trials of 1829 with the most credit?

Q. Historically, where did 'Piepowder Courts' hear pleas?

Q. There are three divisions of the High Court of Justice in England and Wales; the Family Division and the Chancery Division are two, what is the third?

21 STARTER

Q. First propounded by the British scientist James Lovelock in 1969, what name, taken from that of the Greek Earth goddess, is given to the theory that the earth functions as a single self-regulating organism in which all living matter interacts to sustain the whole?

BONUS QUESTIONS

Three questions on woodcarvers:

Q. What did the Italian woodcarver Geppetto fashion from a piece of wood, according to a nineteenth-century children's story?

Q. Which wooden structure was the work of the woodcarver Epios?

Q. Which Northumberland-born wood engraver illustrated several natural history books, including the two-volume *History of British Birds*, one of Britain's swans being named after him?

22 STARTER

Q. In 1997, of which senior Conservative politician did Anne Widdicombe say, 'he has something of the night about his character'?

BONUS QUESTIONS

Three questions on chemistry:

Q. Which American chemist, in 1923, extended the defintion of an acid to that of any compound which, in a chemical reaction, is able to attach itself to an unshared pair of electrons in another molecule?

Q. Which term for a compound formed by an addition reaction is used particularly for those formed by co-ordination between a Lewis acid and a Lewis base?

Q. In 1933, G.N. Lewis became the first person to prepare a pure sample of which compound, which became important in the manufacture of nuclear weapons and the generation of nuclear power?

23 STARTER

Q. Which national holiday is celebrated in Canada on the second Monday of October each year?

BONUS QUESTIONS

Three questons on spacecraft in sci-fi movies:

Q. What was the name of the spacecraft in Stanley Kubrick's film *2001: A Space Odyssey*?

Q. What is the name of the spacecraft in Ridley Scott's 1979 movie *Alien*, a name it shares with the title character of a Joseph Conrad novel?

Q. What was the name of the craft commanded by Han Solo in the 1977 film *Star Wars*?

24 STARTER

Q. What characteristic is displayed by a fruit described as dehiscent?

BONUS QUESTIONS

Three questions on Spain:

Q. The kingdom of Spain comprises 19 autonomous regions, with their own parliaments and governments. Fifteen of these are on mainland Spain, and two are the island groups of the Canaries and the Balearics. In which North African country are the other two?

Q. Which city on the River Tagus was once the capital of Castile, and is now the capital of the Castile-La-Mancha region?

Q. Of which region, once an independent kingdom, is Zaragoza the capital?

25 STARTER

Q. Which scientific discipline would involve the study of a cepheid variable?

BONUS QUESTIONS

Three questions on tragic lovers in literature:

Q. Who were the lovers of classical mythology, whose story is told by Ovid in his *Metamorphoses*, and who were the subject of the play-within-a-play in a Shakespeare comedy?

Q. Which pair of tragic lovers were the subject of Chaucer's longest complete poem and, over 200 years later, of a Shakespeare tragedy?

Q. Who were the twelfth-century French lovers who were secretly married after the birth of their son, but separated shortly after, he to pursue a life of theological scholarship? They were the subject of a poem by Alexander Pope, published in 1717.

26 STARTER

Q. What name is applied to a length of fabric's woven edge designed to prevent fraying?

BONUS QUESTIONS

Q. Which international organization has aims which include community service and charitable works, was founded in 1927 as a 'club for young business and professional men', and has a membership restricted to males under the age of 45?

Q. What word, meaning a seat of distinction, was used by Malory and others for the place reserved for each knight at King Arthur's round table?

Q. Which hotel in Manhattan housed the round table frequented by the writers Dorothy Parker, Robert Benchley and many others?

27 STARTER

Q. 'The Vaseline review' and 'Owl stretching time' were both suggested as alternative titles for which highly successful television programme, first transmitted in 1969?

BONUS QUESTIONS

Three questions on wills and bequests:

Q. Which artist died in 1851 and bequeathed his fortune to the establishment of a charity for 'decayed artists'? After litigation brought by his distant family the will was annulled, and they inherited the estate, although the nation inherited his pictures?

Q. Which of Dickens' novels features the case of Jarndyce and Jarndyce, a long drawn out dispute over an estate?

Q. Whose will, published after his death in 1950, contained a bequest for the founding of a new English alphabet of at least 40 letters?

28 STARTER

Q. Which American president had all of the following named in his honour: the state capital of Wisconsin, an important New York thoroughfare and a major sporting complex in that city?

BONUS QUESTIONS

Three questions on rivers:

Q. The Jhelum, Chenab, Ravi, Beas and Sutlej are the five tributaries of the Indus which flow through which Asiatic region, whose name means 'five rivers'?

Q. Who wrote, in a work of 1653: 'I love any discourse of rivers, and fish and fishing'?

Q. Which river rises in the San Juan mountains of Colorada, and flows through New Mexico; it forms the border between Texas and Mexico for 1300 miles, and empties into the Gulf of Mexico at Brownsville in Texas?

29 STARTER

Q. Some crops, such as certain varieties of peas and potatoes, are termed 'cryophilous', meaning they will not fully flower and seed unless they have experienced what particular condition early in their growth?

BONUS QUESTIONS

Three questions on still life studies:

Q. Which artist, born in 1839 and associated with the Impressionists for part of his career, completed many still life studies including *Still Life With Basket* and *Apples* in the 1890s?

Q. The 1913 work *Still Life with Guitar, Bottle of Bols and Playing Cards* was by which artist?

Q. Which French artist was admitted to the Royal Academy of Painting and

Sculpture in 1728 on the basis of two early still lifes, *The Skate* and *The Buffet*?

30 STARTER

Q. Which American dancer and choreographer, who died in July 1998, was perhaps best known for his *West Side Story* routines, for which he won an Oscar in 1962?

BONUS QUESTIONS

Q. The second magnitude stars Delta, Epsilon and Zeta appear to lie in a straight line, and form part of a bright equatorial constellation. How are they collectively known?

Q. Which British general was the commanding officer of the Second Punjab Cavalry, was awarded the VC for gallantry in 1858, and is now best remembered for his invention of a belt worn by army officers?

Q. What name is given to the low pressure calm latitudes which lie between the belt of north-easterly trade-winds of the northern hemisphere, and the south-westerly trade-winds of the southern hemisphere?

31 STARTER

Q. Which object, first used in London in 1983, derives its nickname 'the Denver boot' from its initial launch in the state capital of Colorado, and has greatly reduced incidents of illegal parking?

BONUS QUESTIONS

Q. What kind of foodstuffs are the Finnish 'pulla' and the Jewish 'challa'?

Q. Which activity would produce a bread-crust bomb?

Q. Which work, translated into English in 1859, contains the lines: 'here with a loaf of bread beneath the bough,/a flask of wine, a book of verse – and thou/beside me, singing in the wilderness'?

32 STARTER

Q. From the Latin for 'to look', what name is given to the medical instrument used to widen bodily passages or cavities for surgery or inspection?

BONUS QUESTIONS

Three questions on names:

Q. In March 1999 Victoria Adams, otherwise known as Posh Spice, gave birth to a son whose first name is the New York district she was staying in when she found she was pregnant – but what is the child's middle name, which he shares with his father?

Q. One of the most influential figures of the nineteenth century, which Briton was born on 12 May 1820, and named after the European city of her birth?

Q. Born about 1489, Antonio Allegri was one of the leading artists of the Renaissance. His works included *Jupiter and Antiope* and *Ecce Homo*. During his life, and since, he has been known by which name, that of the small town near Parma where he was born?

33 STARTER

Q. Which Roman emperor, when fatally ill in 79 AD, is reputed to have said 'vae puto deus fio', or 'woe is me, I think I am becoming a god'?

BONUS QUESTIONS

Q. Which European country has given its name to both a species of lobster and a species of rat?

Q. Which post was held by the Norwegian diplomat Trygve Lie between 1946 and 1952?

Q. Which Norwegian artist was instrumental in establishing the Expressionist movement, his works often reflecting his own traumatic childhood, as in his painting *The Sick Child* from the early 1880s?

34 STARTER

Q. Which eighteenth century Russian army officer was a lover of Catherine the Great, was largely responsible for the construction of the Black Sea fleet and the establishment of the port of Sevastopol, and gave his name to a battleship which was the scene of a notorious mutiny at Odessa in 1905?

BONUS QUESTIONS

Three questions on American judges:

Q. Who is the US Chief Justice who presided over the Clinton impeachment hearings?

Q. Judge John J. Sirica presided in 1973 over the criminal trial following which incident, his comments after passing sentence having far-reaching ramifications?

Q. Which US Chief Justice headed the commission of inquiry into the murder of President Kennedy?

35 STARTER

Q. Samsoe, which is pale yellow with a mild nutty flavour and produced in Denmark, is what type of foodstuff?

BONUS QUESTIONS

Three questions on London squares:

Q. Houses in Gordon Square and Fitzroy Square were the regular meeting places of which group of writers, intellectuals and artists, who acquired their collective name from the district of London where those houses are situated?

Q. In which London square is the central office of the Conservative Party?

Q. Which important art collection was bequeathed to the nation in 1897, and is housed in Hertford House in Manchester Square?

36 STARTER

Q. 'The banana industry', 'Routes to anywhere in mainland Britain by road from Letchworth' and 'Orthopaedic bone cement in total hip replacement' were all rejected as suitable specialist subjects for which quiz show, whose long run on television ended in 1997?

BONUS QUESTIONS

Q. The last serious epidemic of apthous fever in the UK occurred in 1967, resulting in over 100,000 deaths. What is the more common name for aphthous fever?

Q. Similar in appearance to foot and mouth disease, SVD is a notifiable disease in the UK, affecting which animals?

Q. Newcastle Disease is an acute, highly contagious disease of which animals?

37 STARTER

Q. Which high ranking World War II air pilot went on to become a senator, fighting a disastrous campaign for the presidency in 1964 against Lyndon Johnson, during which he promoted his hawkish policies on issues such as Vietnam, and declared his belief that 'extremism in the defence of liberty is no vice'.

BONUS QUESTIONS

Three questions on major ports:

Q. Which port is situated on the Rhine, close to the point where the German, French and Swiss borders meet, and is Switzerland's only major inland port?

Q. Much improved and expanded during World War I, and later developed to accommodate its country's oil exports, what is Iraq's major port on the western bank of the Shatt al-Arab, close to the Persian Gulf?

Q. Which major port of the US eastern seaboard is 200 miles from the open sea, but owes its growth as an international seaport to its sheltered harbourage at the head of Chesapeake Bay?

38 STARTER

Q. Born in Accra in Ghana in 1952, which writer is the author of *Brazzaville Beach, An Ice Cream War* and *Armadillo*?

BONUS QUESTIONS

Three questions on a French scientist:

Q. Which scientist was the son of a French baron and lieutenant of infantry, was born in Picardy in 1744, and proposed one of the earliest, superficially plausible, theories of evolution?

Q. Which word for the study of living organisms was used first by Lamarck in 1802?

Q. Which agronomist, who was the effective 'dictator' of Soviet biology during the Stalin era, revived Lamarckism, dismissing all advances that had been made in classical genetics?

39 STARTER

Q. The church synod of 664 AD, which settled the dispute over the date of Easter, took place in which Yorkshire town, formerly named Streaneshalch?

BONUS QUESTIONS

Three questions on flags:

Q. The national flag of which South American country bears the words *ordem e progresso*, meaning 'order and progress'?

Q. The green flag of which nation is inscribed with the Arabic words, 'there is no God but Allah, and Mohammed is the prophet of Allah'?

Q. Which Central American country's flag is inscribed with the saying *sub umbra floreo*, meaning 'under the shade we flourish'?

40 STARTER

Q. Known as 'ghibli' in Libya, 'zonda' in the Andes and 'chinook' in the North American Rockies, what name is given in the European Alps to the warm and dry, gusty wind that periodically descends the leeward slopes of nearly all mountains and mountain ranges?

BONUS QUESTIONS

Q. Wimbledon Football Club has shared the home ground of Crystal Palace since the 1991-1992 season: with which other club did Palace share Selhurst Park between 1985 and 1991?

Q. Which football league club played its home games at Twerton Park in Bath from 1986 to 1996?

Q. During the redevelopment of Celtic Park in 1994 to 1995, Celtic shared which other Glasgow stadium?

41 STARTER

Q. What name was given in ancient Rome to officials who interpreted signs or 'auspacia' in natural phenomena such as eclipses and meteors?

BONUS QUESTIONS

Three questions on Shakespeare's sonnets:

Q. Who is referred to by the initials 'TT' in the much-debated dedication to Shakespeare's sonnets?

Q. What number is the usual designation of Shakespeare's sonnet which opens: 'Shall I compare thee to a Summer's day'?

Q. In the opening lines of Sonnet 116, to what will the poet 'not ... admit impediments'?

42 STARTER

Q. What word describes an honours examination for degree candidates at Cambridge, and is derived from the three legged stool on which a bachelor of arts sat to deliver a satirical speech?

BONUS QUESTIONS

Three questions on symbolic birds:

Q. Which bird served as an armorial bearing of the Holy Roman Empire and as an emblem of the imperial powers of France, Russian, Austria and Germany?

Q. Which town on the Austrian border was the site of the *berghof*, or 'eagle's nest', where Hitler had his mountain retreat?

Q. 'Eagle day' was the name given by the German military to 13 August, 1940, the date on which they planned to launch which World War II offensive?

43 STARTER

Q. Which mock title for an exalted personage or pompous official was invented in a piece of nonsense verse in 1755 by the actor and dramatist Samuel Foote, to test the actor Charles Mackin's claim that he could memorize anything?

BONUS QUESTIONS

Q. Formerly known as the Trucial States, the United Arab Emirates is a federation of seven states. There are five points for naming two of them, ten points for four and fifteen points for all seven.

44 STARTER

Q. *Curcuma longa* is the Latin name of which member of the ginger family, the powdered root of which can be used as a dyestuff, as a stimulant, as a test for alkalinity and, more commonly, as an essential ingredient of curry powder?

BONUS QUESTIONS

In which English counties are the following hills or ranges of hills:

Q. Purbeck Hills?

Q. Pendle Hill?

Q. Brendon Hills?

45 STARTER

Q. On 23 June 1998, which historical artefact was re-interred, 684 years after its supposed owner led an army to victory over a numerically superior English force, and two years after it was dug up at Melrose Abbey?

BONUS QUESTIONS

Three questions on buildings in ancient Rome:

Q. Which Roman building was begun in 27 BC and since its consecration in 609 has been the Church of Santa Maria rotunda?

Q. Which massive U-shaped structure, of which nothing now remains, was rebuilt by Julius Caesar, and greatly expanded in the fourth century? Its site lies between the Palatine and Aventine Hills.

Q. Originally known as the Flavian Amphitheatre, which building took its present name after the large statue of Vero was erected close by in the Via Sacra?

46 STARTER

Q. President of Eastern Airlines from 1938 to 1959, which businessman is better known for his service in World War I when he was the leading American air ace, shooting down 22 planes and four balloons?

BONUS QUESTIONS

Q. The *Codex Babylonicus Petropolitanus* dates from the tenth century and is the earliest surviving Old Testament text in which language?

Q. Who made the standard Latin translation of the Bible known as the vulgate, which was completed in Bethlehem early in the fifth century?

Q. Which radical English scholar and preacher instigated the first English translation of the Bible, in the second half of the fourteenth century?

47 STARTER

Q. Which colourless oily organic compound has the formula $C_6H_5NH_2$, is an important ingredient in the manufacture of drugs, plastics and, in particular, synthetic dyes, and may either be extracted from coal tar or produced from the reduction of nitrobenzene?

BONUS QUESTIONS

Three questions on political deputies :

Q. Who was deputy leader of the Labour Party to John Smith, became leader *pro tem* on his death, but failed in the subsequent ballots to secure either of the two leadership posts?

Q. Who was the deputy leader of the Liberal Party under David Steel who failed to secure the party leadership of the newly formed Social and Liberal Democrats in July 1988?

Q. Who served as deputy prime minister to Margaret Thatcher between 1989 and 1990?

48 STARTER

Q. Which 'Footsie One Hundred' company was formed by the merger of Grand Metropolitan and Guinness?

BONUS QUESTIONS

Q. For what form of pictorial work is Donald McGill particularly remembered?

Q. The caricaturist Leslie Ward was knighted in 1918. For almost 40 years his distinctive, elongated caricatures appeared in the pages of *Vanity Fair* magazine. What was his pseudonym?

Q. Which artist produced a full-sized cartoon for his depiction of the Battle of Anghiari in 1505, although the wall-painting itself, for the great hall of the Palazzo Vecchio, was never completed?

49 STARTER

Q. Which literary work contains the following diary entry: 'Sunday 14th June 1942. On Friday 12th June, I woke up at 6 o'clock and no wonder. It was my birthday'?

BONUS QUESTIONS

Three questions on young singing successes:

Q. What was the title of the recording which topped the classical music chart in 1998, and was performed by the 12-year-old Charlotte Church?

Q. Which musician and vocalist was born in 1965, and had her first solo album released when she was 11. She became a member of the band 'Exodus' at the age of 14, and had her first international success with 'The Sugarcubes' in the mid-1980s?

Q. In 1962, Ernest Lough was presented with a gold disc for a recording of his made 35 years earlier, when he was a boy soprano. Two Mendelssohn works featured on the recording; one is 'Hear My Prayer', what is the other?

50 STARTER

Q. What is the French equivalent of the Italian 'Giro d'Italie' and the Spanish 'Vuelta a Espana'?

BONUS QUESTIONS

Three questions on gates:

Q. Who, in Roman mythology, was the two-faced god who was the keeper of the gates of heaven?

Q. From which poem, written in the mid-eighteenth century, do these lines come: 'their glowing virtues, but their crimes confined:/forbade to wade through slaughter to a throne,/and shut the gates of mercy on mankind'?

Q. Which French author received the Nobel Prize for literature in 1947, having published *La Porte Etroite*, or *Strait is the Gate*, in 1909?

51 STARTER

Q. The M20 motorway is located entirely within the geographical confines of which county?

BONUS QUESTIONS

Three questions on imprisoned French artists:

Q. Born in 1891, which German-born French artist was a seminal figure in both the Dada and Surrealist movements, and was imprisoned after the German invasion of France in World War II?

Q. Which nineteenth century French Realist painter was imprisoned and fined for his supposed part in the destruction of Napoleon's triumphal column in the Place Vendôme, having been put in charge of art museums during the Paris Commune of 1871?

Q. The painter, sculptor and caricaturist Honoré Daumier served a short term of imprisonment when, in 1832, he produced a cartoon depicting which French monarch as Rabelais's Gargantua?

52 STARTER

Q. *The King's English* and *A Dictionary of Modern English Usage*, first published early in the twentieth century, were both influential books on the correct use of the English language, written by which lexicographer and former school teacher?

BONUS QUESTIONS

Three questions on classical goddesses:

Q. In Roman mythology, Juno was the queen of the gods. Who was the corresponding goddess of Greek myth?

Q. Who was the Roman goddess of the Earth and tillage, identified with the Greek Demeter?

Q. Who was the Greek goddess of wisdom, corresponding to the Roman Minerva?

53 STARTER

Q. The increasingly rare British amphibian *Bufo calamita*, which has a very loud ratchetty croak audible up to a mile away, is commonly known by what name?

BONUS QUESTIONS

Q. Affirming their support for self-determination, free trade, freedom of the seas and disarmament once the defeat of Nazi Germany had been secured, the joint statement made by Churchill and Roosevelt in 1941, following their meetings on warships off Newfoundland, is known by which name?

Q. During the Battle of the Atlantic in World War II, which German battleship was sunk by the Royal Navy west of Brest, three days after it had destroyed *HMS Hood*?

Q. Atlantic City, famous for its casinos and its six-mile boardwalk, is a resort in which US state?

54 STARTER

Q. Called *Gummina* in France, *Brilliantino* in Italy, and *Vaselina* in Mexico, which film celebrated the twentieth anniversary of its release in 1998?

BONUS QUESTIONS

Three questions on spacecraft:

Q. What was the name of the spacecraft in which Alan Shepherd made America's first sub-orbital manned flight in May 1961?

Q. In the sequence of Apollo missions, which number was the designation of the mission which achieved the first manned lunar landing in July 1969?

Q. To date, four American space probes have left our solar system; two of them are Pioneers; what name is shared by the other two?

55 STARTER

Q. Kentucky, Pennsylvania, Virginia and Massachusetts are four mainland American territories which in legal and constitutional terms do not refer to themselves as states, but use what term?

BONUS QUESTIONS

Q. Which fantasy film of 1986 was co-written and directed by Jim Henson, and follows the adventures of a teenage girl called Sarah as she negotiates an intricate maze to rescue her brother from Jareth's castle?

Q. According to Greek mythology, who designed and constructed the Cretan maze or labyrinth of king Minos, which was the lair of the Minotaur?

Q. Less than a month before his death, which inmate of the Maze prison in Northern Ireland won a parliamentary by-election in April 1981 for Fermanagh and South Tyrone?

56 STARTER

Q. The work of the cartoonist Scott Adams, now shown in over 1500 newspapers worldwide, concerns which electrical engineer, who spends most of his time with his computer or his pet dog?

BONUS QUESTIONS

What are the names of the base and derived SI units, which are conventionally abbreviated as follows:

Q. cd?

Q. S?

Q. sr?

57 STARTER

Q. If 'start' is green, 'stop' is red, and 'caution, no passing' is yellow, what is 'finish'?

BONUS QUESTIONS

Q. The North American spider *Latodectus mactans*, of which the larger poisonous female is marked with a characteristic red patch below the abdomen, is known by which common name?

Q. Which poet referred to Queen Victoria in the following lines: 'then 'ere's to the widow at Windsor/an' 'ere's to the stores an' the guns/the men an' the 'orses what makes up the forces/o' missis Victoria's sons'?

Q. According to the Bible story, which pious and beautiful widow volunteered to deliver the beseiged Israelites by murdering the Assyrian captain Holofernes?

58 STARTER

Q. Which Austro-American physicist was awarded the Nobel Prize for physics in 1945 for the discovery of the exclusion principle, whereby no two electrons in an atom can have the same four quantum numbers?

BONUS QUESTIONS

Q. In art or dance, which allegorical theme is referred to by the German term *totentanz*?

Q. Which German painter produced a series of illustrations of the 'dance of death' in Basel in the early sixteenth century?

Q. *The Dance of Death* is the title of a verse play published in 1933 by which British poet?

59 STARTER

Q. In computing, what two-word term describes a method of reasoning used in some expert systems, in which the outcome of an operation can be expressed as a probability rather than a certainty?

BONUS QUESTIONS

Three questions on heresy and religious persecution:

Q. Taking its name from the priest of Alexandria who founded it, which system of Christian theology denied the complete divinity of Christ, and was comdemned as heretical at the council of Nicaea in 325 AD?

Q. *De Heretico Comburendo* was a statute passed by the church in 1401, advocating which method of dealing with heretics?

Q. Many of its members forced to emigrate to North America in order to escape persecution, the Mennonite and Hutterite sects belong to which radical Protestant movement, dating from the sixteenth century?

60 STARTER

Q. Although sounding as if it is derived from Spanish, which American slang term comes from the Japanese for 'squad leader', was adopted by US soldiers during the Korean war and has now come to be used for someone holding a powerful position in an organization?

BONUS QUESTIONS

Q. What name was given to the last of the wars of religion in France fought from 1587 to 1589 between the Roman Catholic Duke of Guise, the Huguenot King of Navarre who was heir presumptive to the throne and the moderate ruler of France assassinated in 1589?

Q. What was the alternative name for the League of the Three Forest Cantons, an inaugural confederation of 1291 from which, through a long series of accessions, Switzerland grew to statehood?

Q. The Dreikaiserbund, or 'Three Emperors League', was an alliance devised by Otto Von Bismarck to isolate France and neutralize the rivalry between Russia and which other of Germany's near-neighbours?

61 STARTER

Q. The name of which surveyor's instrument, usually now consisting of a steel band or tape, is also a unit of measurement constituting 22 yards?

BONUS QUESTIONS

Q. The Town of Sidmouth lies in a hollow in the hills formed by the River Sid in which county?

Q. Queen Victoria's father, who died in Sidmouth in 1820, held which dukedom?

Q. Which British Prime Minister was appointed by George III in 1801 to replace Pitt the Younger, and resigned in 1804, taking the title First Viscount of Sidmouth in the following year?

62 STARTER

Q. In the administrative reorganization of 1975, which Scottish region was created from the former counties of Kincardine, Banff, Aberdeen and most of Moray?

BONUS QUESTIONS

Q. What is the more familiar name for the double portrait of 1533 by Hans Holbein the Younger, entitled *Jean de Dinteville and Georges de Selve*?

Q. Which future American president was appointed US Ambassador to the United Nations in 1971 by Richard Nixon?

Q. In the 1998 film *Elizabeth*, which former footballer played the French Ambassador to the court of Elizabeth I?

63 STARTER

Q. What term means a time of peace and calm, and is derived from the belief that during the nesting period of kingfishers around the winter solstice, the sea always remained calm?

BONUS QUESTIONS

Three questions on Danish astronomers:

Q. Which Danish astronomer observed a supernova in the constellation Cassiopeia in 1572 and proved it was a star?

Q. In 1676, Ole Romer became the first man to make a quantitative measurement of what, his value being about 25 per cent below the modern accepted value?

Q. Which Danish astronomer, who died in 1967, classified types of stars by relating their colour to their absolute brightness and has a diagram of stellar types named in part after him?

64 STARTER

Q. Which French statesman was premier on three separate occasions, was elected president of the republic in 1913, remaining in office until 1920 and had become a member of the Academie Française in 1909?

BONUS QUESTIONS

Three questions on the petroleum industry:

Q. What is the present name of the company founded in 1909 by William Knox d'Arcy as the Anglo-Persian Oil Company?

Q. Between 1970 and 1987, BP acquired which American oil company, founded by John D. Rockefeller?

Q. In August 1998, an intention to merge was announced between BP and which American oil company, with BP as the dominant partner?

65 STARTER

Q. Sacked by Alexander the Great in 330 BC, which ancient city in the Iranian province of Fars was planned by Darius I as the ceremonial capital of his empire?

BONUS QUESTIONS

Three questions on mountains:

Q. The highest point of which mountain was called 'Kaiser Wilhelm Spitze' by the German geographer who first reached it in 1889, but was later renamed Uhuru Peak when the country in which it is found gained independence in 1961?

Q. Which mountain of South Central Alaska is sometimes referred to by its ancient Athabascan Indian name 'Denali', meaning 'the high one', its English name being first applied to it in 1896 by the Prospector William A. Dickey?

Q. The Venezuelan, Colombian, Ecuadorian, Peruvian, Central and Patagonian are the six major subdivisions of which mountain range?

66 STARTER

Q. What German name was given to the 'compromise' of 8 February 1867, which established the dual monarchy of Austria-Hungary?

BONUS QUESTIONS

Q. In the tempering of steel to harden it, what term is used for the rapid cooling of heated metal by immersion in water or oil?

Q. The term quenching is applied to the process of terminating the discharge in which type of radiation detector?

Q. What, according to the Song of Solomon, cannot many waters quench, nor many floods drown?

67 STARTER

Q. Derived from the title of a 1959 novel by Richard Condon, what term describes someone who has been brainwashed by a foreign power to obey orders without thinking?

BONUS QUESTIONS

Q. A sudden increase in wind-speed of 8 metres per second or more, to a peak of speed 11 metres per second or more, lasting for one minute or more, was adopted in April 1962 by the World Metereological Organization as the definition of what?

Q. Of which Welsh MP did Winston Churchill say in 1945 that 'unless [he] changes his policy and methods ... he will be as great a curse to this country in time of peace as he was a squalid nuisance in time of war'?

Q. The oily unsaturated hydrocarbon squalene, an important intermediate in the synthesis of cholesterol, was originally found in oil obtained from the liver of which fish?

68 STARTER

Q. Chu Yuan-Chang, a rebel leader who captured Nanking in 1356 and unified China, ruled as the Hung-Wu emperor and founded which dynasty of Chinese rulers with a name meaning 'bright'?

BONUS QUESTIONS

Of which three Beatles songs are these the opening lines:

Q. 'It was twenty years ago today...'

Q. 'In the town where I was born...'

Q. 'Picture yourself in a boat on a river...'

69 STARTER

Q. What is the name for the fee charged by a restaurant for serving wine that customers have bought elsewhere?

BONUS QUESTIONS

Q. Which scientist was knighted by Queen Victoria for the invention of the telegraph receiver, which he called the mirror galvanometer, but is best remembered for the absolute temperature scale that bears his name?

Q. Which Polish-born physicist invented the alcohol thermometer in 1709 and the mercury thermometer in 1714, but is best remembered for the thermometric scale he invented, still in common use in North America?

Q. Which eighteenth century French scientist invented the cupola furnace for melting Grey Iron, a method of making porcelain and also devised the thermometric temperature scale bearing his name?

70 STARTER

Q. Which word refers to a flavouring ingredient of puddings, and is also used in computer terminology for a basic, no frills system or software?

BONUS QUESTIONS

Q. The dung beetle (*Scarabaeus sacer*) was sacred to which ancient people?

Q. The popular name for which beetle originated in the Middle Ages, when it was considered sacred to the Virgin Mary?

Q. Which great nineteenth century scientist and agnostic, when asked what he knew about God, is said to have said 'the creator, if he exists, has a special preference for beetles'?

71 STARTER

Q. Belonging to the genus *Iphisaurus* and sometimes mistakenly referred to as a snake, which type of lizard is so named because of its fragile tail that can be easily broken off?

BONUS QUESTIONS

Three questions on doctors who became writers:

Q. Who created his best-known character while waiting for patients at his surgery in Southsea, where he began practising in 1882?

Q. Best known as a dramatist, which Russian writer qualified as a doctor in 1884 and supported his family with earnings from comic writing until he began to make a name for himself with more serious works?

Q. Which idealistic young doctor, who practised with Doctor Cameron in the Scottish village of Tannochbrae, was created by A.J. Cronin, himself a qualified doctor?

72 STARTER

Q. Which word, used as a noun for a circuitous course, and as a verb meaning to wander at random, was originally the name of a river of ancient Phrygia with just such a winding course?

BONUS QUESTIONS

Three questions on cutting criticism:

Q. Which playwright, actor, and songwriter, referring to a play featuring a child actor, said, 'two things should be cut; the second act and the child's throat'?

Q. Which monarch gave her opinion of *King Lear* thus, 'a strange, horrible business, but I suppose good enough for Shakespeare's day'?

Q. Which well-known Victorian librettist described Henry Irving's *Hamlet* as 'funny without being vulgar'?

73 STARTER

Q. The Duke of Plaza-Toro who 'led his regiment from behind – he found it less exciting', is a Spanish grandee in which Gilbert and Sullivan operetta?

BONUS QUESTIONS

What do the following symbols in general use in mathematics mean?

Q. An exclamation mark after an integer or letter denoting an integer?

Q. The letters upper case 'I' lower case 'm', followed by a letter denoting an unknown or variable?

Q. The Greek letter capital pi followed by a symbol denoting a sequence of unknowns?

74 STARTER

Q. The full title of *Rasselas* by Samuel Johnson reveals him to be the son of the emperor of which country?

BONUS QUESTIONS

Three questions on teams in the 1998 World Cup:

Q. In the 1998 World Cup, the names of which country's squad all ended in either 'ev' or 'ov'?

Q. Eighteen of the 22 members of which country's squad had names ending in 'vic'?

Q. The names of eleven members of which country's squad had names ending in the letter 'u'?

75 STARTER

Q. What is meant by describing something as potable?

BONUS QUESTIONS

Q. In 1955, following a treaty signed by the four Allied powers, which country was re-established as a sovereign, independent state having the same borders as on 1 January 1938?

Q. What is the English translation of the local German name for Austria?

Q. Who was controversially elected President of Austria in 1986, remaining in that office until 1992?

76 STARTER

Q. Equating $\frac{d^2y}{dx^2} = 0$ is the usual method of finding which point on a curve, $y = f(x)$ at which the concavity of the curve changes?

BONUS QUESTIONS

In which cities are the following detectives principally based?

Q. Val McDermid's Kate Brannigan?

Q. Lindsay Davis's Marcus Didius Falco?

Q. Ellis Peters' Brother Cadfael?

77 STARTER

Q. Which city is the capital of Japan's northernmost island, Hokkaido, and was the venue for the 1972 Winter Olympics?

BONUS QUESTIONS

Three questions on textiles which take their names from towns:

Q. What is the present-day name of the city in Turkey after which angora, the fine, soft wool from goats and rabbits is named?

Q. Which Middle Eastern capital city gives its name to a material, now usually linen or cotton, woven with a pattern?

Q. Which coarse cotton fabric, used in the twentieth century for casual summer attire, was originally made in the town in Northern Kerala from whence it derives its name?

78 STARTER

Q. What term, derived from the Greek word for 'putrid', is used to describe organisms such as truffles, yeasts and some orchids which absorb soluble organic nutrients from dead plant or animal matter?

BONUS QUESTIONS

Three questions on the Lake District:

Q Which Lakeland valley gives its name to a sequence of volcanic rocks which stretches north-east to south-west across central parts of the Lake District?

Q. In the Lake District, Friar's Crag was purchased as a memorial to Canon Rawnsley, one of the co-founders of which organization?

Q. What is the particular claim to fame of Styhead Tarn which lies above the head of Borrowdale?

79 STARTER

Q. Developed by the British and used in both world wars, what particular type of explosive device was the Mills Bomb?

BONUS QUESTIONS

Q. Which avian term for a person who advocates confrontation rather than conciliation is said to have been coined by Thomas Jefferson in 1798?

Q. To which genus of birds do the so-called true hawks belong?

Q. Bob Hawke, who was Prime Minister of Australia from 1983-1991, was the leader of which political party?

80 STARTER

Q. From the Latin for 'depository', which verb means to remove from someone's possession until a dispute or debt has been settled?

BONUS QUESTIONS

Three questions on religious structures:

Q. Which raised structure in a church takes its name from the Latin for 'stage'?

Q. In its simplest form a platform with three steps, what is the name of the pulpit from which the sermon is delivered in a mosque?

Q. Also called the almemor, what is the name in Jewish synagogues of the raised platform with a reading desk from which, in the Aashkenazi ritual, the Torah and Haftarah are read on the Sabbath and on festivals?

81 STARTER

Q. Which two-word Latin term indicated the peace imposed within the British empire by the strength of imperial power and was a version of a similar phrase for the order imposed on Europe by ancient Rome?

BONUS QUESTIONS

Q. Which transport company was set up in 1980 by Brian Souter and his sister Ann Gloag, with their father's financial help, running buses from Aberdeen to London?

Q. Which actor first achieved stardom as the Ringo Kid in the 1939 western *Stagecoach*?

Q. Which essayist wrote, in his *Table Talk* of 1821: 'you will hear more good things on the outside of a stagecoach from London to Oxford, than if you were to pass a twelve-month with the undergraduates, or heads of colleges, of that famous university'?

82 STARTER

Q. Perhaps used when a private address is not available, a facility for holding mail until collected by the recipient is denoted by which French term?

BONUS QUESTIONS

Q. What is the relevance of the following dates to the British royal family; 3 June 1937, 20 November 1947 and 29 July 1981?

Q. Which Flemish artist painted *The Peasant Wedding* in 1565, and *The Wedding Dance* in 1566?

Q. Whose first opera, *The Midsummer Marriage*, premiered at Covent Garden in 1955?

83 STARTER

Q. Which ancient religion, with no historical founder, supreme being or sacred scriptures, is also known as 'kami no michi' or 'the way of the gods'?

BONUS QUESTIONS

Q. What is the connection between Malchus on the eve of Christ's crucifixion, and Vincent Van Gogh on Christmas Eve 1888?

Q. The claim by Captain Jenkins in 1738 that his ear had been severed seven years earlier, resulted in war between Britain and which nation?

Q. Which English poet, in his poem 'Esther's Tomcat' of 1960, wrote of the eponymous animal: 'continual wars and wives are what/have tattered his ears and battered his head'?

84 STARTER

Q. The high-speed transport system in which an electrically powered train glides above a track is known as maglev, a shortening of which two words?

BONUS QUESTIONS

Q. Although the word can be applied to any slender nematode, what is the common name for the human parasite *Enterobius vermicularis*?

Q. One of the standard British screw threads before metrication was often abbreviated to BSW; the BS stood for British Standard. What did the W stand for?

Q. According to Greek myth, who gave Theseus the length of thread which enabled him to find his way out of the labyrinth after slaying the Minotaur?

85 STARTER

Q. 'Organic architecture', in other words the marriage of building and landscape, was the aim behind 'Falling Waters', the Kaufman house in Pennsylvania. Which architect designed it?

BONUS QUESTIONS

Q. Who, in 1954, founded the Holy Spirit Association for the Unification of World Christianity', more usually known as the Unification Church'?

Q. Which Italian-born French astronomer formulated, in 1693, the three rules which accurately described the rotation of the moon?

Q. Which actress spoke the last lines of the 1942 film *Now Voyager*: 'Don't let's ask for the moon! We have the stars'?

86 STARTER

Q. Deriving ultimately from a Greek term meaning, roughly, 'rotten blood', which word refers to a serious condition caused by the presence in the bloodstream of micro-organisms, its associated symptoms including shivering, sweating and pain in the joints?

BONUS QUESTIONS

Three questions on organists:

Q. Now best remembered as a composer of sacred music, who was organist at Waltham Abbey at its dissolution, and from 1545 until his death 40 years later was organist at the Chapel Royal?

Q. Which composer was organist to the Weimar Court between 1708 and 1717, when he was appointed director of music to the court of Prince Leopold of Anhalt-Cöthen?

Q. Who was articled to Haydn Keeton, organist of Peterborough Cathedral in 1910, and became organist at Melton Mowbray in 1914 but is now remembered as a conductor, succeeding Adrian Boult as conductor of the BBC symphony orchestra in 1950?

87 STARTER

Q. On what date is St Distaff's Day, so called because traditionally, once the Christmas festivities ended on Twelfth Night, the women returned to their distaffs or daily occupations on the following day?

BONUS QUESTIONS

Questions on international organizations:

Q. In March 1999, three new member states were admitted to NATO. Five points if you can name all three.

Q. Four countries are members of the EU, but not members of NATO. Five points for three, ten points for all four.

88 STARTER

Q. With a name deriving from a valley in the Grampians, which brimless headgear has a crease down the centre, often with ribbons hanging from the back, and is best known in the tartan version worn by certain Scottish regiments?

BONUS QUESTIONS

Three questions on epitaphs:

Q. Which writer's headstone in the Westminster Cemetery, Baltimore, bears the epitaph 'quoth the raven nevermore'?

Q. Which English poet, who died in 1915, has an epitaph which reads: 'here lies the servant of God. Sub-lieutenant in the English navy who died for the deliverance of Constantinople from the Turks'?

Q. Which of Shakespeare's monarchs has the lines to the Duke of Aumerle: 'of comfort no man speak;/let's talk of graves, of worms, and epitaphs'?

89 STARTER

Q. From old Norse for 'holy', which female first name was reintroduced in the twentieth-century from Scandinavia and Germany?

BONUS QUESTIONS

Three questions on foxes:

Q. What is the name of the fox who is the central character of a number of satirical medieval tales? Caxton printed an English translation of the Flemish versions in 1481.

Q. First published in Latin at Strasbourg in 1559, what is the more popular name for John Foxe's *Actes and Monuments of These Latter Perillous Dayes, Touching Matters of the Church*?

Q. Which American playwright was the author of *The Little Foxes*, first performed in 1939?

90 STARTER

Q. With a name meaning 'intestinal beetle' in allusion to his mother Nandi having been pregnant without being officially married, which African chief took over the Zulus on the death of his father, Senzangakona, in 1816, and went on to found the Zulu empire?

BONUS QUESTIONS

Q. Which term refers to any of a group of chemical compounds, which are an undesirable by-product in the manufacture of herbicides and bactericides? The term has become synonymous with one specific compound, namely 2,3,7,8-TCDD, which is extremely stable and highly toxic?

Q. Atoms of which element are bonded to the carbon atoms in the positions 2,3,7,8 on the benzene rings of 2,3,7,8-TCDD?

Q. Dioxin is formed as an undesirable by-product during the synthesis of the herbicide 2,4,5-T; of which defoliant, used by the US military in Vietnam, is this latter a major active ingredient?

91 STARTER

Q. Which traditional cake takes its name from that of the fine flour used in the recipe and is a rich fruit cake with a layer of marzipan. Usually associated with Easter?

BONUS QUESTIONS

Three questions on religion:

Q. Which religious movement derives its name from the Latin and, ultimately, the Greek words meaning 'elder'?

Q. Which sixteenth-century French theologian is generally accepted as being the founder of Presbyterianism?

Q. Having made an earlier visit in 1536, to which European city was Calvin persuaded to return in 1541 in order to lead the Reformation of the church, this being the city where he largely remained for the rest of his life?

92 STARTER

Q. The tote, a system of betting at racecourses, is an abbreviation of what word?

BONUS QUESTIONS

Q. First implemented by Stalin in 1928 and seen as a model for state control of the economy, what phrase was used to describe the co-ordinated national effort towards fixed industrial, agricultural and economic targets within a fixed time period?

Q. Named after the former German chief of staff, which war plan was put into operation in August 1914, and involved a massive flanking movement through Belgium with the aim of overwhelming the French army?

Q. Who was rewarded with a gift of an emerald tie clip from 'a gracious lady at Windsor' for his part in the recovery of the Bruce Partington plans?

93 STARTER

Q. Which small furry animal may be striped, hooded, hog-nosed or spotted, belongs to the weasel family and usually gives a warning such as stamping or growling before spraying musk from a gland near the base of its tail?

BONUS QUESTIONS

Three questions on the historical context of creative works:

Q. Who was on the British throne when Bach's 'Brandenberg Concertos' were first performed?

Q. Who was on the British throne when Rodin completed his group study *The Burghers of Calais*?

Q. Who was on the British throne when Vermeer painted *Young Girl with a Flute* and *The Letter*?

94 STARTER

Q. The name of which American journalist is considered the source of a mild expletive or expression of surprise, although he is also noted for having edited the *New York Herald*, commissioned Stanley to find Livingstone, and popularized the game of polo in the USA?

BONUS QUESTIONS

Three questions on London theatres:

Which London theatres derive their names, either directly or indirectly, from the following:

Q. The god of music and poetry, who was also the son of Zeus and Leto?

Q. The patron saint of innkeepers and reformed drunkards, who became Bishop of Tours in the fourth century?

Q. Which theatre's name is that of a British actor, who made his Old Vic debut in 1921, and was knighted in 1953? He died in May 2000.

95 STARTER

Q. Thought to have originated in *Private Eye* magazine in the 1960s, when it was used to describe the lapses of the then Foreign Secretary George Brown, which three-word phrase serves as a euphemism for being drunk?

BONUS QUESTIONS

Three questions on observations on war:

Q. What did the American politician Hiram Johnson define as 'the first casualty of war' in a speech to the US Senate at the end of the First World War?

Q. Who, in a 1938 speech on the subject of war, said '... there are no winners, but all are losers'?

Q. Which historian, in his 1963 history of the First World War, wrote that it had been 'imposed on the statesmen of Europe by railway timetables. It was an unexpected climax to the railway age'?

96 STARTER

Q. Who is being described? Born the son of a vicar in 1772, he incurred massive debts from his debauched behaviour and left Cambridge without a degree. A brief stint in the army saw him discharged on a plea of insanity. He formulated but abandoned a plan to build a utopian society in Pennsylvania, and in 1797 formed a lifelong friendship with William Wordsworth?

BONUS QUESTIONS

Three questions on sisters:

Q. Which star cluster in constellation Taurus is named after the seven sisters of Greek myth, the daughters of Atlas and Pleione, who were transformed into stars?

Q. Which novel of 1872 features the sisters Dorothea and Celia Brooke?

Q. What is the surname of the musical sisters Andrea, Sharon and Caroline?

97 STARTER

Q. What word derives from the Greek for 'water' and 'labour', and refers to the process of growing plants in sand, gravel or liquid, without soil and with added nutrients?

BONUS QUESTIONS

Three questions on unknowns:

Q. Who was given the epithet 'The Great Unknown' by his publisher James Ballantyne because his novels written between 1814 and 1827 were published anonymously?

Q. The body of the unknown soldier is buried in Westminster Abbey, but in the USA the bodies of three unknown American soldiers are similarly honoured at the national cemetery in which site in Virginia?

Q. Which English poet and satirist, in his 'Ode on solitude' of 1717, wrote: 'thus let me live, unseen, unknown / thus unlamented let me die'?

98 STARTER

Q. Whose first book was an autobiographical account of his love affair with a football club, and was followed by a novel about an obsession with music and a third entitled *About A Boy*?

BONUS QUESTIONS

Q. In medieval law, felonies were defined as crimes of sufficient gravity for the offender to lose his right to own what?

Q. Now often used to denote rowdy confusion or chaos, what word was historically applied to malicious injury that impaired or destroyed the victim's capacity for self-defence?

Q. 'Grand larceny' was a term in use in England before 1827 to describe theft of property above what value?

99 STARTER

Q. Which Christian statement of faith is accepted as authoritative by both Western and Eastern churches, is used principally in the eucharist, and begins 'we believe in one God, the Father, the Almighty, Maker of Heaven and Earth, of all that is seen or unseen'?

BONUS QUESTIONS

Three questions on European cities:

Q. In which European capital, located on the Danube, were the ancient city walls replaced in 1857 by the Ringstrasse, a broad boulevard encircling the old city?

Q. In which European city, located at the head of Lake Ijssel, does the 'old church' occupy a site which has been the location of a church since 1300?

Q. As well as in Paris, there is another Arc de Triomphe in Northern Europe. It can be found in the same city as the 'Grand Place'. Which city?

100 STARTER

Q. Which British retail chain has its origins in a single shop in Brighton which opened in 1976, and has grown into a multinational enterprise with over 1600 stores in 48 countries?

BONUS QUESTIONS

Three questions on prisoners:

Q. In 1998, it was announced that a cell in the Tower of London would be opened to the public as part of the Millennium celebrations. Who was its most famous occupant, imprisoned between April and July 1534?

Q. Robert Stroud, who died in 1963, spent the last 54 years of his life in prison. During this time he carried out scientific research, and published a noted work of scholarship in 1943. What was his nickname?

Q. Who was arrested in November 1660 for preaching without a licence, spending most of the next 12 years in prison, during which time he wrote several books on religious themes?

101 STARTER

Q. Which British soldier led the relief of Cawnpore and Lucknow in 1857, and has given his name to the neck-flap at the back of the traditional cap worn by soldiers in the French Foreign Legion?

BONUS QUESTIONS

Three questions on mythical lands:

Q. In Norse mythology, what was the name of the heaven at the centre of the universe in which Valhalla was situated?

Q. What was the name of the mythical land beyond land's end that, according to Spenser, was the birthplace of Tristram and, according to Tennyson, was the scene of King Arthur's death?

Q. What was the mythical Celtic land of youth beyond the western sea, populated by the 'tuatha dé danann', 'the people of the goddess Danu'?

102 STARTER

Q. What abbreviation refers to the currently fashionable district of Manhattan which forms a triangular area to the south of Canal Street?

BONUS QUESTIONS

Q. Which annual payment derives its name from the fact that, until 1831, the salaries of judges and civil servants were paid from the allowance, although now it refers to the amount allowed by parliament for the Royal Family's household expenses?

Q. In which operetta by Gilbert and Sullivan does the lord high executioner boast that he has 'a little list'?

Q. Which documentary work, first published in 1982, has appeared under two titles, one a 'list', the other an 'ark'?

103 STARTER

Q. C_6H_5OH is the chemical formula for which white, soluble substance used as a disinfectant and in the production of drugs, weedkillers and synthetic resins?

BONUS QUESTIONS

Three questions on publishers' emblems, or colophons:

Q. Which long-established publishing house has a sailing ship as its colophon?

Q. Although published by various houses since its establishment in 1768, the *Encyclopaedia Britannica* retains which colophon, indicative of its geographic roots?

Q. Which publishing house, founded in Cambridge in 1844, uses the initial letter 'M' as a colophon?

104 STARTER

Q. Which distinguished British mountaineer, asked in 1923 why he proposed to climb Mount Everest, replied 'because it's there'?

BONUS QUESTIONS

Three questions on film adaptations of cartoon strips:

Q. Which actor played Obelix in a French film adaptation of the cartoon strip *Asterix the Gaul*, released in France in 1999?

Q. Which actor played Popeye in a 1980 Hollywood adaptation of the cartoon strip?

Q. In the first film adaptation of *The Flintstones*, John Goodman played Fred Flintstone; who played Barney Rubble?

105 STARTER

Q. Having worked as a bricklayer and then as an actor, which English dramatist is believed to have been the first to oversee the publication of a collected edition of his own plays, which appeared in 1616, including *The Alchemist* and *Bartholomew Fair*?

BONUS QUESTIONS

Q. From the Latin 'to refuse', what name was given, mainly in the sixteenth and seventeenth centuries, to Roman Catholics and others who would not attend Church of England services?

Q. What term was applied to churchmen who depended upon reason to establish the moral certainty of Christian doctrines rather than tradition, especially seventeenth century Anglican clerics whose beliefs and practices were viewed by conservatives as unorthodox?

Q. Latitudinarians were the precursors of which movement in the nineteenth century Church of England that eschewed narrow expressions of doctrine as practiced by high churchmen on one hand and low churchmen on the other?

106 STARTER

Q. Which adverising slogan was devised by B.J. Kidd of the Ayer Agency of Chicago, on behalf of De Beers Consolidated Mines, in an attempt to boost sales of engagement rings? A variation on the slogan was used by Ian Fleming for the title of a novel of 1956.

BONUS QUESTIONS

Q. Who rose to prominence while conducting the English National Opera in the 1980s and in June 1999 replaced Kent Nagano as music director of the Hallé Orchestra?

Q. Which liqueur's name is derived from the Italian for elder, as that was its original flavouring ingredient, although it is now aniseed-flavoured, traditionally served with a coffee bean and set alight?

Q. Which sweet liqueur has a name derived from Scottish Gaelic for 'satisfying drink'?

107 STARTER

Q. What first was achieved by the French footballer Lucien Laurent in the nineteenth minute of a match on Sunday 13 July 1930 against Mexico?

BONUS QUESTIONS

Q. Elected since 1866, The Lower House of the Tynwald, The Isle of Man Parliament, is known by what name thought to derive from a Norse word for 'chosen'?

Q. *The House of the Seven Gables*, Nathaniel Hawthorne's novel of a jinxed family, is said to have been inspired by his own family history as his great-grandfather allegedly presided over what proceedings and was cursed by one of his victims?

Q. 'House of Fun' reached number one in Britain in 1982 for which group?

108 STARTER

Q. In which ship did Captain Scott set sail on his doomed expedition to the South Pole in 1911?

BONUS QUESTIONS

Three questions on American history:

Q. Which doctrine was first put forward in the USA in 1798 by James Madison and Thomas Jefferson, who claimed that states had the right to prevent the application of federal laws within their borders if they felt them to be unconstitutional?

Q. The Missouri compromise of 1820 aimed to exclude what from all parts of the Louisiana purchase north of latitude 36 degrees 30 minutes, although it would still be allowed in Missouri?

Q. What appropriate name was given to an act of 1862 that hoped to encourage settlement of the American west by giving a farm of 160 acres to any citizen being over 21 or the head of a family?

109 STARTER

Q. In which military formation were officers forbidden to compromise their dignity by smoking Virginia cigarettes, reversing in the waltz, carrying parcels in public or wearing brown shoes east of Ascot?

BONUS QUESTIONS

Q. In the card game solo whist, how many tricks are required to achieve an 'abondance' or 'royal abondance' call?

Q. When W.B.Yeats wrote 'nine bean-rows will I have there', to what place was he referring?

Q. Which detective solved the 'Nine Tailors' mystery in the novel by Dorothy L. Sayers?

110 STARTER

Q. Sinn Fein is the name of the nationalist party in Northern Ireland, but what is the literal meaning of Sinn Fein?

BONUS QUESTIONS

Q. What was the title of the 1933 novel, set in the Tibetan lamasery of Shangri-La, where inmates enjoyed perpetual youth?

Q. Who, in his 1877 work *The Lost Chord*, put music to the poem by Adelaide Anne Proctor as a tribute to his late brother?

Q. What is the name of the palace built by Satan in Book One of Milton's *Paradise Lost*?

111 STARTER

Q. Which two words are the Spanish for 'strained pineapple', and in English refer to a drink usually made from pineapple juice, rum and coconut?

BONUS QUESTIONS

Three questions on drownings:

Q. According to Greek mythology, who drowned while swimming the Hellespont to meet his lover hero, a priestess of Venus?

Q. In August 1875 Captain Matthew Webb, the first person to swim the Channel, was drowned while attempting another, more dangerous, swim at which location?

Q. Who was the secretary of state for war who was drowned when *HMS Hampshire* went down in 1916?

112 STARTER

Q. Created by Axel Springer, which German mass-circulation tabloid newspaper is dedicated to democracy and reconciliation, and was inspired by the post-war *Daily Mirror*?

BONUS QUESTIONS

Three questions on the Balearic Islands:

Q. Each of the Balearic Islands speaks its own distinctive dialect, derived from which language, spoken particularly in the Barcelona region of Spain?

Q. Puerto de la Salina is the only port, and San Francisco Javier the principal town, on which of the Balearic Islands?

Q. On which of the Balearic Islands are the Taulas to be found, these being megalithic structures from the pre-Roman era, believed to be supports for even larger structures no longer in existence?

113 STARTER

Q. Which British fashion designer is associated with the logo of a five petalled daisy?

BONUS QUESTIONS

Q. Which disease is caused by an increase in pressure within the eye as a result of blockage of the flow of aqueous humour?

Q. Sandstones, which have a sufficient colour of the mineral glauconite in them to give a greenish tinge to the unweathered rock, are known by what name?

Q. 'Glaucous', 'little' and 'common' are among the less common members of which family of sea-birds that nest in Britain?

114 STARTER

Q. What is the sum of the interior angles in a pentagon?

BONUS QUESTIONS

Three questions on British rivers:

Q. Which river, approximately 170 miles long, has the tributaries the Soare, the Dove and the Derwent?

Q. Which river, approximately 130 miles long, rises on the eastern slopes of Plynlimmon and is joined by the Elan near Rhayader?

Q. Which river is Scotland's longest at 118 miles, and rises on the northern slopes of Ben Lui, with headwaters called the Fillan and the Dochart?

115 STARTER

Q. Which philosopher, in his *Discourse* of 1637, came to the conclusion that he did indeed exist, since the very act of doubting required a doubter?

BONUS QUESTIONS

Q. The birthstone for December, which semi-precious gemstone is sky-blue or blue-green in colour, and is a form of hydrated copper and aluminium phosphate?

Q. In one of the world's first hard-rock mining operations, the ancient Egyptians obtained turquoise from which peninsula?

Q. Indicating the route by which it was transported to Europe, the name 'turquoise' is French for what?

116 STARTER

Q. Of which two words is 'modem' a contraction?

BONUS QUESTIONS

Three questions on lens defects:

Q. What name is given to the defect of a spherical lens or mirror, in which the rays of light from an object come to a focus in slightly different positions as a result of the curvature of the lens or mirror?

Q. Which defect of lenses, including the eye, is caused by the curvature being different in two mutually perpendicular planes, so that rays in one plane may be in focus while those in the other are out of focus?

Q. What name is given to the abberation of a lens or mirror, in which the image of a point lying off axis has a comet-shaped appearance?

117 STARTER

Q. 'Fax me', 'page me' and 'be my icon' are inscriptions which have recently appeared on which sweets, first available in 1954 when 'hey daddio' and 'be true' were among the featured legends?

BONUS QUESTIONS

The following lines are excerpts from the national anthems of various countries; in each case, name the country:

Q. 'Over Thrace the sun is shining, Pirin looms in purple glow'

Q. 'Land of mountains, land of streams, land of fields, land of spires, land of hammers, with a rich future'

Q. 'Your message, oh imam, of independence, freedom is inscribed on our souls. Oh martyrs your cries echo in the air of time'

118 STARTER

Q. What form of protection is enshrined in the Berne Convention, which was first signed in 1886?

BONUS QUESTIONS

Three questions on astronomy:

Q. Which American astronomer, who died in 1953, is credited with providing the first evidence of the expansion of the universe?

Q. What term is used for the displacement of spectral lines of stellar objects towards longer wavelengths, which gives evidence of the expansion of the universe?

Q. In 1925, Hubble introduced a classification scheme for galaxies recognizing three main types, 'elliptical' denoted by the letter 'E', 'spiral' denoted by 'S' and which type, denoted by 'SB'?

119 STARTER

Q. In Greek mythology, what name refers both to an attic goddess of fertility, and the personification of divine anger at human presumption?

BONUS QUESTIONS

Q. Which classic film of 1949 opens with the line: 'I never knew the old Vienna before the war, with its Strauss music, its glamour and easy charm'?

Q. Which film depicts love as a merry-go-round, has music by Oscar Straus, was set in Vienna in 1900, and was based on a play called *Der Reigen* by Arthur Schnitzler?

Q. What is the 'Riesenrad'? built in the late 1890s in Vienna's Prater Park, it features in the film *The Third Man*?

120 STARTER

Q. For what symbolic reason was nineteen-year-old Yoshinori Sakai chosen to light the Olympic flame at the opening of the Tokyo Games in 1964?

BONUS QUESTIONS

Three questions on pseudonymous French writers:

Q. What was the pseudonym used by the French dramatist Jean-Baptiste Poquelin, born in 1622?

Q. Born in 1873, which novelist's four *Claudine* novels were first published under her husband's pen name, Willy?

Q. Under what name did the teenaged Françoise Quoirez publish her novel *Bonjour Tristesse* in 1954?

FINAL

1 STARTER

Q. What is the popular name for Ranunculales, the order of plants comprising approximately 3000 annual and perrenial species?

BONUS QUESTIONS

Q. Built on the instructions of Bishop Erghum at the end of the fourteenth century, which cast iron mechanical device in Salisbury Cathedral is believed to be one of the oldest working examples of its kind in the world?

Q. Which of Christopher Marlowe's tragic heroes has the lines: the stars move still, time runs, the clock will strike/the devil will come...'?

Q. An isotope of which rare metallic element was first employed in the 1950s in the so-called atomic clock, now giving a level of accuracy of better than one second in a million years?

2 STARTER

Q. In heraldry, what name is given to a cross in the shape of a letter X, one form of which is sometimes known as Saint Andrew's cross?

BONUS QUESTIONS

Three questions on British towns and cities:

Q. Which British city contains an area known as the New Town, laid out on classical lines by the architect James Craig in the second half of the eighteenth century?

Q. Which town in the south of England was formerly a popular spa resort, and has a thoroughfare known as 'The Pantiles', which acquired the name after the street was paved in the early 1700s?

Q. Many ancient English towns and cities have had streets or districts known as 'The Shambles', the one in York being perhaps the best-known extant example. What trade or craft was carried out in shambles?

3 STARTER

Q. What is the principal protein found in blood plasma?

BONUS QUESTIONS

Q. In classical mythology, how were Aglaia, Thalia and Euphrosyne collectively known?

Q. Born in 1757, which Italian sculptor created a celebrated group study of the Three Graces?

Q. In which classic film western did Grace Kelly play the Quaker bride of a western lawman?

4 STARTER

Q. Which monk founded the monastry at Monte Cassino, where he established a rule of life which stressed communial living and the daily balance of prayer, work and study, a rule that was to be adopted by most western monasteries?

BONUS QUESTIONS

Three questions on collections of poetry:

Q. Which American poet's works were published in the 1850s and early 1860s in anthologies entitled *Leaves of Grass*?

Q. Which English poet's work has been published in collections entitled *The Hawk in the Rain*, *Lupercal* and *Moortown*?

Q. Which Welsh poet's work has been collected in the volumes *Song at the Year's Turning*, *Poetry for Supper*, and *Not That He Brought Flowers*?

5 STARTER

Q. For which actress did George Bernard Shaw create the role of Eliza Doolittle in *Pygmalion*, the actress also being famous for her observation that 'it doesn't matter what you do in the bedroom as long as you don't do it in the street and frighten the horses'?

BONUS QUESTIONS

Three questions on cities and their rivers:

Q. Which major French port is situated on the River Loire, about 30 miles from its mouth?

Q. Which Asian capital city has a name which means roughly mouth of the muddy river, and is situated at the confluence of the River Kelang and the River Gombak?

Q. What is the major city at the mouth of the Volga Delta, about 60 miles from the Caspian Sea?

6 STARTER

Q. Born in 1810, which German composer's works include four symphonies, a piano concerto and numerous chamber pieces; his later years were dogged by increasing mental illness, and he died in 1856, two years after a suicide attempt?

BONUS QUESTIONS

Q. Joan, wife of the Black Prince and only daughter of Edmund Plantagenet, was known by what epithet?

Q. Also called 'the fair maid', Margaret, granddaughter of Alexander III of Scotland and acknowledged as his heir, was the daughter of the king of which country?

Q. Fair maid of February was a once popular name for which flower?

7 STARTER

Q. Which sporting metaphor is used for making unheralded alterations to terms and considerations already agreed?

BONUS QUESTIONS

Three questions on teeth:

Q. Which alternative name for the premolars indicates that they have two points?

Q. What term is popularly used for the canine teeth in the upper jaw?

Q. Hutchinson's teeth, which have a notched edge, are characteristic of which disease when acquired congenitally?

8 STARTER

Q. What term is applied to a restraint on the expansion of an economy as a result of government taxation policy, whereby a rise in inflation causes a larger proportion of a wage earner's income to be paid in tax?

BONUS QUESTIONS

Q. What is the title of Joseph Conrad's debut novel published in 1895, the central character, Captain Tom Lingard, appearing in two of the author's future works *An Outcast of the Islands* and *The Rescue*?

Q. Which eighteenth-century novelist, playwright and poet wrote the lines, 'when lovely woman stoops to folly/and finds too late that men betray,/what charm can soothe her melancholy,/what art can wash her guilt away?'

Q. According to Edward Gibbon what was little more than the register of the crimes, follies and misfortunes of mankind?

9 STARTER

Q. The nineteenth century American lawyer and anthropologist, Lewis Henry Morgan, lived with and was adopted into which tribe of North American Indians, now mainly found in the north eastern United States and eastern Canada?

BONUS QUESTIONS

Q. British troops serving in which country towards the end of World War II were considered to be the forgotten army as many people felt the war to be over following VE Day?

Q. Who was supreme allied commander in South-East Asia who reassured the Burmese troops with the words, 'you are not the forgotten army – nobody's even heard of you!'?

Q. Of which British island, having strong links with his great-grandmother, was Mountbatten made governor in 1965 and Lord Lieutenant nine years later?

10 STARTER

Q. Which measure, originally the reach of the outstretched arms, is now defined as 1.8 metres or 6 feet and is used as a unit of depth of water?

BONUS QUESTIONS

Q. Which English mezzo-soprano studied at the Mozarteum in Salzburg, made her operatic debut in 1956 and in 1971 created the role of Kate Julian, written especially for her, in Benjamin Britten's *Owen Wingrave*?

Q. The English civil engineer Benjamin Baker, in a series of articles published in 1867, discussed the application of the cantilevers used in his designs for which Scottish bridge, completed in 1890?

Q. In 1970, James A. Baker ran whose campaign for the US Senate, ten years later directing the same man's campaign for the presidential nomination in the Republican primaries?

11 STARTER

Q. In electricity and magnetism, magnetic field strength is conventionally denoted by the letter 'H', but which property is denoted by the letter 'B'?

BONUS QUESTIONS

Three questions on religious themes:

Q. Followers of which religious faith were given their present name in Antioch in Asia Minor, when some of its leading figures moved there in the first century?

Q. In Bunyan's *Pilgrim's Progress*, what was Christian's ultimate destination when he set off from the city of destruction?

Q. Who founded the Christian Science religious movement in Boston in 1879?

12 STARTER

Q. What, in a media context, have come to be referred to as 'red tops'?

BONUS QUESTIONS

Q. What name was given to the social reform and literary movement, which was founded by Ludolf Wienborg, Karl Gutzkow and Theodor Mundt in the 1830s?

Q. Born in 1720, who was known as the Young Chevalier?

Q. What payments were reduced by about 70 per cent under the terms of the Young Plan of 1929-30, sometimes described as 'too little, too late'?

13 STARTER

Q. *Vultur gryphus*, a bird native to South America with a wing span reaching 10 metres, is better known by what name?

BONUS QUESTIONS

Three questions on acts of parliament and the Anglican Church:

Q. Which act of 1534 set aside papal authority, and established the monarch as head of the Church of England?

Q. Which act of 1673 directed that all holders of public office had to be communicants of the Church of England?

Q. Which act of 1701 prohibited Roman Catholics from acceding to the throne, or the heirs to the throne from marrying Roman Catholics?

14 STARTER

Q. Either warlike or festive, the Corroboree is a traditional dance ceremony associated with native people of which country?

BONUS QUESTIONS

Three questions on fictional doctors:

Q. Which doctor was created by Max Brand for a series of successful novels, first adapted for the screen in 1937? The character later became the basis of a successful television series.

Q. Which former anaesthetist and assistant editor of the *British Medical Journal* created Dr Simon Sparrow for a successful series of novels, beginning with *Doctor in the House*?

Q. Which author created Dr Finlay, the subject of two successful television series, one in the 1960s and one in the 1990s?

15 STARTER

Q. The path to the well at the top of a hill in the village of Kilmersdon in Somerset is to be restored in memory of which lovers, immortalized in nursery rhyme?

BONUS QUESTIONS

Q. Which actress was born Anna Maria Italiano in New York in 1931, had her first major success as Anne Sullivan in *The Miracle Worker* in 1962, and appeared as Mrs Robinson in *The Graduate*, and Mrs Kendal in *The Elephant Man*?

Q. Bancroftian is the commonest form of which disorder, caused by a nematode living principally in the lymph nodes and vessels, which is usually transmitted to humans by the mosquito *Culex fatigans*?

Q. What is the name of the legal system of the church, which was formalized mainly by the papal bureaucracy from the twelfth century, and substantially revised in 1604 for the Church of England by Richard Bancroft, Archbishop of Canterbury?

16 STARTER

Q. In philosophy, what name, derived from the Greek for 'take', is given to a proposition put forward in the course of an argument, often accompanied by its own proof?

BONUS QUESTIONS

Three questions on names of political parties:

Q. Which words have been added to the name of the political party 'Plaid Cymru', presumably to make it more appealing to non-Welsh speakers?

Q. What name was adopted by the Communist Party of Great Britain in 1991, coinciding with their decision to concentrate on political debate rather than contesting elections?

Q. Under what name did the Social Democratic Party and the Liberal Party jointly campaign between 1981 and 1987?

17 STARTER

Q. *Ivanov*, first performed in Moscow in 1887, was the first full length play by which writer?

BONUS QUESTIONS

Q. In metallurgy, what name is given to a permanent change in the physical dimensions of a metal caused by the application of a continuous stress and, in geology, to the slow downward movement of particles on slopes covered with loose, weathered material?

Q. Who, in his *Poems for Children*, wrote: 'Hi! handsome hunting man /fire your little gun. /bang! now the animal /is dead and dumb and done./nevermore to peep again, creep again, leap again,/eat or sleep or drink again, oh, what fun!'?

Q. Which group took their name from a track on the Talking Heads album *True Stories*, and had a top ten hit in 1993 with 'Creep'?

18 STARTER

Q. Said to have been coined by R.B. McCallum, an Oxford don, from the Greek word for the pebble which Athenians dropped into an urn to vote, what term is used for the study of political elections?

BONUS QUESTIONS

Q. Which of the Scottish islands is to the immediate south-west of Jura, is the southernmost of the Inner Hebrides, and is known for its whisky distilleries?

Q. Which island in Strathclyde region shares its name with the kyles, or straits, separating it from the mainland?

Q. Which kyle is separated from Skye by Kyle Akin?

19 STARTER

Q. Which type of small, dried grape derives its name from the Greek city of Corinth, the centre for its export?

BONUS QUESTIONS

Q. Whose portrait was painted twice by Jacques-Louis David, in 1810, 'distributing the eagles' and, in 1812, 'in his study'?

Q. Who, in his poem 'Don Juan', wrote that he 'was reckon'd, a considerable time/the grand napoleon of the realms of rhyme'?

Q. Which Italian sculptor's statue of Napoleon clothed only in a fig leaf can be seen at Apsley House in London?

20 STARTER

Q. Noting that the sun's rays fell vertically at the summer solstice in Aswan and at an angle of about seven degrees from the vertical at Alexandria some 500 miles north-west at the same time and date, what, in the third century BC, did Eratosthenes of Cyrene calculate to within about 10 per cent of the value accepted by modern astronomers?

BONUS QUESTIONS

Q. Which country was incorporated into Nazi Germany in March 1938 under the name Ostmark?

Q. Which German word, meaning 'union', was used for the annexation of Austria by Germany on 13 March 1938?

Q. Who resigned as chancellor of Austria on 11 March 1938, two days before Hitler proclaimed the Anschluss?

21 STARTER

Q. Running parallel to the Protestant Shankhill Road, the area around which main thoroughfare is the chief Catholic district of Belfast?

BONUS QUESTIONS

Three questions on ferromagnetism:

Q. Apart from iron, name any two of the elements which display ferromagnetism at normal room temperatures.

Q. What name is given to the regions within a ferromagnetic material, within which all the atomic magnetic moments are aligned, but between which the alignment may vary?

Q. Which French physicist gives his name to the temperature above which a ferromagnetic substance loses its ferromagnetism and becomes paramagnetic?

22 STARTER

Q. Former diplomat and mastermind Sir David H. Gunt, who died in July 1998, wrote the speech delivered by Harold Macmillan in Cape Town in 1960 containing which memorable line?

BONUS QUESTIONS

Three questions on ballet music:

Q. Although not particularly associated with ballet music, which composer wrote the music for the ballet *Les Petit Riens* in 1778, and was the composer of *Idomeneo* in 1781, which includes ballet sequences?

Q. Choreographed by Fokine and first performed in 1911, the ballet *Petrushka* is the story of a puppet who comes to life. Who wrote the music for the ballet?

Q. Who choreographed the ballet based on Mahler's 'Song of the Earth', which premiered in 1965, five years before he became director of the Royal Ballet?

23 STARTER

Q. Which Italian dish derives its name from a term meaning a knot in a piece of wood, and consists of small dumplings, usually made of potato or semolina flour?

BONUS QUESTIONS

Q. Born around 1450, the Dutch painter Jerome van Aeken, whose works include *The Seven Deadly Sins* and *The Garden of Earthly Delights*, was better known by what name?

Q. Invented by Fritz Haber and developed for industrial use by Carl Bosch, the Haber-Bosch process is a method of producing ammonia by the reaction of nitrogen with what?

Q. Which component of the fuel combustion system of a motor car was jointly invented by Robert Bosch and G. Honold in 1902?

24 STARTER

Q. For the measurement of distances, which landmark is the official centre of London?

BONUS QUESTIONS

Q. In the Odyssey, which nymph detained the hero for seven years on her island of Ogyvia, until Zeus ordered her to release him?

Q. Which American singer/songwriter, who died when his experimental plane crashed into the sea off California in 1997, wrote a song called 'Calypso' for his album *Windsong*, in honour of Jacques Cousteau?

Q. Calypso and Telesto, which share the orbit of Tethys, are satellites of which planet?

25 STARTER

Q. Floria is the first name of which operatic heroine, who commits suicide by throwing herself from the battlements of the Castel Sant Angelo in Rome?

BONUS QUESTIONS

Q. Which word is a corruption of the word 'business', and refers to a simplified language containing vocabulary from two or more languages?

Q. What word was coined in the 1960s for a type of French that contains many English loan words, and was adopted by Miles Kington to describe the schoolboy French of Britons abroad?

Q. Who invented the term 'newspeak' for a simplified version of English, which could not express concepts such as 'all men are created equal', because the concept of equality was 'crimethink'?

26 STARTER

Q. Derived from the Latin for 'little brain', what is the name of the lower posterior part of the brain, whose function is to co-ordinate voluntary movements and maintain balance?

BONUS QUESTIONS

Q. Often used as a toast, what is the Welsh for 'good health'?

Q. What is the third person singular present subjunctive of the Latin verb prodesse, meaning to be of use? It is often used as a salutation in drinking healths.

Q. From the Norwegian for 'bowl', what term is used by Scandinavians as a friendly exclamation before drinking?

27 STARTER

Q. First noticed by Aristotle, which fallacy is illustrated by the question, 'have you stopped beating your wife yet'?

BONUS QUESTIONS

Q. Of which island in the Mediterranean is Palermo the capital?

Q. Which Italian composer's opera *Les Vépres Siciliennes*, or 'The Sicilian Vespers', was commissioned for the Great Exhibition of Paris in 1855?

Q. Which composer, born in Catania, Sicily, in 1801, is best remembered for the operas *Norma* set in ancient Gaul, and *I Puritani*, ultimately derived from Scott's *Old Mortality*?

28 STARTER

Q. Hash fudge was the most celebrated recipe in whose cook book, published in 1954, eight years after the death of her lover, Gertrude Stein?

BONUS QUESTIONS

The following adjectives are all used in botany, and all of them derive from the shape of a piece of weaponry. In each case, from which piece of weaponry does the adjective derive.

Q. Sagittate?

Q. Hastate?

Q. Peltate?

29 STARTER

Q. What can be found on Mount Hopkins in Arizona, or Mount Licke in Texas and on Mount Wilson in California?

BONUS QUESTIONS

Three questions linked by a name:

Q. Starting work at NATO as a minute taker in 1980 after having gained a doctorate in 1978 for his thesis on the role of the intellectuals in mobilizing public support for the First World War, who was NATO's chief spin doctor during the Kosovo crisis?

Q. Which politician had a long affair with Katharine, the wife of William Henry O'Shea, finally marrying her in June 1891, four months before his death?

Q. The Shea Stadium in Flushing in the borough of Queens is the home of which baseball team?

30 STARTER

Q. An oneiroscopist is an interpreter of what?

BONUS QUESTIONS

Q. Equal to one lumen per square metre, what is the SI unit of illuminance?

Q. Used as a rocket propellant, what is abbreviated to lox?

Q. Derived originally from Old Norse, lax is a word for which fish?

31 STARTER

Q. Sweyn Forkbeard, who was King of Denmark from about 987 to 1014, was the father of which King of Denmark and England?

BONUS QUESTIONS

Three questions on sports cars:

Q. Which dancer was accidentally strangled when her scarf caught in the wheel of a Bugatti sports car she was planning to buy?

Q. Which ill-fated make of sports car was used for time travelling in the *Back To The Future* films?

Q. Which of the James Bond films, the fourth in the series, features a pre-titles sequence in which Bond takes off from a balcony with a portable jet pack, and lands beside his waiting Aston Martin DB5?

32 STARTER

Q. Supposedly originally designed so that divinity students could be spotted nipping into brothels, red gowns are worn by students of which Scottish university?

BONUS QUESTIONS

Q. When he wrote the score for Otto Preminger's *Anatomy of a Murder*, which jazz orchestra leader became the first black composer commissioned to write a major film soundtrack?

Q. Ellington himself was an accomplished performer on which instrument, having been taught to play it as a child by a Miss Clinkscales?

Q. Ellington's suite 'Such Sweet Thunder' was a musical portrait of characters created by which playwright?

33 STARTER

Q. *The Countess's Morning Levée*, part of the *Marriage à la Mode* series, was painted by which British artist between 1743 and 1745?

BONUS QUESTIONS

Q. What is the more common name for the grasslike plants of the family Cyperaceae, found in wet regions and including some bulrushes and cotton grass?

Q. In Keats' poem 'La Belle Dame Sans Merci', what line follows, 'the sedge is wither'd from the lake'?

Q. Three new towns have been built in the north east since the Second World War. Washington and Peterlee are two; which is the third, situated in Sedgefield?

34 STARTER

Q. Characterized by supple, low-slung bodies, finely moulded heads, long tails that aid them in balance and specialized teeth and claws, which is the smallest member of the animal family Felidae?

BONUS QUESTIONS

Q. Although La Paz is the government capital of Bolivia, which city, formerly called Chuquisaca, is the country's judicial and legal capital?

Q. Antonio Jose de Sucre, after whom the Bolivian city is named, was a revolutionary born in Cumana, New Granada in 1795 and considered the most able of the generals of which Venezuelan-born statesman?

Q. Bolivar's victory at the battle of Boyaca in 1819 achieved the liberation of New Granada; how was the territory renamed?

35 STARTER

Q. Which term for the class of chemical compounds whose molecular structure includes one or more planar rings joined by covalent bonds, was first applied to a group of hydrocarbons isolated from coal tar and distinguished by their odours?

BONUS QUESTIONS

Three questions on people born in Derbyshire:

Q. Which aeronautical engineer was born in Ripley in Derbyshire in 1887, his achievements including the development of the R100 airship, the Wellington bomber, and the so-called bouncing bombs?

Q. Which English novelist was born in Shirley in Derbyshire in 1872, his works including *Wolf Solent* in 1929, and *A Glastonbury Romance* in 1939?

Q. Which pioneer of tourism was born at Melbourne in Derbyshire in 1808, his first organized excursion being a trip for teetotallers from Leicester to Loughborough?

36 STARTER

Q. A musical note with the time value of one sixteenth of a howle note is known as a what?

BONUS QUESTIONS

Three questions on maths:

For the following functions f(x) what, in each case, is the simplest form of the derivative f-(x)'?

Q. sec x?

Q. tan-¹x?

Q. coth x?

37 STARTER

Q. What word can mean a sharp tap or blow, an unforseen phenomenon, especially in economics, expected to be temporary, and the image of an object on a radar screen?

BONUS QUESTIONS

Three questions on trade names:

Q. Marmite, the yeast spread first produced at Burton-on-Trent in 1902, takes its name from the French word for which object, prominently featured as the company trademark?

Q. The French word for parsley which has become a trademark of Ronchetti, who discovered a method of adding bleach to soap, became the name of which household product?

Q. The name of which product derives from a combination of the French word for rice, and part of the name of its inventor, Lacroix, who manufactured it from 1796?

38 STARTER

Q. A trichromat is a person who has normal what?

BONUS QUESTIONS

Three questions on haircuts:

Q. Lord Petre's infamous advance to Lady Anabella Fermour, in which he cut off a tress of her hair, was the inspiration for which mock heroic poem of 1712?

Q. After Delilah had cut off his hair and sapped his strength, Samson was taken as a prisoner to which Philistine city?

Q. Whose haircut, by the fashionable Beverly Hills crimper 'Christophe', took place aboard Air Force One' on 22 May 1993, causing the runways of Los Angeles airport to be closed for over half an hour?

39 STARTER

Q. In the Roman Catholic Church, what name is given to the book containing the complete service for Mass throughout the year?

BONUS QUESTIONS

Three questions on armaments:

Q. The name of which light sub-machine gun, used by the British army in World War Two, is derived from its designers, R. V. Shepherd and H. J. Turpen, and the small arms factory at Enfield where it was manufactured?

Q. Which artillery officer lends his name to the exploding bullet-filled shell that he devised in 1784?

Q. Nicknamed Black Jack, which US army general was Chief of Staff from 1921 to 1924, and shares his name with the land-based missile with a nuclear warhead deployed by the United States in West Germany from 1983?

40 STARTER

Q. What name is given to a short verse composition so constructed that the initial letters of the lines, taken consecutively, form one or more words?

BONUS QUESTIONS

Q. Which publication is Britain's oldest women's weekly magazine, founded in 1885 by Thomas Gibson Bowles, with the declared aims of covering, quote, 'the whole field of womanly action', and serving 'to be at once a valuable friend and a delightful companion'?

Q. Who directed in the 1938 comedy thriller *The Lady Vanishes*?

Q. *Lady Susan* is an early work by which English novelist, born in 1775?

41 STARTER

Q. The Greek god of the underworld, whose name Hades means 'the invisible', was most commonly called what, meaning 'the rich'?

BONUS QUESTIONS

Three questions on British history:

Q. Lord Chancellor from 1658, Edward Hyde, first Earl of Clarendon became the father-in-law of which monarch?

Q. What was the broad purpose of a series of measures, including the Corporation Act and the Act of Uniformity, generally referred to as the Clarendon Code, passed by the Cavalier parliament from 1661 to 1665?

Q. Clarendon, near Salisbury in Wiltshire, lends its name to the Constitutions of Clarendon – declarations of royal rights over the English church – promulgated there in 1164 by which monarch?

42 STARTER

Q. From the German derivation of the word, what was originally carried in a haversack?

BONUS QUESTIONS

Three questions on the gothic novel:

Q. Published in 1765 under the pen name of *Unophrio Muralto*, supposedly a medieval Italian canon, which fictional work is generally regarded as the first of the true gothic novels?

Q. Which remote and mysterious castle in the Apennines is the setting for the fourth and best known novel of Mrs Ann Radcliffe?

Q. *The Mysteries of Udolpho* has a dramatic effect upon Catherine Moreland during a visit to the medieval home of the Tilney family, in which novel by Jane Austen?

43 STARTER

Q. The phenomenon whereby, when subjected to mechanical pressure, positive electric charge appears on one side of certain non-conducting crystals and negative charge on the opposite side, is known as what?

BONUS QUESTIONS

Q. Knole, near Tunbridge Wells in Kent, was the family home of which gardener and writer, born in 1892?

Q. Vita Sackville-West was married in 1913 to which diplomat and biographer, with whom she spent several years living in Persia?

Q. In the surrounds of which Tudor house near Maidstone did Sackville-West and Nicholson create their influential garden designs?

44 STARTER

Q. *The Less Deceived* and *High Windows* are collections of verse by which writer, who turned down the poet laureateship after the death of his friend, John Betjeman, in 1984?

BONUS QUESTIONS

Three questions on America:

Q. Which American state shares its name with that of the purchase of 1803 when, for 15 million dollars, America purchased from France the largest area ever added to its territory at one time?

Q. What name is given to the French-speaking descendants of the eighteenth-century dissidents who settled in Louisiana after their exile from Nova Scotia?

Q. By which nickname is the state of Louisiana now also known?

45 STARTER

Q. A prolate spheroid is generated by rotating an ellipse about its major axis; what name is given to the figure obtained by rotating an ellipse about its minor axis?

BONUS QUESTIONS

Three questions on political movements:

Q. Giovane Italia, the Young Italy movement, was founded in 1831 by which patriot and nationalist?

Q. Killed fighting the Bolsheviks in Turkestan, which politician and soldier led the revolt in 1908 that resulted in the rebellion of the Young Turks against Sultan Abd-ul-Hamad II?

Q. Agitating for the repeal of the Act of Union, which magazine was the principal publication of the 'Young Ireland' movement?

46 STARTER

Q. The site of which ancient city includes the 'processional way', which runs north-east from the temple of Marduk and through the Ishtar Gate, which guarded the city's northern side?

BONUS QUESTIONS

Three questions on cinema and clothing:

Q. Which actress became known as 'the sarong girl', after the costume designer Edith Head adapted the garment for her first feature film appearance, in *The Jungle Princess* in 1936?

Q. Which American actress popularized the baby doll, a skimpy night-dress she wore in the 1956 film of the same name?

Q. Which actress briefly popularized the women's fashion of wearing loose-fitting men's clothes, a look which took its name from her eponymous screen role of 1977?

47 STARTER

Q. The 'Saunders and Roe Number One', or S.R.- N1, was launched in 1959 and was the first full-sized practical version of which method of transport?

BONUS QUESTIONS

Three questions on zoology:

Q. Otherwise known as 'mutualism', which term in zoology derives from the Greek for 'to live together', and describes a relationship, usually between members of two different species, in which both parties benefit in some way and neither is disadvantaged?

Q. What loose form of symbiosis is known as iniquilinism?

Q. What is the essential difference between parasitic symbionts known as endoparasites, and those termed ectoparasites?

48 STARTER

Q. What name derives from that of a British explorer and statesman, born in 1781, and is given to a parasitic growth largely confined to the forests of Malaysia, notable for bearing the world's largest flower with a smell comparable to rotting flesh?

BONUS QUESTIONS

Q. The most efficient cycle of operations for a reversible heat engine is named after which French engineer, who conceived it early in the nineteenth century?

Q. The Carnot cycle involves two pairs of reversible expansion and compression processes; which types of processes are they?

Q. What is the efficiency, expressed as a percentage, of a Carnot engine which takes in heat at 600 degrees kelvin and gives it out at 300 degrees kelvin?

49 STARTER

Q. In August 1998, the Garrick Club was placed in the enviable position of having to decide how to distribute a £40 million payment from the Disney Corporation for the rights to use which character, the club having been left a share of the rights by the author?

BONUS QUESTIONS

Q. Belonging to the Tupi-Guarani family, Guarani is the most widely spoken language in which South American country?

Q. Traditionally spoken by indigenous farmers, Amharic is the native tongue of about 60 per cent of the population of which African country?

Q. Persian, or Dari, and Pushto are the official languages of which republic in south-western Asia?

50 STARTER

Q. Born around 1547, Nicholas Hilliard was a leading exponent of which form of portrait painting, his notable subjects including Queen Elizabeth I, Sir Walter Raleigh and Sir Philip Sidney?

BONUS QUESTIONS

Three questions on the European Space Agency:

Q. The European Space Agency, established in 1975, has its headquarters in which capital city?

Q. What name was given to the ESA rocket launching system, used to put the planetary probe Giotto into orbit in July 1985 to rendezvous with Halley's Comet?

Q. Which ESA probe, launched in 1997, is named after a seventeenth-century Dutch astronomer?

51 STARTER

Q. What are the Swedish OMX, the Swiss SMI, the Russian RTS, and the French CAC 40?

BONUS QUESTIONS

Three questions on a twentieth-century dramatist:

Q. The play submitted to BBC radio under the title *The Boy Hairdresser* was broadcast in 1964 as *The Ruffian on the Stair*, and was an early play by which dramatist?

Q. For which offence were Joe Orton and his partner Kenneth Halliwell imprisoned in 1962?

Q. Which of Joe Orton's plays was first produced in 1969, two years after his death, and includes the psychiatrist Doctor Prentice among its characters?

52 STARTER

Q. Which severe medical condition is specific to pregnancy and is characterized by raised blood pressure, swelling of the ankles or fingers, and the presence of protein in urine?

BONUS QUESTIONS

Q. What name was given to the style of art particularly in vogue from about 1890 until the First World War, and based on the sinuous, asymmetrical lines of natural forms?

Q. Which London store, founded in 1875, was instrumental in popularizing Art Nouveau, but first specialized in oriental wares, a fact reflected in a roofline frieze showing goods travelling by camel and elephant towards an image of Britannia?

Q. Who began selling toys in London in 1760, calling his outlet 'Noah's Ark'?

53 STARTER

Q. The Russian hero Alexander Yaroslavich incorporated the name of which river into his own name, after his victory over the Swedes on the river's banks in 1240; it flows west through the Russian Federation from Lake Lagoda to the Gulf of Finland, passing through St Petersburg?

BONUS QUESTIONS

Q. In the apocryphal book *The History of Susanna*, which prophet is said to have delivered Susanna from charges of adultery by speaking separately to the two elders who accused her and demonstrating their untruthfulness?

Q. According to the Old Testament apocrypha, which Babylonian god was exposed by Daniel to be no more than an image which the prophet destroyed?

Q. In Shakespeare, which character is described as 'a Daniel come to judgement'?

54 STARTER

Q. Dating from 1898, which annual British publication gives an illustration and technical details of every significant ship in every navy of the world?

BONUS QUESTIONS

Q. *Kosmos* is the major work of which German naturalist and geographer, born in 1769, who explored South America with Aimé Bonpland and Central Asia with Eherenberg?

Q. The Humboldt current, flowing northwards along the west coast of South America, is otherwise known by the name of which country?

Q. Who was awarded the Nobel Prize for literature shortly after the publication of his novel *Humboldt's Gift* in 1975?

55 STARTER

Q. In 1842, which physician wrote the first major histological description of the kidney, the capsule surrounding the glomerulus being named in his honour?

BONUS QUESTIONS

Three questions on mythology:

Q. In Greek mythology, Aphrodite is married to which god?

Q. Harmonia is generally said to have been the daughter of Aphrodite, the issue of her adulterous relationship with which son of Zeus?

Q. Fathered by Anchises – a member of the royal line of Dardania – which Trojan leader was born to Aphrodite on Mount Ida?

56 STARTER

Q. Which composer and Wolverhampton Wanderers fan is credited with writing the first football chant when he set to music 'banged the leather for goal', as the winning goal in the 1893 cup final was described to him by Dora Penny?

BONUS QUESTIONS

Q. In *A Midsummer Night's Dream* Puck reckoned he could put a girdle round the earth in what length of time?

Q. 'Forty Years On', the title of the Harrow School song, was used by which playwright for his work of 1968?

Q. According to a rhyme based on a real-life trial in Massachusetts in 1893, who: 'took an axe and gave her mother forty whacks'?

57 STARTER

Q. Which imperial unit of area is equal to 4046.86 square metres?

BONUS QUESTIONS

Q. What collective name is used to refer to the seven major English kingdoms which were in existence at the end of the seventh century?

Q. Which King of Mercia briefly established himself as King of the English, the first major minting of Anglo-Saxon silver pennies being among his achievements?

Q. Lying on the River Itchen and formerly the capital of England under Alfred the Great, which city was a major centre of the Wessex Anglo-Saxon kingdom?

58 STARTER

Q. Which three word phrase describes the distance, equivalent to less than three-quarters of a mile, prescribed by Jewish tradition as the maximum to be travelled on a certain day of the week?

BONUS QUESTIONS

Three questions on philosophers:

Q. Born in 1588 to an impoverished family in Wiltshire, which philosopher, mathematician and linguist was the author of *Leviathan*, first published in 1651?

Q. Which philospher served in the Peloponnesian war with Sparta, and was charged in 399 BC with neglecting the established gods and introducing new divinties?

Q. *La Nausée*, published in 1938, was the first novel by which philosopher?

59 STARTER

Q. Officially designated 'free and Hanseatic', which German city is sited on the River Elbe, is the second most populous in Germany after Berlin, and features the notorious Reeperbahn as the principal street in its red-light district?

BONUS QUESTIONS

Q. Sometimes a symptom of inner ear disease, what name derives from the Latin for 'turning around', and is given to the disabling sensation in which the affected individual feels that either he or his surroundings are in a state of constant movement?

Q. Having many causes, the medical symptom characterized by persistent buzzing or ringing sounds in the ear is known by which name?

Q. Caused by a build-up of fluid within the inner ear and often accompanied by bouts of deafness, vertigo and tinnitus, endolymphatic hydrops is more commonly known by which medical term?

60 STARTER

Q. Who is the eponymous hero of Ivan Goncharov's novel of 1855, whose name has passed into the Russian language as a symbol of passivity and inertia?

BONUS QUESTIONS

Three questions on Latin terms:

Q. Which two-word Latin term literally means 'bounteous mother', was applied by the Romans to several goddesses including Ceres, and has been used in English to mean one's old school or university, which were regarded as having fostered their alumni?

Q. The dura mater is the tough, outer membranous envelope of the spinal chord and which organ of the human body?

Q. Born in 1732, which Austrian composer's works include the Stabat Mater, described in *Grove's Dictionary* as 'a treasury of refined and graceful melody'?

61 STARTER

Q. What is the length of the hypotheneuse of a right-angled triangle, whose other two sides are of lengths eight units and fifteen units respectively?

BONUS QUESTIONS

Q. Also known as the quill pig, which New World rodent presents its rear when approached and, if attacked, uses its strong tail against its assailant?

Q. Who wrote the provocatively pro-British *Life and Adventures of Peter Porcupine* while living in the United States in 1796, and later, as a radical journalist back in Britain, wrote *Rural Rides*, which appeared in the political register from 1821?

Q. Nicknamed the flying porcupine by Luftwaffe pilots, what sort of aircraft was the Sunderland, manufactured by Short Brothers and operational with coastal command throughout World War II?

62 STARTER

Q. Who reciprocated her lover's gift of Walt Whitman's *Leaves of Grass* with *Vox*, a novel about telephone sex?

BONUS QUESTIONS

Q. In rowing, what term is used to describe the turning of an oar or paddle so that the blade is horizontal, in order to move it forward or backward with the minimum air or water resistance?

Q. In boxing, which weight comes between featherweight and flyweight?

Q. When archers still used real feathers on their arrows, what name was given to the central of the three feathers, spaced 120 degrees apart on the shaft to stabilize it in flight, although the feather was not necessarily from a male bird?

63 STARTER

Q. Which island was formerly a Carthaginian colony known as Eivissa, it is now part of the autonomous community of Spain co-extensive with the Baleares province, and lies some 50 miles south-west of Mallorca?

BONUS QUESTIONS

Three questions on quotations about sex:

Q. Which English biographer and conscientious objector, when asked by a military tribunal what he would do if he saw a German soldier about to violate his sister, reportedly answered 'I would try to get between them'?

Q. George Mikes, in his 1946 book *How to be an Alien'*, wrote that continental people have sex lives, the English have – what?

Q. In her journal, Alice, Lady Hillingdon, supposedly wrote in 1912, on the sound of her husband approaching her bedroom: 'I lie down on my bed, close my eyes, open my legs and...' do what?

64 STARTER

Q. Diego Colon, who received the hereditary titles of viceroy of the Indies in 1511, was the eldest son of whom?

BONUS QUESTIONS

Three questions on variations of English:

Q. In which Scottish city is Kelvinside, which has given its name to an affected, hypercorrect imitation of received pronunciation since early this century?

Q. Taken from a type of stew, what name is given to the variety of English spoken on Merseyside, and also the inhabitants?

Q. The English spoken in which university city, as opposed to that spoken by the townspeople, was considered 'the best' English usage early this century, although it later became regarded as affected?

65 STARTER

Q. Which two-word term is used for an economic system in which the activities of firms and the allocation of productive resources is determined by government direction rather than market forces, the term 'planned economy' also being used for such a system?

BONUS QUESTIONS

Three questions on islands:

Q. Bathurst and Melville Islands are home to the Tiwi people who belong to which indigenous group, having preserved their homeland more successfully than their mainland counterparts?

Q. The Kiriwina or Trobriand Islands are coral formations in the Solomon Sea of the southwestern Pacific, lying some 90 miles north of the southeastern tip of which large island country?

Q. Torshavn, on Stromo Island, is the capital of which group of islands, a self-governing region within the Kingdom of Denmark?

66 STARTER

Q. What word derives in part from the German for education, and refers to a novel which specifically deals with its protagonist's youth and development?

BONUS QUESTIONS

Q. The occasion on which a ram's horn is sounded as a call to repentance and spiritual renewal, Rosh Hashana, is a Jewish festival marking which event?

Q. What name is given to the four-day festival which marks the Chinese new year?

Q. Tet is a three-day celebration marking the new year in which Asian country?

67 STARTER

Q. Of what is pharology the study, the word being derived from the name of an island off Alexandria, on which one of the seven wonders of the ancient world stood?

BONUS QUESTIONS

Three questions on drugs that have found alternative uses:

Q. Popularized as a controversal cure for impotence, what condition was the drug Viagra originally designed to treat?

Q. The drug Diamox, with the generic name acetazolomide, is licenced to help treat glaucoma and epilepsy, and has a side effect which helps mountaineers cope with what?

Q. The drug Minoxidil, originally developed to treat hypertension, has been sold under the proprietary name Regaine as a cure for what?

68 STARTER

Q. Which American politician made four runs for the presidency, having declared 'segregation now! segregation tomorrow! segregation forever!' in his inaugural address as Governor of Alabama in 1963, although he later recanted of such views; he died in September 1998?

BONUS QUESTIONS

Three questions on classical music:

Q. Of which of his works did Debussy say, 'you will say that the ocean does not exactly wash the Burgundian hillside and my seascapes might be studio landscapes'?

Q. 'Sunrise' is the best known episode of which tone poem by Richard Strauss, which was freely composed after the book by Friedrich Nietzsche?

Q. A cheerful pot-pourri of student songs was Brahms' own description of which overture, composed in 1880?

69 STARTER

Q. In engineering, what property of a substance is measured by the Brinell test?

BONUS QUESTIONS

Q. Formerly a teacher at Mount Holyoke College, which American-born writer was the author of *The Hotel New Hampshire* in 1981?

Q. Which jazz trumpeter and vocalist was a pioneer of west coast 'cool' jazz, and died in a fall from a hotel window in Amsterdam in 1988, during the making of a film about his life entitled *Let's Get Lost*?

Q. According to the song by 'The Eagles', 'you can check out any time you like, but you can never leave...' – which hotel?

70 STARTER

Q. Placing particular emphasis on inner motivation and psychological truth, what term is applied to the approach to acting popularized by the actor, director and teacher Lee Strasberg, which he based on ideas advanced by Stanislavsky in *An Actor Prepares*?

BONUS QUESTIONS

Three questions on musical instruments:

Q. First described in the late fifteenth century, the sackbut was developed from the medieval trumpet probably in Burgundy, and was an early form of which instrument?

Q. Born in Scotland in 1732, John Broadwood trained as a cabinet maker before becoming one of the greatest early manufacturers of which instrument, his early square models in the mid-1770s being based on those by Zumpe?

Q. Also associated with clarinets and oboes, Theobald Boehm made several improvements to which instrument in the mid-nineteenth century, changing the conical bore to the one now in general use, making fingering easier and so producing a more even tone?

71 STARTER

Q. 'Olbers' paradox', named after the German astronomer who discussed it in a work of 1826, concerns itself with which simple question?

BONUS QUESTIONS

Q. Its name said to have been chosen at random from a French dictionary, which modern art movement was founded at Zurich around 1916, partly as a reaction against the disillusionment engendered by World War I?

Q. *Pagoda Fruit* and *Eggboard* are among the works of which Strasbourg-born sculptor, a founder of Dadism who often collaborated with his wife, Sophie Tauber?

Q. The American anti-art magazine *291* was edited by which Dada painter, best known for his influential mechanistic style and his erotically charged imagery evident in such works as *I see again in memory, my dear Udnie*?

72 STARTER

Q. Forming part of the Saint Lawrence seaway, the Welland Ship Canal opened in 1933 to link Lake Erie and Lake Ontario, thus allowing shipping to bypass which geographical feature?

BONUS QUESTIONS

Three questions on woods and their uses:

Q. What name is usually given to the wood of any of several tropical hardwood timber trees, including the family Meliaceae, which is of a reddish-brown colour when mature, much used in making furniture?

Q. Which American timber, the true form of which is produced by four species of *carya*, has been used in the manufacture of lacrosse sticks because it can withstand the strain of hard play?

Q. Which European species of maple, especially those with a wavy grain, provides the traditional wood for violins?

73 STARTER

Q. In analytical chemistry, the brown ring test is used to determine the presence of which substances?

BONUS QUESTIONS

Q. According to the proverb, what is a dish that tastes better cold?

Q. Revenge is described as the dish which people of taste prefer to eat cold in which Ealing film comedy of 1949, involving the serial killing of an aristocratic family?

Q. Which English poet wrote: 'sweet is revenge – especially to women', in his work *Don Juan*, published between 1819 and 1824?

74 STARTER

Q. What is the Spanish for 'good night'?

BONUS QUESTIONS

Three questions on acronyms used in computing:

Q. A measure of computing speed and power which became increasingly common during the 1980s, what does the acronym MIPS represent?

Q. Which expression, often abbreviated to a four letter acronym, originated as computer jargon to imply that what emerges from a system is dependent on the quality of material entering it?

Q. What words are represented by the acronym MIDI, being an electronic device enabling equipment such as synthesizers to be connected to computers and used simultaneously?

75 STARTER

Q. Born in Stockholm in 1688, which Christian mystic and scientist worked as an assessor for the College of Mines, and was the author of *Opera Philosophica et Mineralia*, which represented a mixture of metallurgy and metaphysical speculation on the creation of the world; after his death, his followers formed the 'Church of the New Jerusalem'?

BONUS QUESTIONS

Q. Which monument on a hill outside Pretoria commemorates the battle of Blood River and the achievements of the first Dutch farmers in leaving the British Cape colony in Southern Africa and moving to the interior during the 1830s?

Q. The 500th anniversary of the death of which Portuguese prince is commemorated by the Monument to the Discoveries in Lisbon, erected in 1960?

Q. The Memorial to the Disappeared bears the names of those who went missing in detention, at one end of its 180 foot length, whilst those executed for political beliefs are at the other end; it was erected in which South American city, in remembrance of the coup of 1973?

76 STARTER

Q. 'Knight', 'Officer', 'Commander', 'Grand Officer' and 'Grand Cross' are the five grades or ranks of which honour, awarded in France for civil and military service, and created by Napoleon I in 1802?

BONUS QUESTIONS

Three questions on figures in Greek literature:

Q. In Aeschylus' play *Seven against Thebes*, the rival claimants to the throne are the sons of whom?

Q. Tiresias, the seer of Thebes who plays a prominent part in the Oedipus cycle of legends, suffers from which physical handicap?

Q. Who was the faithful daughter of Oedipus, who accompanied her blinded father into exile and took care of him in Colonus?

77 STARTER

Q. Which 'first' was achieved by seventeen-year-old Daniel Alter on 19 May 1999, when he began sitting on a folding chair outside the Mann Village Theater in Westwood, Los Angeles?

BONUS QUESTIONS

Three questions on remedies:

Q. *Desperate Remedies* was in 1871 the first published novel by which author, for which he deliberately adopted the popular formula of the sensation novel?

Q. The words 'a desperate disease requires a dangerous remedy' have been attributed to which soldier and Catholic convert, born in 1570?

Q. What did Walter Raleigh describe as 'a sharp remedy, but a sure one for all ills'?

78 STARTER

Q. What word derives from the Italian for 'follows', and was popularized by disc jockeys referring to two or more pieces of music played back to back with a smooth transition between them?

BONUS QUESTIONS

Three questions on Alaska:

Q. Prudhoe Bay has been the centre of drilling activities since the discovery of petroleum deposits on Alaska's north slope in 1968, and is an inlet of which sea?

Q. The trans-Alaskan oil pipeline links Prudhoe Bay to which ice-free port 800 miles to the south?

Q. Valdez was the principal settlement affected when the oil tanker *Exxon Valdez* ran aground in March 1989, in which stretch of water?

79 STARTER

Q. For what primary purpose are tartrazine and carotene added to food products?

BONUS QUESTIONS

Three questions on place names with political associations:

Q. Which street in Whitechapel was the scene of confrontations between police and anti-fascists attempting to prevent Oswald Mosley's British Union of Fascists from marching through predominantly Jewish areas of London?

Q. What was the name of the urban district council in Derbyshire which refused to implement the 1972 Housing Act, causing individual councillors to be surcharged and barred from office?

Q. In a so-called mutiny in 1914, at which military training camp in County Kildare did British cavalry officers threaten to resign if ordered to coerce Ulster into accepting home rule?

80 STARTER

Q. Having an important role in regulating the sleep cycle and determining seasonal breeding patterns in some mammals, which gland, situated above the third ventricle of the brain, synthesizes the hormone melatonin?

BONUS QUESTIONS

Identify the following planets from a selection of their statistics:

Q. Siderial period, 164.79 years, mass relative to earth, 17.2, number of satellites, 8.

Q. Equatorial diameter, 12,104 kilometres, axial tilt 177 degrees, number of satellites, nil.

Q. Siderial period, 29.46 years, axial period 10.66 hours, mass relative to earth, 95.17.

81 STARTER

Q. Which Anglican clergyman established the Samaritans in Britain in 1953?

BONUS QUESTIONS

Three questions on time:

Q. During the late 1870s, the Scottish-born civil engineer Sir Sandford Fleming played a prominent role in establishing which worldwide system of uniform time zones?

Q. What is the basic unit of coordinated universal time, which is the international basis of civil and scientific time?

Q. The caesium-beam atomic frequency used to regulate the speaking clock is generated at the National Physical Laboratory in Teddington, but from which town in Warwickshire do BT then transmit it?

82 STARTER

Q. Active in Paris at the end of the nineteenth century, the group of painters calling themselves 'Les Nabis' were particularly influenced by the mystic content and intense colour that characterized the work of which French artist?

BONUS QUESTIONS

In each case, identify these former medical students from their descriptions:

Q. After studying medicine at Moscow University and qualifying in 1884, he practised very little except during the cholera epidemic of 1892–1893 but was elected fellow of the Moscow Academy of Science in 1900 by which time his work as a playwright was starting to be recognized?

Q. Born in 1934, he qualified as a doctor at Cambridge University before making his directorial debut in 1962 at the Royal Court with *Under Plain Cover*, a play by John Osborne?

Q. This fashion designer initially studied medicine in Milan, and then worked for Nino Cerruti before setting up his own company in 1975?

83 STARTER

Q. What name is given to the parallel of about 66 degrees 32 minutes south, which marks the southernmost point at which the sun can be seen during the southern hemisphere's winter solstice?

BONUS QUESTIONS

Q. What first came into force in Britain in January 1904 when registration cost £1, and Earl Russell queued all night to acquire the first London one?

Q. The first annual suffix letter on number plates appeared in January of which year?

Q. What fundamental alteration was made to number plates in August 1983?

84 STARTER

Q. 'Stooge Viller', 'Doc Hump' 'Boris Arson' and 'The Mole' are among the adversaries of which fictional detective, created in 1931 by the American cartoonist Chester Gould?

BONUS QUESTIONS

Q. *Ad valorem* taxes, often preferred because their real value is not eroded by inflation, are proportional to what?

Q. Carbon tax, designed to reduce world output of carbon dioxide, is a proposed levy on the use of what type of materials?

Q. Which tax is designed to counter the loss of revenue from inheritance taxes through people transferring their wealth to others while still alive?

85 STARTER

Q. From 1981 until 1992, Heng Samrin led the puppet government of which Asian republic?

BONUS QUESTIONS

Q. At the Sydney Olympics, Denise Lewis won gold for Britain in the heptathlon. Of the seven disciplines contained in the heptathlon, name three for 5pts, five for 10pts and all seven for the full 15.

86 STARTER

Q. Originally an image of a saint or other holy person, particularly in the orthodox church, what term is now used for a much-admired person or a small picture on a computer screen?

BONUS QUESTIONS

Q. Organic compounds containing the group $CONH_2$ and inorganic compounds containing the ion NH_2- ($NH2$ minus), are known as what?

Q. Excreted by mammals, what is the more common name for the crystalline compound, carbamide?

Q. Used in insect repellents, by what abbreviation is diethyl toluamide commonly known?

87 STARTER

Q. Known around the turn of the century as 'bottled madness' and banned in France from 1914, which green liquor is traditionally based on a distillate of the herb wormwood?

BONUS QUESTIONS

Three questions on suffixes:

Q. Which seven letter suffix, from the Latin 'to fold', is used to denote a number of identical copies?

Q. Which four letter suffix comes from the Latin for 'head', and denotes the number of heads, or origins, of certain muscles of the body?

Q. Which four letter suffix, from the Latin for 'oar', is used to denote a galley with a given number of banks of oars?

88 STARTER

Q. Found in the mountainous regions of western North America, noted for its ferocious temperament and sometimes referred to as the 'silvertip', what is the more familiar name of any of about 80 sub-species of *Ursus horribilis*?

BONUS QUESTIONS

Three questions on cinematic vampires:

Q. Who played the vampire in pursuit of Isabelle Adjani in Werner Herzog's 1979 film *Nosferatu, Phantom Der Nacht*?

Q. Dracula, played by George Hamilton, flees from the communists and settles in New York in which 1979 spoof?

Q. In Bram Stoker's *Dracula*, released in Britain in 1993, who portrays vampire hunter Professor Abraham van Helsing?

89 STARTER

Q. The name of which French neurologist is associated with a disorder characterized by involuntary tics and the compulsive utterance of obscenities?

BONUS QUESTIONS

In which plays by Terence Rattigan do the following lines occur:

Q. 'elle a des idées au-dessus de sa gare'?

Q. 'the boy is plainly innocent. I accept the brief'?

Q. 'were you medaillon or goulash'?

90 STARTER

Q. What shape are the faces of a regular dodecahedron?

BONUS QUESTIONS

Q. Which English naval commander was given charge of the grand fleet on the outbreak of World War I, and was described by Winston Churchill as 'the only man on either side who could lose the war in an afternoon'?

Q. Of which Russian politician, who represented his country at the Potsdam Conference, did Churchill say, 'I have never seen a human being who more perfectly represented the modern conception of a robot'?

Q. Who in 1931 was referred to by Churchill as 'the boneless wonder sitting on the treasury bench'?

91 STARTER

Q. In English law, which division of the High Court deals with such matters as the administration of the estates of deceased persons, the execution of trusts, the enforcement of land sales and foreclosures of mortgages?

BONUS QUESTIONS

Three questions on spices:

Q. Which spice is the berry of the climbing vine *Piper nigrum*, and may be black, white or green?

Q. Which Chinese spice has a flavour similar to aniseed and resembles a flower in shape, with five to ten 'petals' acting as seed pods?

Q. In October 1997, on the steps outside the Albert Hall, the Spice Girls each read a line from Laurence Binyon's 1914 poem 'For the Fallen', to launch an appeal for which organization?

92 STARTER

Q. Piled on top of each other by legendary giants in order to reach the abode of the gods, which pair of mountains in Thesally in Greece are now used in a phrase meaning to heap one trouble upon another?

BONUS QUESTIONS

Three questions on astronomy:

Q. In 1931, the American engineer Karl Jansky discovered an extra-terrestrial source of what, giving rise to a new form of astronomy?

Q. What term describes the shape of the dish used in most radio telescopes, including the one at Jodrell Bank?

Q. Which technique used in radio astronomy is often referred to by the initials VLBI?

93 STARTER

Q. Princess Charlotte Augusta, who died in childbirth following her marriage to Leopold of Saxe-Coburg, was the only child of which British monarch?

BONUS QUESTIONS

Three questions on terms used in literature:

Q. Deriving from the Greek for 'depth', what word describes a passage intended to be solemn and impressive but which fails due to a textual incongruity, as in Wordsworth's lines: 'the piteous news, so much it shocked her /she quite forgot to send the doctor'?

Q. Which word means a repetition of two or more identical vowel sounds, as in John Masefield's *Sea Fever*: 'and a grey mist on the sea's face and a grey dawn breaking'?

Q. Which word means a figure of speech which opposes or contrasts ideas, and is demonstrated by John Milton in *Paradise Lost* with the line 'better to reign in hell, than serve in heaven'?

94 STARTER

Q. Which artist and illustrator, born in 1872, became known for his drawings of fantastic and elaborate contraptions designed to perform simple tasks, such as raising a hat or boiling an egg?

BONUS QUESTIONS

Q. Bertolt Brecht's play *The Resistible Rise of Arturo Ui* is a parable of Hitler's rise to power, and is set in which American city?

Q. Known as Big John, which building was the first in Chicago to exceed 1000 feet?

Q. Known for his work in both theatre and film, who directed and choreographed the musical *Chicago*, in its first run in New York in 1975?

95 STARTER

Q. What word is the Greek for 'navel', and is given to the sacred stone in the Temple of Apollo at Delphi, which was thought to mark the central point of the Earth?

BONUS QUESTIONS

Three questions on English castles:

Q. Which castle, five miles north-east of Rotherham, was built around 1180, and has the oldest surviving circular keep in England?

Q. The excellently preserved Muncaster Castle, built in about 1300 with nineteenth-century reconstructions, lies one mile east of which Cumbrian village, famous for its railway?

Q. In which English county is Caister Castle?

96 STARTER

Q. Which twelfth-century German abbess is particulary remembered as a composer of sacred music, recordings of her works having featured in the classical music charts in recent years?

BONUS QUESTIONS

Q. Beginning in 1902 to mark the coronation of Edward VII and Queen Alexandra, which annual procession takes place in St Helier in Jersey on the second Thursday in August?

Q. 'The Flowers of the Forest' is a Scottish lament for those who fell at which sixteenth-century battle?

Q. Which Hans Anderson character, named 'Tommelise' in the Danish original, is found sitting in a flower inside a grain of barley, and eventually marries the king of the flower-angels?

97 STARTER

Q. What term means to prolong or enlarge life, and refers to the dietary regime of organically grown wholefoods, much influenced by Zen Buddhism, in which the principles of yin and yang are said to be in balance?

BONUS QUESTIONS

Three questions on flowers in Shakespeare:

Q. In *A Midsummer Night's Dream*, who describes a bank 'whereon the wild thyme blows/where oxlips and the nodding violet grows/quite over-canopied with lush woodbine/with sweet musk roses and with eglantine'?

Q. According to Ophelia in *Hamlet*, 'rosemary is for remembrance'; which flowers are for thought?

Q. 'When daises pied and violets blue/and lady smocks are silver white,/and cuckoo buds of yellow hue, do paint the meadow with delight,' are lines from a song closing which of Shakespeare's comedies?

98 STARTER

Q. The former prime ministers Harold Wilson and James Callaghan both chose to be known by their middle names. Wilson's first name was James: what was Callaghan's?

BONUS QUESTIONS

Q. Fined $100, the Dayton biology teacher John T. Scopes was accused in 1925 of teaching Darwinism to his pupils, contrary to the law of which American state?

Q. Tennessee, Arkansas and Mississippi, where the teaching of evolutionary theory was prohibited, form a major part of the south-central American region of religious fundamentalism known by which nickname?

Q. In 1960, Fredric March and Spencer Tracy starred in which film, directed by Stanley Kramer and based on the trial of John T. Scopes?

99 STARTER

Q. Considered to be the first colony of ancient Rome and situated at the mouth of the Tiber on Italy's western coast, which ancient town was the capital's major port during the period of the empire?

BONUS QUESTIONS

Three questions on fine art:

Q. By what name is the Italian painter Michelangelo Merisi better known, the name being that of the town where he spent much of his early life? Born around 1571, his works caused a sensation because of his use of peasant or low-life models for works on a devotional theme?

Q. Which painter, born in Seville in 1599 but of Portuguese origin, was much influenced by Caravaggio? One of his most famous works, *Las Meninas*, depicts the Infanta Margareta Teresa and her retinue of ladies and dwarfs.

Q. Which painter, born around 1617, became Seville's leading artist after Velasquez's departure for Madrid? He became particularly known for a series of sentimentalized depictions of beggar boys.

100 STARTER

Q. Which name means 'night monster' in Hebrew, and refers to a female demon of Jewish folklore; in the Talmud, she is the first wife of Adam, who was dispossessed by Eve?

BONUS QUESTIONS

Q. What age was William Pitt when he became Britain's youngest prime minister in 1783?

Q. Of the 24 letters in the Greek alphabet only three have names that do not end in a vowel; epsilon is one, name either of the other two.

Q. Letters of the Greek alphabet referred to as bayer letters have been largely superseded by flamsteed numbers as a system of identifying what?

101 STARTER

Q. Which nineteenth-century physicist gives his name to the earthed screen of metal wire or 'cage' which surrounds an electrical device to shield it from external electric fields?

BONUS QUESTIONS

Q. Germany had four African colonies at the outbreak of World War I. German East Africa and German South West Africa were two; name either of the other two, both in West Africa.

Q. In 1960 Moise Tshombe led the secession of Katanga province from which newly independent country in west-central Africa?

Q. President Nimeiry became leader of which north-east African country in 1971, being overthrown in a bloodless coup in April 1985?

102 STARTER

Q. Gheg and Tosk are the main dialects of which language spoken mainly in the Balkans?

BONUS QUESTIONS

What was the occupation of each of the following biblical characters:

Q. Rahab, whose house was built into the wall of Jericho but who was spared when the city was captured?

Q. Demetrius, leader of a group of craftsmen who sold miniatures of the goddess Artemis, but rioted against Paul when it seemed his Christian preaching would threaten their business?

Q. According to Luke's Gospel, what was the occupation of Levi, whom Jesus called to follow him, and who held a banquet for Jesus at his house, along with others of the same occupation?

103 STARTER

Q. In Greek legend, the hundred eyes of the giant Argus were placed in the tail of which bird?

BONUS QUESTIONS

Three questions on wines:

Q. Which term is used in the UK for red wines of Bordeaux, and derives ultimately from the Latin for 'clear'?

Q. Which region in the Bordeaux wine area lies between the rivers Garonne and Dordogne, sometimes referred to as 'the two seas', and is chiefly known for its light, dryish white wines?

Q. Which region to the south of Bordeaux, within the area of Graves, produces a sweet white wine with a deep golden colour, made from grapes that have been left to shrivel on the vine?

104 STARTER

Q. In which battle was Richard III killed in 1485?

BONUS QUESTIONS

Three questions on the deaths of writers:

Q. Which English writer died on 18 January 1936, just two days before George V?

Q. Name either of the British writers whose deaths on 22 November 1963 were largely forgotten as news of John F. Kennedy's assassination came through.

Q. St George's Day, 1616 saw the death of Shakespeare. The previous day had seen the death of which Spanish writer, whose best-known work was supposedly penned in prison and first published in 1605?

105 STARTER

Q. In the children's nursery rhyme, what did the crooked man buy with his crooked sixpence?

BONUS QUESTIONS

Q. The 1963 Halsbury Report recommended the adoption of what, an idea that was accepted in 1966 by the British Government although it was not to come into force until February 1971?

Q. Which master of the rolls gave his name to a report of 1963, the result of a judicial inquiry which found that there had been no disclosure of official secrets in the Profumo case?

Q. What name is given to a clause frequently inserted in marine insurance policies to provide cover for a variety of risks that are not covered by perils at sea?

106 STARTER

Q. In *The Devil's Dictionary*, what did Ambrose Bierce define as 'that period in time in which our affairs prosper, our friends are true and our happiness is assured'?

BONUS QUESTIONS

Q. In designating the electronic structure of an atom, which letter comes next in the sequence s, p, d ...?

Q. What is the maximum number of electrons that can be contained in the f-subshell of an atom?

Q. The f-block elements in the periodic table with atomic numbers from 58, cerium, to 71, lutetium, are known as lanthanides; what name is given those with atomic numbers from 90, thorium, to 103, lawrencium?

107 STARTER

Q. Alexandrina was the first Christian name of which British monarch?

BONUS QUESTIONS

Three questions on the great outdoors:

Q. Swirral Edge leads down to Red Tarn after leaving the summit of which Cumbrian mountain?

Q. Which British mountain can be ascended by way of the Pyg Track, so called because it crosses Bwlch-Y-Moch, the pass of the pigs?

Q. From the Derbyshire village of Edale, a path leads westwards to a slope called Jacob's Ladder, and eventually over which peak?

108 STARTER

Q. The 'distemper of gentlemen' was how Lord Chesterfield described which disease, characterized by severe inflammation of the extremities, and caused by the deposit of salts of uric acid in the joints?

BONUS QUESTIONS

Three questions on triple alliances:

Q. In 1668, which country joined England and the Dutch republic in a triple alliance against France?

Q. An alliance between Britain and France, agreed in September 1717, became triple when the united provinces joined, lending their support to France's rivalry with which king of Spain?

Q. From 1882 to 1914, which country formed a triple alliance with Germany and Austria-Hungary?

109 STARTER

Q. The mother of which screen heart-throb chose his name because she was standing in front of a Renaissance masterpiece when she felt the first *in utero* kick?

BONUS QUESTIONS

Q. What name was given to Garibaldi's expedition of May 1860 in which the Bourbon kingdom in Sicily was overthrown?

Q. First held in 1927 but abandoned 30 years later after a number of fatalities, which Italian motor race was so named because it was about 1000 miles in length?

Q. Which European country is known as the land of a thousand lakes because approximately 10 per cent of its area is covered by them?

110 STARTER

Q. What is the second derivative with respect to 'X' of the function X squared times 2?

BONUS QUESTIONS

Three questions on currencies:

Q. In which European state, other than Switzerland, is the Swiss franc the unit of currency?

Q. In which European state, which has its own franc, is the Belgian franc also legal tender?

Q. Which two European states, other than France, use the French franc as their currency?

111 STARTER

Q. Elizabeth Dakin, the wife of a London coffee merchant, in about 1848, invented which simple coffee-making device, still in use 150 years later?

BONUS QUESTIONS

Q. Which twelfth-century chronicler brought the figure of Arthur into European literature in his *Historia Regum Britanniae*?

Q. Who, according to Geoffrey, founded the city of Leicester and subsequently divided his kingdom between his two ungrateful daughters?

Q. The *Historia* begins with the settlement of Britain by Brutus the Trojan; who, supposedly, was Brutus's great-grandfather, the subject of a Roman epic?

112 STARTER

Q. *Cimex lectularius*, a species of nocturnal parasite rarely seen in Britain for 60 years, has made a comeback in Cambridge; how is this blood-sucking insect that bites humans while asleep, and has a characteristic oily smell, commonly known?

BONUS QUESTIONS

Q. Also called the Kipchak Khanate, the western part of the Mongol empire which flourished from the mid-thirteenth century to the end of the fourteenth century was also known by what name, originally coined by the Russians?

Q. *The Golden Bowl*, first published in 1904, was the last major novel by which American-born writer?

Q. The golden rule is a name given to which fundamental principle of Christian ethics, stated in the gospel of St Matthew chapter 7 verse 12?

113 STARTER

Q. In a letter to her brother, Edward, which novelist describes her work as, 'the little bit ... of ivory on which I work with so fine a brush, as produces little effect after much labour'?

BONUS QUESTIONS

Q. What word for a regular remuneration derives from the salt money paid to Roman soldiers?

Q. From the Latin for 'to weigh', what term is used for a fixed payment or salary, particularly that of a clergyman?

Q. What word meaning the amount of money picked up by a boxer for a fight, is also used in the United States for a woman's handbag?

114 STARTER

Q. Japanese inventor Pumpei Yokoi, who died in October 1997, is best remembered as the chief designer of which electronic toy that sold 60 million units world wide and established Nintendo as the world's leading computer game developers?

BONUS QUESTIONS

Q. Which politician was played by Anthony Sher in the film *Mrs Brown*?

Q. Which earl, who was three times prime minister, did Disraeli succeed in 1868 when he first became premier?

Q. Using funds provided by the Rothschild family, in what enterprise did Disraeli purchase shares in 1875, overriding recommendations from the foreign office?

115 STARTER

Q. In legal terminology, what is a 'next friend'?

BONUS QUESTIONS

Q. What term for the uncoordinated quivering contraction of muscle usually refers to the condition in which the atria in the heart beat very rapidly and are not synchronized with the ventricular beat?

Q. Fibrin, the matrix on which a blood clot develops, is formed from the soluble protein, fibrinogen, by the catalytic action of which enzyme?

Q. Which protein, the major protein constituent of white fibrous tissue, such as skin, bone and all connective tissue, is produced in cells called fibroblasts?

116 STARTER

Q. Which orchestral interlude in Rimsky-Korsakov's opera *The Legend of Tsar Sultan* depicts the metamorphosis of a prince into an insect?

BONUS QUESTIONS

Q. From the old French for 'the twittering of birds', which six-letter word has now come to mean the specialized terminology of a particular profession or occupation?

Q. Which five-letter French word, of unknown origin, is used for the jargon of a class, originally that of thieves and rogues?

Q. Which four-letter word can mean the specialized vocabulary of thieves, politicians, or lawyers, to speak in a wheedling or hypocritical manner, and also an inclination from the vertical or horizontal?

117 STARTER

Q. The QAPF diagram is used in the classification of which naturally-occurring objects?

BONUS QUESTIONS

Three questions on keyboards:

Q. Which standard keyboard design in Britain and the United States was originally laid out to slow typists down so that the keys wouldn't jam, the design taking its name from the first six keys on the top row?

Q. Which keyboard layout, developed in the 1930s and named after a lecturer at the Univeristy of Washington, is designed so that the most commonly used keys are in the centre?

Q. In English-speaking countries, which nine-word sentence is often used in word processing language handbooks to test fonts, because it contains all 26 letters of the alphabet?

118 STARTER

Q. A mullion is the vertical bar dividing the lights of a window; what is the name of the horizontal bar serving the same purpose?

BONUS QUESTIONS

In the novels of Charles Dickens, what are the final fates of the following villains:

Q. Uriah Heep in *David Copperfield*?

Q. Daniel Quilp in *The Old Curiosity Shop*?

Q. Wackford Squeers in *Nicholas Nickleby*?

119 STARTER

Q. In the Christian calendar, which festival is usually celebrated forty days after Easter day?

BONUS QUESTIONS

Q. Which four chemical elements are common to the 20 or so amino acids that occur naturally in proteins?

Q. In addition to the four elements previously mentioned, the amino acids cysteine, cystine and methionine all contain which element?

Q. The amino acid thyroxine, which occurs only in the hormone protein thyroglobulin, contains atoms of which element in addition to the four base elements?

120 STARTER

Q. Which mathematical game, played on an infinite two-dimensional grid of squares, was invented by the mathematician John Conway?

BONUS QUESTIONS

Q. Largely formulated by American astrophysicist Frank Drake, and first discussed in 1961 at a conference held at the National Radio Astronomy Observatory in Green Bank, West Virginia, the 'green bank equation' purports to give the number of TAC's in the Milky Way. What do the initials TAC stand for?

Q. Percival Lowell, who predicted the existence of the planet Pluto, was a champion of the theory that intelligent life once existed on which planet of the solar system?

Q. For the film ET, the extraterrestrial, Steven Spielberg specified that the alien should have a rear like Donald Duck, and devised the face by pasting the eyes and forehead of which physicist on to a photograph of a newborn baby?

First Round Answers

1 STARTER

A. *Suffragettes*

BONUS QUESTIONS

A. *Kiwi*

A. *Emu*

A. *Rhea*

2 STARTER

A. *Bill Gates*

BONUS QUESTIONS

A. *River Severn*

A. *Tintern Abbey*

('Lines composed a few miles above Tintern Abbey', 1798)

A. *(Second-hand) books*

3 STARTER

A. *Magma is found beneath the Earth's crust; lava is magma that has appeared at the Earth's surface*

BONUS QUESTIONS

A. *Echidna*

A. *Melusina / Melusine / Melisande*

A. *Macbeth*

4 STARTER

A. *Tea*

BONUS QUESTIONS

A. *Sebum*

(secreted by sebaceous glands)

A. *Earwax*

A. *Saliva*

5 STARTER

A. *Prime (number)*

BONUS QUESTIONS

A. *Wrestling*

A. Women In Love

A. *Jacob*

6 STARTER

A. *Grand Guignol*

BONUS QUESTIONS

A. *Lara Croft*
A. *Julie Christie*
A. *Trinidad*

7 STARTER

A. *Ultrasound*

BONUS QUESTIONS

A. *(Rebecca) Becky Sharp*
  (in *Vanity Fair* by Thackeray)
A. *Jane Eyre*
A. The Wolves of Willoughby Chase

8 STARTER

A. *Dennis Bergkamp*

BONUS QUESTIONS

A. *'... your right to say it.'*
  (generally attributed, but actually said by S.G. Tallentyre)
A. *'...to invent him.'*
A. *'Virginity'*

9 STARTER

A. *'... with malice aforethought'*

BONUS QUESTIONS

A. *Duke of Wellington (boeuf Wellington)*
A. *(Count Paul) Stroganoff*
A. *(Vicomte de) Chateaubriand*

10 STARTER

A. *New Zealand*

BONUS QUESTIONS

A. *Sievert*
A. *Decathlon*
A. *Casey Jones*

11 STARTER

A. *Staccato*

BONUS QUESTIONS

A. *Boudicca / Boadicea*
A. *Iceni*
A. *Ben Jonson*

12 STARTER

A. *Donatella*

BONUS QUESTIONS

A. *(Compagnie internationale des) wagon-lits (et des grands express Européens)*

A. *Orient Express (express d'orient)*

A. *(Marshal Ferdinand) Foch*

13 STARTER

A. *Royalty*

BONUS QUESTIONS

A. Gone With The Wind

A. *Atlanta*

A. *First black performer to win an Academy Award/Oscar*

14 STARTER

A. *Survivors of the atomic bombs dropped on Hiroshima and Nagasaki*

BONUS QUESTIONS

A. *Caricature*

A. *Georg Grosz*

A. *Doctor Syntax*
   (The Tours of Doctor Syntax, 1812-20)

15 STARTER

A. *Jupiter's great red spot*

BONUS QUESTIONS

A. *Timothy*

A. *Philemon*

A. *Letters to the Corinthians*

16 STARTER

A. *A piano*

BONUS QUESTIONS

A. *Bioluminescence*

A. *Luciferin*

A. *Photophore*

17 STARTER

A. *Dr Benjamin Spock*

BONUS QUESTIONS

A. *Id est*

A. *Indo-European*

A. *Internet Explorer*

18 STARTER

A. *Joan of Arc*
(la pucelle = the maid)
BONUS QUESTIONS
A. *1964, 1966*
A. *1970, 1974, 1974, 1979*
A. *1983, 1987*

19 STARTER

A. *Roof*
BONUS QUESTIONS
A. *Bob Marley*
A. *Elephant dung*
A. *Oklahoma*
(the song 'Oh What a Beautiful Morning', from *Oklahoma!*)

20 STARTER

A. *Blue*
BONUS QUESTIONS
A. *First woman official/linesman/assistant referee (at a league match)*
A. *(English) Derby*
A. *Boxing match (professional)*
(at Caesar's Palace, Streatham)

21 STARTER

A. *Melatonin*
BONUS QUESTIONS
A. *Half crown*
A. *(Decimal) half penny*
A. *Steel*

22 STARTER

A. *Daiquiri*
BONUS QUESTIONS
A. *DNA*
A. *Plane tree*
A. *Carl Linnaeus*
(also called Carl Linne)

23 STARTER

A. *Metonym*
BONUS QUESTIONS
A. *Montserrat*
A. *George Washington*
A. *Southern Alps*

24 STARTER

A. *Youth hostels*

BONUS QUESTIONS

A. *'(Bring me my) arrows of desire!'*

A. *Sam Peckinpah*

A. *Graham Norton*

25 STARTER

A. *Crony*

BONUS QUESTIONS

A. *The field of the cloth of gold*
   (camp du drap d'or)

A. *Cambodia*

A. *Vincent van Gogh*

26 STARTER

A. *Pituitary gland*

BONUS QUESTIONS

A. *'So Long Frank Lloyd Wright'*

A. *The Pet Shop Boys*

A. *Tom Jones*

27 STARTER

A. *Virginia Woolf*

BONUS QUESTIONS

A. *Alum*

A. *Sand*

A. *Former pupil/graduate of school, college*

28 STARTER

A. *Rolls Royce*

BONUS QUESTIONS

A. *Bombay*

A. *Madras*

A. *Poona*

29 STARTER

A. *In the deep ocean floors*

BONUS QUESTIONS

A. *Abraham Lincoln*

A. *Basketball*

A. *Ozark Mountains (or plateau)*

30 STARTER

A. *Allotments*
BONUS QUESTIONS
A. Toys
A. *Oliver Sachs*
A. *(Hunter) 'Patch Adams'*

31 STARTER

A. *Rheostat (or potentiometer)*
BONUS QUESTIONS
A. Hyperion
A. *Percy Bysshe Shelley*
A The Excursion

32 STARTER

A. *The six days of the creation*
BONUS QUESTIONS
A. *Titanium dioxide*
A. *Deodorant/anti-perspirant*
A. *(Artificial) suntan products*

33 STARTER

A. *AA*
   (Automobile Association)
BONUS QUESTIONS
A. *France*
   (Louis XVII, son of Louis XVI, was never crowned)
A. *Sweden*
A. *Denmark*

34 STARTER

A. *Gouache*
BONUS QUESTIONS
A. *Copper and zinc*
A (Cardinal) Thomas Wolsey
A. *He made himself red hot and hugged his victims to death*

35 STARTER

A. The Sunshine Boys
BONUS QUESTIONS
A. *Sir Francis Walsingham*
A. *Daniel Defoe*
A. *George Smiley*

36 STARTER

A. *As bait*
   (it is a red earthworm)
BONUS QUESTIONS
A. *Frederick Soddy*
A. *Helium*
A. *Economics (he was the author of* Cartesian Economics*)*

37 STARTER

A. *A portable tent*
BONUS QUESTIONS
A. *Tippoo's tiger*
A. *Georges Clemenceau*
A. *Winston Churchill*

38 STARTER

A. *The Countryside Alliance*
BONUS QUESTIONS
A. *Dr Manette*
A. *David Copperfield*
   (the prisoner is Uriah Heep)
A. *The Fleet Prison*

39 STARTER

A. *Gannet*
BONUS QUESTIONS
A. *Dolman*
A. *Box pleat*
A. *Yoke*

40 STARTER

A. *Violas*
BONUS QUESTIONS
A. *Connecticut   Maine*
   Massachusetts   New Hampshire
   Rhode Island   Vermont

41 STARTER

A. *Chitin*
BONUS QUESTIONS
A. *House of Keys*
A. *The Salem witch trials*
A. *Madness*

42 STARTER

A. *Domino theory (effect)*
(accept falling domino principle)
BONUS QUESTIONS
A. *Pearls*
A. *Canton (Guangzhou)*
A. The Good Earth

43 STARTER

A. *Cape Wrath*
BONUS QUESTIONS
A. *Chaos*
A. *The creation*
A. *Edward Lorenz*

44 STARTER

A. *Cleopatra*
BONUS QUESTIONS
A. *Simple plurality*
A. *Additional member*
A. *Proportional representation*

45 STARTER

A. *Ski jumping*
BONUS QUESTIONS
A. *Le Corbusier*
A. *Mies Van Der Rohe*
A. *Frank Lloyd Wright*

46 STARTER

A. *Leghorn*
BONUS QUESTIONS
A. *Berwick Rangers*
A. *Chester City*
A. *Derry City*

47 STARTER

A. *Leviathan*
BONUS QUESTIONS
A. The Merchant of Venice
(spoken by Antonio, the merchant)
A. Julius Caesar
(spoken by Flavius)
A. All's Well That Ends Well
(spoken by the Countess of Rousillon)

48 STARTER

A. £21
(£24 - £3)
BONUS QUESTIONS
A. *Aborigines*
A. *Tasmania*
A. *Evonne Goolagong*

49 STARTER

A. *Cantor*
(accept chazan [yiddish for cantor])
BONUS QUESTIONS
A. *Alpaca*
A. *Astrakhan*
A. *Chenille*

50 STARTER

A. *Croon*
BONUS QUESTIONS
A. *Women's Institutes*
A. *Llanfair P. G.*
A. *Posed for a nude calendar*

51 STARTER

A. *Sublimation*
BONUS QUESTIONS
A. *Abraham*
A. *Joe Orton* (in Loot)
A. *Herbert Samuel*

52 STARTER

A. *Riviera*
BONUS QUESTIONS
A. *Charles Goodyear*
A. *John Boyd Dunlop*
A. *Michelin*

53 STARTER

A. *Climate/climatic regions*
BONUS QUESTIONS
A. *Finings*
A. *Hop*
(*humulus lupulus*)
A. *Wort*

54 STARTER

A. *Stirling Bridge*
BONUS QUESTIONS
A. *Currants*
A. *Spike Milligan*
A. *Q*

55 STARTER

A. *Astrology*
BONUS QUESTIONS
A. *Jitterbug*
A. *V-1*
A. *Immortality*

56 STARTER

A. *Joseph Haydn*
BONUS QUESTIONS
A. *Acceleration due to gravity*
   (accept just gravity)
A. *Ten (metres per second squared)*
A. *At the poles*

57 STARTER

A. A Burnt Out Case
BONUS QUESTIONS
A. *Cow*
A. *Aurgelmir/Ymir (accept either)*
A. *Ireland*

58 STARTER

A. *Assignats*
BONUS QUESTIONS
A. Irma La Douce
A. *Cynthia Payne*
A. The Best Little Whorehouse In Texas

59 STARTER

A, *Eight*
   (then: five, four, nine, one, seven, six, ten, three, two)
BONUS QUESTIONS
A. *B.B. King*
A. *The Drifters*
A. *Carole King*

60 STARTER

A. *Claymore*
(Gaelic: claidheamh mor)
BONUS QUESTIONS
A. *Hypermetropia/hyperopia*
A. *Hyperglycaemia*
A. *Graves' Disease*
(accept Basedow's Disease/thyrotoxicosis)

61 STARTER

A. *Nominative*
BONUS QUESTIONS
A. *Gloucester*
A. *Winchester*
A. *Worcester*

62 STARTER

A. *'(He's a) dedicated follower of fashion'*
BONUS QUESTIONS
A. *Ithaca*
(in modern Greek = Ithaki)
A. *Corfu*
A. *Lawrence Durrell*

63 STARTER

A. *Statics*
BONUS QUESTIONS
A. *Slavic*
(accept 'Slavonic')
A. *Armenian*
A. *Yiddish*

64 STARTER

A. *Revoke*
BONUS QUESTIONS
A. *Opening of the Welsh Assembly*
A. *Alun Michael*
A. *Ron Davies*

65 STARTER

A. *Depth charge*
BONUS QUESTIONS
A. *Richard E. Grant*
A. *The Detainees*
A. *Alan Titchmarsh*

66 STARTER

A. *Electrum*
BONUS QUESTIONS
A. *Her name is never mentioned*
A. *Martha*
   (her brother was Lazarus)
A. *Miriam*

67 STARTER

A. *Edward Alleyn*
BONUS QUESTIONS
A. *(Joseph Von) Fraunhofer*
A. *Sodium*
A. *(Anders Jonas) Angström*

68 STARTER

A. *T'ai Chi Chuan (or T'ai Chi)*
BONUS QUESTIONS
A. *Canute/Knut*
A. *Turnstone*
A. *Ruff*

69 STARTER

A. *Gunpowder*
BONUS QUESTIONS
A. *Parliamentary Commissioner for Standards*
A. *Deputy Leader of the Labour Party*
A. *Piano*

70 STARTER

A. *They are craters on the planet Mercury*
BONUS QUESTIONS
A. *Ann Packer*
   (Ian and David Brightwell)
A. *(John and Sheila) Sherwood*
A. *Sally Gunnell*

71 STARTER

A. *Diazepam*
   (benzodiazepine + am)
BONUS QUESTIONS
A. *The Jacobite Rebellion*
   (the second Jacobite rebellion)
A. *Sand*
A. *Vancouver*

72 STARTER
A. *Port Salut*
BONUS QUESTIONS
A. *Ultraviolet radiation*
A. *Johann Ritter*
A. *Ergosterol*

73 STARTER
A. *Aztec*
BONUS QUESTIONS
A. *Sagittarius*
A. *Castor and Pollux*
A. *Leo*

74 STARTER
A. *Nuremberg Rally (of 1934)*
BONUS QUESTIONS
A. *Birds' eggs*
A. *Leda*
A. *Love*
   (in tennis)

75 STARTER
A. *Wave power*
BONUS QUESTIONS
A. *Maine*
A. *Cat*
A. *Manchester City*

76 STARTER
A. *25 March*
BONUS QUESTIONS
A. *Voice of America*
A. *Jane Horrocks*
A. The Barber Of Seville

77 STARTER
A. *'Poster'*
BONUS QUESTIONS
A. *Thomas Telford*
A. *Britannia Bridge*
A. *(Gustave) Eiffel*

78 STARTER
A. *The Sphinx*
BONUS QUESTIONS
A. *Rochdale*

A. *(Lord George Gordon) Byron*
A. *Michael Owen*

79 STARTER

A. *The 'Road' films, with Bob Hope and Bing Crosby*
BONUS QUESTIONS
A. *Headline (rate of inflation)*
A. *Mortgage (interest) payments*
A. *Harmonized index (of) consumer prices*

80 STARTER

A. *Damascening*
BONUS QUESTIONS
A. *Pegasus*
A. *Hero ([or Heron] of Alexandria)*
A. *Trevi Fountain*

81 STARTER

A. *Sir Roger Hollis*
BONUS QUESTIONS
A. *Fish*
A. *John Betjeman*
A. *Jeanette Winterson*

82 STARTER

A. *Manila*
   (Philippines)
BONUS QUESTIONS
A. *Second marriage*
A. *Women preaching*
   (or 'a woman's preaching')
A. *Lord Chesterfield*

83 STARTER

A. *Contingency fees*
BONUS QUESTIONS
A. *Spiel*
A. *Chatter*
   (accept chat)
A. *Patter*

84 STARTER

A. Titanic
BONUS QUESTIONS
A. *Russia*
A. *(Glenn T.) Seaborg (Seaborgium)*
A. *(Lise) Meitner*

85 STARTER
A. *Beaumarchais*
BONUS QUESTIONS
A. *Swansea*
A. *Armagh*
A. *St David's*

86 STARTER
A. *Karl Marx*
BONUS QUESTIONS
A. *Ideal point*
A. *George Berkeley*
A. *Rupert Everett*

87 STARTER
A. *Société Anonyme*
BONUS QUESTIONS
A. Amsterdam
A. Enduring Love
A. The Innocent

88 STARTER
A. *Lagoon*
BONUS QUESTIONS
A. *Chris Isaak*
A. *Annie Nightingale*
A. *Margaret Lockwood*

89 STARTER
A. *Deliquescence*
BONUS QUESTIONS
A. *Haydn*
A. *William Walton*
A. *Edward Elgar*

90 STARTER
A. *The Queen*
BONUS QUESTIONS
A. *Simon*
A. *Cyrene*
A. *Judas Iscariot*

91 STARTER
A. *Shin splints*
(it can also be caused by myositis, muscle tear or periotitis)
BONUS QUESTIONS
A. *Montana*
A. *The broad (padded) shoulder look*
A. *Clematis*

92 STARTER

A. *Holy Loch*

BONUS QUESTIONS

A. *Sir Antony Jay*

A. *Halemprice*
(in the *New Statesman*)

A. *Francis Urquhart*

93 STARTER

A. *The Pledge of Allegiance*

BONUS QUESTIONS

A. *Grout*
(not mortar; grout is a mortar, but the term is not specific to the material as above)

A. *Eggshell*

A. *Laminates*

94 STARTER

A. *Notifiable*

BONUS QUESTIONS

A. *Canon*

A. *'Sumer Is Icumen In'*
(accept 'Cuckoo song')

A. *Johann Sebastian Bach*

95 STARTER

A. *Ostracism*

BONUS QUESTIONS

A. *Ch'i*

A. *Phoenix*

A. *Yorkshire*

96 STARTER

A. *Cornea*

BONUS QUESTIONS

A. *Associate professor*

A. *Regius professor*

A. *Emeritus*

97 STARTER

A. *The first crusade*
(accept 'crusades')

BONUS QUESTIONS

A. *Field*

A. *Fly*

A. *Halyard/halliard/haulyard*

98 STARTER

A. *Elgar*
BONUS QUESTIONS
A. *The peasants' revolt/Wat Tyler's revolt (rebellion)*
A. *Jacquerie*
A. *The Philippines*

99 STARTER

A. *The Lord's Prayer*
BONUS QUESTIONS
A. *'Little Voice'*
A. *Captain Darling*
A. *Captain James Cook*

100 STARTER

A. *Ten years*
(a vice-president can serve up to two years after succeeding an incumbent president, and then a further two terms on election. Should a vice-president succeed in mid-term for over two years he can only stand for one more term)
BONUS QUESTIONS
A. *Thomas de Quincey*
A. *W.B. Yeats*
A. *E.M. Forster*

101 STARTER

A. *Panacea*
BONUS QUESTIONS
A. *Krakatoa East Of Java – when it actually lies to the west*
A. *Mount Rushmore*
A. *Hamlet*

102 STARTER

A. *Brazil*
BONUS QUESTIONS
A. *Deltoid*
A. *Eye*
A. *Sartorius*

103 STARTER

A. *Ely*
BONUS QUESTIONS
A. *October*
A. *February*
A. *July*

104 STARTER

A. *Textured Vegetable Protein*
BONUS QUESTIONS
A. A Midsummer Night's Dream
(spoken by Puck)
A. Titus Andronicus
(spoken by Lucius)
A. The Tempest
(Prospero, in the epilogue)

105 STARTER

A. *David Hockney*
BONUS QUESTIONS
A. *Erik Satie*
A. *Miss Havisham*
A. *Everton*

106 STARTER

A. *(Venetian) gondoliers*
BONUS QUESTIONS
A. *Gustav Mahler*
A. *Oskar Kokoschka*
A. *Walter Gropius*

107 STARTER

A. *Viscount Hailsham and Lord Hailsham*
BONUS QUESTIONS
A. *Roman à clef*
A. *Roman fleuve*
A. *Roman à thèses*

108 STARTER

A. *Mexico*
BONUS QUESTIONS
A. *John Newlands*
A. *Dmitri Mendeleyev*
(Element 101 having been named Mendelevium)
A. *Henry Moseley*

109 STARTER

A. *Alien*
BONUS QUESTIONS
A. *The Rambler*
A. *Blackwood's Magazine*
A. *Sir George Newnes*

110 STARTER
A. *Witchcraft*
BONUS QUESTIONS
A. *Proteus*
A. The Apple Cart
A. *Neptune*

111 STARTER
A. *J.R.R. Tolkein*
BONUS QUESTIONS
A. *Buckinghamshire*
A. *Viscount (Arthur Hamilton) Lee of Fareham*
A. *Medmenham Abbey*

112 STARTER
A. *King Kong*
BONUS QUESTIONS
A. *Jennings*
   (John Christopher Timothy Jennings)
A. *Malory Towers*
A. *Arthur Marshall*

113 STARTER
A. *'My Way'*
BONUS QUESTIONS
A. *Sir Francis Beaumont*
A. *Philip Massinger*
A. *John Ford*

114 STARTER
A. *Herman Melville*
   ('Moby Dick', chapter 17)
BONUS QUESTIONS
A. *Eustasy*
A. *The pharynx*
A. The Return Of The Native

115 STARTER
A. *Rayon*
BONUS QUESTIONS
A. The Waste Land
A. The Love Song of J. Alfred Prufrock
   (accept Prufrock)
A. *Ash Wednesday*

116 STARTER

A. *The mean distance of the Earth from the sun*
BONUS QUESTIONS
A. *San Francisco*
A. *Nob Hill*
A. *Japanese*

117 STARTER

A. *Legate*
BONUS QUESTIONS
A. *Francis (François) I*
A. *Palace of Versailles*
A. *I.M. Pei*
  (Ieoh Ming Pei)

118 STARTER

A. *Ukraine*
BONUS QUESTIONS
A. *Leonardo da Vinci*
A. *Kaiser Wilhelm II*
A. *Rin Tin Tin*

119 STARTER

A. *The Church of Jesus Christ of the Latter Day Saints*
  (accept Mormons)
BONUS QUESTIONS
A. *(Sir Thomas) Malory*
A. *US (singles) tennis championship*
A. *Andrew Irvine*

120 STARTER

A. *Jiminy Cricket*
BONUS QUESTIONS
A. *Philippe Starck*
A. *Arne Jacobsen*
A. *Finnish*

SECOND ROUND ANSWERS

1 STARTER
A. *Ruth Rendell*
BONUS QUESTIONS
A. *Four*
A. *Span*
A. *Chain*
(also accept Gunter's chain, from English mathematician Edmund Gunter, 1581-1626)

2 STARTER
A. *A series of cave paintings*
BONUS QUESTIONS
A. *Radio 4*
A. *World Service*
A. *Home Service*

3 STARTER
A. *Pogrom*
BONUS QUESTIONS
A. *Addison's Disease*
A. *The Spectator*
A. *Secretary of State*

4 STARTER
A. *Argon*
BONUS QUESTIONS
A. *Wynton Marsalis*
A. *Dorothy Parker*
A. *Weird sisters/three witches*

5 STARTER
A. *Air passenger duty*
BONUS QUESTIONS
A. *Zero tolerance*
A. *Ronald Reagan*
A. *Bob Dylan*

6 STARTER
A. *Ballroom dancing*

BONUS QUESTIONS
A. *Vaclav Havel*
A. *Presemyslid/Premyslid*
A. *(Good King) Wenceslas*

7 STARTER
A. *Lahore*
BONUS QUESTIONS
A. *Ems telegram*
A. *Jameson raid*
A. *Mexico*

8 STARTER
A. *Dross*
BONUS QUESTIONS
A. *Henry Kissinger*
A. *Le Duc Tho*
A. *Shuttle diplomacy*

9 STARTER
A. *Carmelites*
BONUS QUESTIONS
A. *Philip, Duke of Edinburgh*
A. *(Edmund) Blackadder*
A. *Tweed*

10 STARTER
A. *The Liberty Bell*
BONUS QUESTIONS
A. *The Cherry Orchard*
A. *George Washington*
A. *Cyanide*

11 STARTER
A. *The Yangtze*
BONUS QUESTIONS
A. *Louis Pasteur*
A. *Albert Einstein*
A. *Harpo Marx*

12 STARTER
A. *Michael Owen*
BONUS QUESTIONS
A. *Huntsman/hunter (style)*
A. *Der Freischutz*
A. *Esau*

13 STARTER
A. *Swahili*
BONUS QUESTIONS
A. *William Shakespeare*
A. *Titian*
A. *John Blow*

14 STARTER
A. *The livre*
BONUS QUESTIONS
A. Ring of the Nibelung
A. *Bayreuth*
A. Gotterdammerung

15 STARTER
A. *Taurus*
BONUS QUESTIONS
A. Oliver Twist
A. Tess of the D'Urbervilles
A. Middlemarch

16 STARTER
A. *Raoul Wallenberg*
BONUS QUESTIONS
A. *Tandoori*
    (the oven being the tandoor)
A. *Tikka*
A. *(Fried) bread*

17 STARTER
A. *Belgium*
BONUS QUESTIONS
A. *Volley*
A. *Pam*
A. *John McEnroe*

18 STARTER
A. *Modesty Blaise*
BONUS QUESTION
A. *Associative (law)*
A. *Distributive (law)*
A. *Commutative (law)*

19 STARTER
A. *Robert Dudley, Earl of Leicester*
BONUS QUESTIONS
A. *Antoni Gaudi*

A. *Matthew Arnold*
A. Decline and Fall

20 STARTER

A. *The mouse*
BONUS QUESTIONS
A. *Clinker*
   (nb: not cinders, which still has combustible matter in it)
A. *Overlapping*
   (external planks overlapping downwards and secured with clinched copper nails)
A. *Tobias Smollett*

21 STARTER

A. *Haggadah or aggadah*
BONUS QUESTIONS
A. *Sicily*
A. *Guiseppe Verdi*
A. *Vincenzo Bellini*

22 STARTER

A. Utopia Limited
BONUS QUESTIONS
A. *Saccharin*
A. *Cyclamates*
A. *Aspartame*

23 STARTER

A. *Piranha*
BONUS QUESTIONS
A. *Northern Line*
A. *Amersham*
A. *Central Line*

24 STARTER

A. *Nigeria*
BONUS QUESTIONS
A. *D.H. Lawrence*
A. *Anthony Burgess*
A. *Stephen King*

25 STARTER

A. *Thomas Hood*
BONUS QUESTIONS
A. *Dante Gabriel Rossetti*
A. *Bela Lugosi*
A. *Humphrey Bogart*

26 STARTER

A. *Beginners' All-Purpose Symbolic Instruction Code*
BONUS QUESTIONS
A. *Oklahoma*
A. *Merle Haggard*
A. *Rod Steiger*

27 STARTER

A. *It fixes the colour*
BONUS QUESTIONS
A. *Westward Ho!*
A. *Ben Jonson*
A. *Carnoustie*

28 STARTER

A. *David Lloyd George*
BONUS QUESTIONS
A. *Sir Jack Hobbs*
A. *Jim Laker*
A. *Peter May*

29 STARTER

A. *Peritoneum*
BONUS QUESTIONS
A. *Pedigree*
A. *'Common law' marriage/non-legal union*
A. *Parish registers*

30 STARTER

A. *Pediment*
BONUS QUESTIONS
A. *(Glasgow) Govan*
A. *Gregor Fisher*
A. *(Sir) Alex Ferguson*

31 STARTER

A. *Pedagogue*
BONUS QUESTIONS
A. *Jack the Ripper*
A. *Matches*
A. *The* Star

32 STARTER

A. *Ship money*
BONUS QUESTIONS
A. *Bob Willis*

A. *Harold Larwood*
A. *Chris Read*

33 STARTER

A. *The pobble ('The Pobble Who Has No Toes')*
BONUS QUESTIONS
A. *Beirut*
A. *Damascus*
A. *Baghdad*

34 STARTER

A. *Learning behaviour*
   (the 'skinner box')
BONUS QUESTIONS
A. *Straits of Messina*
A. *Scylla and Charybdis*
A. Much Ado About Nothing

35 STARTER

A. *Ascension Day/Holy Thursday*
BONUS QUESTIONS
A. *Lurid*
A. *Livid*
A. *Vivid*

36 STARTER

A. *(Lord) David Owen*
BONUS QUESTIONS
A. *Itchycoo Park*
A. *MacArthur Park*
A. *Phil Daniels*

37 STARTER

A. *Peridot*
   (a form of chrysolite)
BONUS QUESTIONS
A. *Polaris*
A. *Ursa Minor*
   (accept little bear)
A. *North Pole*

38 STARTER

A. *The BFG – Big Friendly Giant*
BONUS QUESTIONS
A. *Medway*
   (a Kentish man is born west of the Medway)
A. *Applause*
A. *Limestone*

39 STARTER

A. *Internal Revenue Service*
BONUS QUESTIONS
A. *Fidel Castro*
A. *Ernesto 'Che' Guevara*
A. *The Bay of Pigs*

40 STARTER

A. *Lord Scarman (Leslie George Scarman)*
BONUS QUESTIONS
A. *Farad*
A. *Avogadro (constant/number)*
A. *Magnetic flux*

41 STARTER

A. *Christianity*
BONUS QUESTIONS
A. *Donatello*
A. *Michelangelo*
A. *(Gian Lorenzo) Bernini*

42 STARTER

A. *Oxidation state or number*
BONUS QUESTIONS
A. *Chess*
A. *Norsemen (not Vikings, who were a later race)*
A. *(Howard) Staunton*

43 STARTER

A. *Pelagius*
BONUS QUESTIONS
A. *Alto*
A. *Soprano*
A. *Baritone*

44 STARTER

A. *Tartaric acid*
   (accept dihydroxybutanedioic acid)
BONUS QUESTIONS
A. *Chandler*
A. *Strangers On A Train*
   (co-written with Czenzi Ormonde, from the novel by Patricia
   Highsmith)
A. *(Geographical) poles*
   (accept polar motion)

45 STARTER

A. *Chicane*
BONUS QUESTIONS
A. Santa Maria
(Columbus' flagship on his first voyage to America)
A. *25 December*
A. Niña *and* Pinta

46 STARTER

A. The Likely Lads
BONUS QUESTIONS
A. *Daisywheel*
A. *Hal (9000)*
(in 2001: *A Space Odyssey*)
A. *Aster*
(*aster tripolium*)

47 STARTER

A. Titus Alone
BONUS QUESTIONS
A. *Brick Lane*
A. *Augustus*
A. *The Tate Gallery, London*
(now housed at The Tate Modern)

48 STARTER

A. *Charles de Gaulle*
BONUS QUESTIONS
A. *All People That On Earth Do Dwell*
A. *Geoffrey Boycott*
A. *Prague*

49 STARTER

A. *Barcelona*
BONUS QUESTIONS
A. *Anatoly Karpov*
A. *John Stuart Mill*
A. *Daniel Barenboim*

50 STARTER

A. *Ernie*
(Electronic Random Number Indicator Equipment)
BONUS QUESTIONS
A. *India pale ale*
A. *Ice beer*
A. *Pilsen*

51 STARTER
A. *Tomato*
BONUS QUESTIONS
A. *Hover mower/Flymo*
A. *LCD (liquid crystal display)*
A. *Pill/medicine bottles*

52 STARTER
A. *Mornington Crescent*
BONUS QUESTIONS
A. *Afghan hound*
A. *Sir Richard (Francis) Burton*
A. *Khyber Pass*

53 STARTER
A. *Venoms*
   (accept parenteral poisons)
BONUS QUESTIONS
A. *French chalk*
A. *Shellac*
A. *Embroidery*

54 STARTER
A. *Bandwidth*
BONUS QUESTIONS
A. *Venice*
A. *Helena Bonham-Carter*
A. *Clarinet*

55 STARTER
A. *Minus 460 (degrees)*
BONUS QUESTIONS
A. *Mother Goose (rhyme)*
A. *Maurice Ravel*
A. *(Clarence Seward) Darrow*

56 STARTER
A. *Bernadette Devlin*
BONUS QUESTIONS
A. *Georgia*
A. *Slovakia*
A. *Slovenia*

57 STARTER
A. *Slate*
BONUS QUESTIONS
A. *(The ceiling of) the Sistine Chapel*

A. *Pope Julius II*
A. *The chapel was used by cardinals for the election of new popes*
(John Paul I in August. John Paul II in October)

58 STARTER

A. *Skywave*
BONUS QUESTIONS
A. *Silverfish*
A. *Photographic or sensitized printing paper*
A. *William Wordsworth*

59 STARTER

A. *Harry Houdini (Erik Weisz)*
BONUS QUESTIONS
A. *Tom Sutherland*
A. *Terry Anderson*
A. Some Other Rainbow

60 STARTER

A. *Charlemagne/Charles the Great*
BONUS QUESTIONS
A. *Chlorofluorocarbons*
A. *Polychlorinated biphenyls*
A. *Hexachlorobenzene*

61 STARTER

A. *Knesset*
BONUS QUESTIONS
A. *George Bernard Shaw*
A. *Thomas Jefferson*
A. *Warren Harding*

62 STARTER

A. *Augeas/Augeias/Augias*
BONUS QUESTIONS
A. *Albrecht Dürer*
A. *The Jumblies*
A. *Rodolfo*
(in Puccini's *La Boheme*)

63 STARTER

A. *Impedance*
BONUS QUESTIONS
A. *Inigo Jones*
A. *ICI*
A. *The London Marathon*

64 STARTER

A. *Angelica*
BONUS QUESTIONS
A. *Double bass*
A. *Holland*
A. *Sioux*

65 STARTER

A. *Geneva*
BONUS QUESTIONS
A. *C. Auguste Dupin*
A. *Nero Wolfe*
A. *Philip Marlowe*

66 STARTER

A. *Israel*
BONUS QUESTIONS
A. *Blood groups*
A. *The Zulus*
A. *The monmouth rebellion of 1685*

67 STARTER

A. The Dream of Gerontius
BONUS QUESTIONS
A. *Buster Keaton*
A. *The* African Queen
A. *A sledge/sled*

68 STARTER

A. *Maris (Crane)*
   (ex-wife of Frazier's brother Niles)
BONUS QUESTIONS
A. *Elastic (collision)*
A. *All (100 per cent)*
A. *One half (50 per cent)*

69 STARTER

A. *Sikh*
BONUS QUESTIONS
A. *Henry III*
A. *Henry VI*
A. *Edward VI*

70 STARTER

A. *Jimmy White*

BONUS QUESTIONS
A. *Niagara Falls*
A. *The Rock of Gibraltar*
A. *Ayers Rock/Uluru*

71 STARTER

A. *Annealing*
BONUS QUESTIONS
A. *Captain Marvel*
A. *Abraham Lincoln*
A. *The* Nautilus

72 STARTER

A. *Sintering*
BONUS QUESTIONS
A. *Sir Peter Maxwell Davies*
A. *John Ruskin*
A. *Ingmar Bergman*

73 STARTER

A. *Tricky*
BONUS QUESTIONS
A. *The Seven Weeks War*
A. *The Franco-Prussian War*
A. *The American Civil War*

74 STARTER

A. *Nana*
BONUS QUESTIONS
A. *Court fool/court jester*
A. *The bishop*
A. *Sam Shepard*

75 STARTER

A. *Galen*
BONUS QUESTIONS
A. *Siddons*
A. *David Garrick*
A. *Joshua Reynolds*

76 STARTER

A. *(Joseph) Sheridan Le Fanu*
BONUS QUESTIONS
A. *Espalier*
A. *Pollarding*
A. *Coppicing*

77 STARTER
A. *Gabriel Faure*
BONUS QUESTIONS
A. *That of Diana, Princess of Wales*
A. *The metronome*
A. *Hovis (from* hominis vis*)*

78 STARTER
A. *Judaism*
BONUS QUESTIONS
A. *Richard Bright*
    ('Bright's disease')
A. *Otters*
A. *George Frideric Handel*

79 STARTER
A. *Hyperparasite*
BONUS QUESTIONS
A. *Copenhagen*
A. *Michael Frayn*
A. *The Duke of Wellington*

80 STARTER
A. *Muck*
BONUS QUESTIONS
A. *Henry the First*
A. *Robert the Bruce/Robert I*
A. *Edward VI*
    (son of Henry VIII)

81 STARTER
A. *Uranium*
BONUS QUESTIONS
A. *French*
    (a corruption of 'dixieme', meaning one tenth)
A. *Plonk*
A. *Skive*
    (the French: esquiver)

82 STARTER
A. *Juventus*
BONUS QUESTIONS
A. *(Spenser's)* The Faerie Queene
A. *Cardinal*
A. *The child of a ruler born after its father's accession*

83 STARTER

A. *Grind your teeth*
BONUS QUESTIONS

A. *Boxing*
(the mark scratched in the earth to which the boxer had to return 30 seconds after a knockdown)

A. *Football*
(the diagram of numbered squares which allowed listeners to radio commentaries to follow the game. If developing play broke down and the ball ended up in the penalty area it was 'back to square one')

A. *Horse racing*
(a jockey with a commanding lead can relax his pull on the reigns and win with his hands down)

84 STARTER

A. *Linoleum*
BONUS QUESTIONS

A. Twelfth Night

A. King Lear

A. Richard II

85 STARTER

A. *'You're the top'*
(the lyrics of Cole Porter's 'You're the Top', from *Anything Goes*)
BONUS QUESTIONS

A. *(The court of the) Star Chamber*

A. *Tomás de Torquemada*

A. *Room 101*

86 STARTER

A. *39 units*
BONUS QUESTIONS

A. *(The old course) at St Andrews*

A. *Horatius (Cocles)*

A. *Mersey*

87 STARTER

A. *Beer*
BONUS QUESTIONS

A. *Coleridge*
(*The Ancient Mariner*)

A. *Byron*
('She Walks in Beauty')

A. *Shelley*
('To Night')

88 STARTER

A. *Pietà*
BONUS QUESTIONS
A. *Teutonic*
A. *Belgium*
A. *Russia*

89 STARTER

A. *Liver*
BONUS QUESTIONS
A. *Tosca*
A. *Norma*
A. *Rigoletto*

90 STARTER

A. *Duffel*
(the duffel coat)
BONUS QUESTIONS
A. *Wrestling*
A. *Menzies Campbell*
A. *Sebastian Coe*

91 STARTER

A. *Rocket/roquette*
BONUS QUESTIONS
A. *She*
(accept, she-who-must-be-obeyed)
A. *Charles Aznavour*
A. *Notting Hill*

92 STARTER

A. *Jo Brand*
BONUS QUESTIONS
A. *Gatcombe Park*
A. *David Ricardo*
A. *Adam Smith*

93 STARTER

A. *Soap operas*
BONUS QUESTIONS
A. *Lenin*
A. *Stalin's*
A. *Ice breaker*

94 STARTER

A. *Dana (International)*
(the transsexual winner of the Eurovision Song Contest)
BONUS QUESTIONS
A. The Taming of the Shrew
A. Emma
A. Les Liaisons Dangereuses (Dangerous Liaisons)

95 STARTER

A. *Sheffield*
BONUS QUESTIONS
A. *Troll*
A. *Edvard Grieg*
A. *The three billy goats gruff*

96 STARTER

A. *George III*
BONUS QUESTIONS
A. *Eric Satie*
A. *Little Lord Fauntleroy*
A. *Yves Saint Laurent*

97 STARTER

A. *Wave guides*
BONUS QUESTIONS
A. *Geoffrey Robinson*
A. *John Prescott*
A. *Morse*

98 STARTER

A. Whisky Galore
BONUS QUESTIONS
A. *Coral*
A. Lord of the Flies
A. *Ariel*

99 STARTER

A. *Phi beta kappa*
BONUS QUESTIONS
A. *Georgetown*
A. *Venezuela*
A. *Ecuador*

100 STARTER
A. *Nimrod*
BONUS QUESTIONS
A. *£500*
A. *Five per cent*
A. *Tony Blair*

101 STARTER
A. *Walter Cronkite*
   (Walter Leland Cronkite Jr)
BONUS QUESTIONS
A. *Ergot*
   (accept *claviceps purpurea*; technically this is the fungus and ergot the disease caused by it, but ergot is also generally used to describe the fungus)
A. *Carlsberg*
A. The Third Man

102 STARTER
A. *The Arc de Triomphe*
BONUS QUESTIONS
A. *Wesley Clark*
A. *Rome*
A. *(Captain Meriweather) Lewis*

103 STARTER
A. *Elvis Presley*
BONUS QUESTIONS
A. *Anatomy*
A. *(Sir Joshua) Reynolds*
A. *(Vincent) Van Gogh*

104 STARTER
A. *Tuna*
BONUS QUESTIONS
A. *Kurds*
A. *Saladin*
A. *Emma Nicholson (Baroness Nicholson of Winterbourne)*

105 STARTER
A. *The Universe*
   (Hubble's Constant is the ratio of the speed of recession of a galaxy to its distance from the observer)
BONUS QUESTIONS
A. *Prague*
A. *Marienbad*
A. *Budweis*

106 STARTER

A. *Borneo*
BONUS QUESTIONS
A. *FM/VHF*
A. *Digital (radio)*
A. *300*

107 STARTER

A. *Phwoar*
BONUS QUESTIONS
A. *(Sir Simon) Rattle*
A. *Wilfrid Owen*
A. *John Lennon*

108 STARTER

A. *Velvet*
BONUS QUESTIONS
A. *(Ehud) Barak*
A. *(Sir Max) Mallowan*
   (he married Agatha Christie)
A. *Muhammad*

109 STARTER

A. *Denmark*
BONUS QUESTIONS
A. *Ramblers' Association*
A. *Kinder Scout*
A. *Michael Meacher*

110 STARTER

A. *Homer Simpson*
   (in the cartoon series *The Simpsons*)
BONUS QUESTIONS
A. Anna Of The Five Towns
A. *Shirley*
A. *Sir Walter Scott*

111 STARTER

A. *Panzer*
BONUS QUESTIONS
A. *The General Synod (of the Church of England)*
A. *Vienna*
A. *John Harrison*

112 STARTER

A. *Joyce Grenfell*
BONUS QUESTIONS
A. *Waterloo*
A. *Barcelona*
A. *Mons*

113 STARTER

A. *Henrik Ibsen*
BONUS QUESTIONS
A. *Kangaroo (Island)*
A. *Goat Island*
A. *The Bahamas*

114 STARTER

A. *François Rabelais*
BONUS QUESTIONS
A. *Golden handcuffs*
A. *Golden handshake*
A. *Golden parachute*

115 STARTER

A. *Japan*
BONUS QUESTIONS
A. *File Transfer Protocol*
A. *Protocol of the learned elders of Zion / or Protocols of Zion*
   (due to translation difficulties, accept any reasonable answer that
   includes the words 'protocol(s)' and 'Zion')
A. *(Rudolf) Carnap*

116 STARTER

A. *Horses (also asses, mules)*
   (glanders is also known as farcy)
BONUS QUESTIONS
A. *Matthew Modine*
A. *Spartacus*
A. *Barry Lyndon*

117 STARTER

A. *Hacienda*
BONUS QUESTIONS
A. *The lump*
A. *Karl Marx*
A. She Stoops To Conquer

118 STARTER

A. *Cain*

BONUS QUESTIONS

A. *Sir Walter Scott*

A. *Anthony Armstrong-Jones (Lord Snowdon)*

A. *Franklin Delano Roosevelt*

119 STARTER

A. *Vinland*

BONUS QUESTIONS

A. *Or gate*

A. *Nand (not and)*

A. *Exclusive or (xor)*

120 STARTER

A. *Oxfordshire*
  (Northamptonshire also borders Oxfordshire)

BONUS QUESTIONS

A. *Moonshine*

A. *George Burns*

A. Hair

QUARTER-FINAL

1 STARTER

A. *Symposium*
BONUS QUESTIONS
A. *Dame Peggy Ashcroft*
A. *Buddy Holly*
A. *Roofing slate*

2 STARTER

A. *Tanaiste*
BONUS QUESTIONS
A. *Boron*
A. *(Thermal) neutrons*
A. *Glass or pyrex or borosilicate glass*

3 STARTER

A. *Siesta*
BONUS QUESTIONS
A. *James Madison*
A. *Great Britain*
   (accept England)
A. *Gerrymandering*

4 STARTER

A. *Clinometer*
BONUS QUESTIONS
A. *Rex Harrison*
A. *Ringo Starr*
A. *Robbie Coltrane*

5 STARTER

A. *Heligoland/Helgoland*
BONUS QUESTIONS
A. *Thérèse Raquin*
A. *Germinal*
A. *J'accuse/I accuse*

6 STARTER

A. *(Michelangelo) Antonioni*
BONUS QUESTIONS
A. *Aurora*

A. *Aurora australis*
A. *St Petersburg*

7 STARTER

A. *(John Maynard) Keynes*
BONUS QUESTIONS
A. *Bodhran*
A. Riverdance
A. *Orange order (loyalist) marches*

8 STARTER

A. *Tunisia*
BONUS QUESTIONS
A. *Gangrene*
A. *Buerger's (disease)*
A. *(Honoré de) Balzac*

9 STARTER

A. *Fire-damp*
BONUS QUESTIONS
A. *(Joseph) Priestley*
A. *(Jean Jacob) Schweppe*
A. *Coca-Cola*

10 STARTER

A. *Jerome K. Jerome*
BONUS QUESTIONS
A. *Bastille*
A. *Spandau*
A. *Lubyanka*

11 STARTER

A. *Jesuits or the Society of Jesus*
BONUS QUESTIONS
A. *(Lord Anthony) Lambton*
A. *(Sir) Peregrine Worsthorne*
A. *A worm*
  ('The Song of the Lambton Worm')

12 STARTER

A. *Mastodon*
BONUS QUESTIONS
A. Cube
A. Sphere
A Pi

13 STARTER

A. *Sergey Prokofiev*
BONUS QUESTIONS
A. *Platinum*
A. *Iridium*
A. *Catalytic converters*

14 STARTER

A. *Lenin*
BONUS QUESTIONS
A. *'Elementary, my dear Watson'*
A. *'The white heat of technology'*
(He actually said: 'the Britain that is going to be forged in the white heat of this revolution.')
A. *'The green shoots of recovery'*
(He said: 'the green shoots of economic spring are appearing once again.')

15 STARTER

A. Gay News
(not *Gay Times*, which is a later publication)
BONUS QUESTIONS
A. *Hawaii*
A. *Sandwich Islands*
A. *Mexico*

16 STARTER

A. *Trench fever*
BONUS QUESTIONS
A. *(Charles) Fourier*
A. *Mormons*
A. *Paris Commune*

17 STARTER

A. *Fermatt's Last Theorem*
BONUS QUESTIONS
A. *Pancake race*
A. *'Amazing Grace'*
A. *WIlliam Cowper*

18 STARTER

A. Corpus delicti
BONUS QUESTIONS
A. *Forked (or cleft)*
A. *King Lear*

A. *Mrs Mary Wilson*

19 STARTER
A. *8, 9 and 10*
BONUS QUESTIONS
A. *Luddites*
A. *Lord Byron*
A. *Charlotte Brontë*

20 STARTER
A. *Abbey Road (recording studios)*
BONUS QUESTIONS
A. *Bursa(e)*
A. *Ottoman Empire*
A. *Shepherd's purse*

21 STARTER
A. *Francis Bacon*
BONUS QUESTIONS
A. *Koine*
A. *Demotic (Greek)*
A. *Katharevusa (Greek)*

22 STARTER
A. *United States of America*
BONUS QUESTIONS
A. *17 (units)*
A. *25 (units)*
A. *29 (units)*

23 STARTER
A. *Gerald Ratner*
BONUS QUESTIONS
A. *Schnauzer*
A. *Weimaraner*
A. *Rottweiler*

24 STARTER
A. *Doughnutting*
BONUS QUESTION
A. *Macrophages*
A. *(Competitive) exclusion principle*
A. *Artificial insemination*

25 STARTER

A. *0.36*
BONUS QUESTIONS
A. *Blackpool*
A. *Stratford-upon-Avon*
A. *Glyndebourne*

26 STARTER

A. *Andy Pandy*
BONUS QUESTIONS
A. *(Common) ash*
A. *Norse (accept Scandinavian, Viking)*
A. *Bark*

27 STARTER

A. *36*
    (15 reds with accompanying black each time + 6 colours)
BONUS QUESTION
A. *Whips*
A. *Baronesses-in-Waiting*
A. *Chairman of Ways and Means*

28 STARTER

A. *£26.25*
BONUS QUESTIONS
A. *The tea ceremony*
A. *Franco Zeffirelli*
A. *Roses*

29 STARTER

A. *Noggin the Nog*
BONUS QUESTIONS
A. *Mark Twain*
A. *Dave Swarbrick*
A. *Bob Hope*

30 STARTER

A. *'Bestseller'*
BONUS QUESTIONS
A. *Sidney and Beatrice Webb*
A. *Professor Anthony Giddens*
A. *Mick Jagger*

31 STARTER

A. *The fates/moerae*
BONUS QUESTIONS
A. *Michael Jackson*
A. *Mikhail Gorbachev*
A. *Monica Lewinsky*

32 STARTER

A. *Accommodation*
BONUS QUESTIONS
A. *Solipsism*
A. *Phenomenalism*
A. *Existentialism*

33 STARTER

A. *Electret*
BONUS QUESTIONS
A. *Martin Chuzzlewit*
A. *Mr Micawber*
A. Dombey and Son

34 STARTER

A. *Kingdom*
BONUS QUESTIONS
A. *Canal boats*
 (accept barges as the technically incorrect but popular term)
A. *To take goods from larger vessels to the shore*
 (accept loading/unloading)
A *An engine*

35 STARTER

A. *Vindaloo*
 (the Portuguese being *vin d'alho*)
BONUS QUESTIONS
A. *Percy Bysshe Shelley*
A. *W.B. Yeats*
 ('The Secret Rose')
A. *'The Ballad of Reading Gaol'*
 (by Oscar Wilde)

36 STARTER

A. *Amman*
BONUS QUESTIONS
A. *Albania*
A. *Bulgaria*
A. *Yugoslavia*

37 STARTER

A. *Stonehenge*
BONUS QUESTIONS
A. *Joe DiMaggio*
A. *'Mrs Robinson'*
A. *Ernest Hemingway*

38 STARTER

A. *Vladivostock*
BONUS QUESTIONS
A. *Christo*
A. *Brigitte Bardot*
A. *Colorado*

39 STARTER

A. *William Beveridge*
BONUS QUESTIONS
A. Whistle Down The Wind
A. *Robert Burns*
A. *Canary Islands*

40 STARTER

A. *Blood-letting*
   (accept opening/puncturing vein etc)
BONUS QUESTIONS
A. *Bermuda*
A. *David (Lord) Waddington*
A. *Won an olympic gold medal*

41 STARTER

A. *Murder*
BONUS QUESTIONS
A. *840 million*
A. *One quarter of a mile (0.25 miles)*
A. *Four million miles per hour*

42 STARTER

A. *Helena*
BONUS QUESTIONS
A. *William Hague*
A. *Richmond*
A. *Secretary of State for Wales*

43 STARTER

A. *The zither*
BONUS QUESTIONS
A. *Costa Rica*

A. *Oscar Arias (Sanchez)*
A. *Panama*

44 STARTER

A. *Astatine*
(formerly called alabamine or anglo-helvetium)
BONUS QUESTIONS
A. *Elephant and Castle*
A. *Clare Short*
A. *Denmark*

45 STARTER

A. *Salmon*
BONUS QUESTIONS
A. *J.M. Barrie*
A. *Edwin Lutyens*
A. *The Serpentine*

46 STARTER

A. *Rudolph Valentino*
BONUS QUESTIONS
A. *Chris(topher) Woodhead*
A. *Sheffield*
A. *Palestine*

47 STARTER

A. *Mesozoic*
BONUS QUESTIONS
A. *(St) Aldhelm*
A. *Dorset*
A. *Dad's Army*

48 STARTER

A. *A tontine*
BONUS QUESTIONS
A. *Dar Es Salaam*
A. *La Paz*
A. *Jerusalem*

49 STARTER

A. *Michael Bond*
(creator of Paddington Bear)
BONUS QUESTIONS
A. *Magnesium (no oxidation)*
A. *Pressurised water reactor*
A. *Canada (deuterium and uranium)*

50 STARTER

A. South Park
BONUS QUESTIONS
A. *Sudan*
A. *Franco-Prussian War*
A. *Emmanuel (Manu) Petit*

51 STARTER

A. *Lady Emma Hamilton*
BONUS QUESTIONS
A. *Mathematics*
A. *Archimedes*
A. Good Will Hunting

52 STARTER

A. *Bombay duck*
BONUS QUESTIONS
A. *(7th Duc) de Broglie*
A. *Psi*
A. *(Proportional to the) probability (per unit volume) of locating the particle (at a given point)*

53 STARTER

A. *The Ashes*
BONUS QUESTIONS
A. *Skye*
A. *Bonnie Prince Charlie's*
A. *The cairn terrier*

54 STARTER

A. *Martin Boorman*
BONUS QUESTIONS
A. *Holy Roman Empire*
A. *Byzantine Empire*
A. *Ethelred the Unready*

55 STARTER

A. *Zero*
BONUS QUESTIONS
A. *Kosovo*
A. *Albanian*
A. *Ottoman Turks*

56 STARTER

A. *Subbuteo*
 (from *falco subbuteo*)
BONUS QUESTIONS
A. *Cartilaginous fish*
A. *Shark*
A. *Rays*

57 STARTER

A. *All Saints*
BONUS QUESTIONS
A. *Pumpkin*
A. *Royal Pavilion, Brighton*
A. *Billy Corgan*

58 STARTER

A. *The Moomins/Moomintrolls*
 (created by Tove Jansson)
BONUS QUESTIONS
A. *Call to prayer (made by the muezzin)*
A. *God (Allah) is great*
A. *Five*

59 STARTER

A. *Prince George, The Duke of Kent*
BONUS QUESTIONS
A. *Rubber chicken circuit*
A. *Henry IV (of Navarre)*
A. *Russia*

60 STARTER

A. *It is unfinished*
BONUS QUESTIONS
A. *Caspar Weinberger*
A. *Weak (interactions)*
A. *(Gilbert Harold) Hardy*

61 STARTER

A. The Magic Roundabout
BONUS QUESTIONS
A. *Sinking of the* Titanic
A. *'The Red Flag'*
A. *Turnips 1*

62 STARTER

A. *Tin Pan Alley*
BONUS QUESTIONS
A. *Saturn*
A. *Uranus*
A. *Neptune*

63 STARTER

A. *The Women's FA Cup Final*
BONUS QUESTIONS
A. *Nestorians*
A. *Pylos*
A. *Navarino*

64 STARTER

A. *Not proven*
BONUS QUESTIONS
A. *(Robert) Schumann*
A. *(Gustav) Mahler*
A. *(Sergei) Prokofiev*

65 STARTER

A. *Nitrous acid*
BONUS QUESTIONS
A. *Ghosts*
A. *Gilbert Ryle*
A. *The Police*

66 STARTER

A. *Gladys Aylward*
BONUS QUESTIONS
A. *Eleventh century*
A. *Istanbul*
    (accept Constantinople, which remains part of the title)
A. *Hagia (Saint) Sophia/church of the divine wisdom*

67 STARTER

A. *Marilyn Monroe*
BONUS QUESTIONS
A. *Chloroplast*
A. *CS gas*
A. *Spider plant*
    (accept St Bernard's lily)

68 STARTER

A. *Lemur*
BONUS QUESTIONS
A. *Archie Rice*

A. Luther
A. Inadmissible Evidence

69 STARTER
A. *Leonard Bernstein*
BONUS QUESTIONS
A. *Chess*
A. *Backgammon*
A. *Scotland*

70 STARTER
A. *Queen Christina of Sweden*
BONUS QUESTIONS
A. *Isle of Dogs*
A. *Canary Islands*
A. *Skye*

71 STARTER
A. *Synchronized swimming*
BONUS QUESTIONS
A. *Texas*
A. *California*
A. *Arizona*

72 STARTER
A. *Eleven*
(six doubles, four trebles, one accumulator)
BONUS QUESTIONS
A. *Totty*
(not bimbo, which has a different origin and was originally a term for a man)
A. *Samuel Johnson*
A. Swallows and Amazons

73 STARTER
A. *Field-day*
BONUS QUESTIONS
A. *Mckenzie (man/friend)*
A. *'Eleanor Rigby'*
A. *Swingometer*

74 STARTER
A. *Tara*
BONUS QUESTIONS
A. The Merry Wives of Windsor
A. *The Barsetshire or Barchester Chronicles/novels*
A. Middlemarch

75 STARTER

A. *Glycogen*
BONUS QUESTIONS
A. *Bull-bar*
A. *Morris*
A. *Theodore Roosevelt*

76 STARTER

A. *Shinty*
BONUS QUESTIONS
A. *Joseph of Arimathaea*
A. *The vacancy among the 12 apostles (following the death of Judas Iscariot)*
A. *Reuben*

77 STARTER

A. *Salisbury*
   (Robert Arthur Talbot Gascoyne-Cecil, 3rd Marquess of Salisbury. Others: 2nd Earl of Liverpool, 14th Earl of Derby, 4th Earl of Aberdeen, 5th Earl of Rosebery)
BONUS QUESTIONS
A. *David Moorcroft*
A. *Christopher Hampton*
A. *Dance/ballet*

78 STARTER

A. *Peter Ilych Tchaikovsky*
BONUS QUESTIONS
A. *The furies*
A. The Oresteia
A. *T.S. Eliot*

79 STARTER

A. *Jefferson Davis*
BONUS QUESTIONS
A. *Pictographic*
A. *Japanese*
   (Amharic and Cherokee also use the system)
A. *Korean*

80 STARTER

A. *Davy Jones's locker*
BONUS QUESTIONS
A. *Friar Lawrence*
   (in *Romeo and Juliet*)
A. *Arsenic*

A. *Deadly nightshade/belladonna*

81 STARTER
A. *The bell known as Big Ben*
BONUS QUESTIONS
A. *Job*
A. *William Blake*
A. Songs of Innocence and Experience

82 STARTER
A. *Alice*
   (in *Alice's Adventures in Wonderland*)
BONUS QUESTIONS
A. *The winter queen*
A. *1978*
A. *Leontes*

83 STARTER
A. *Jack Charlton*
BONUS QUESTIONS
A. *Tunisia*
A. *Morocco*
A. *(Kwame) Nkrumah*

84 STARTER
A. *The Man Who Broke the Bank at Monte Carlo*
BONUS QUESTIONS
A. *Jacobins (Dominicans were nicknamed Jacobins)*
A. *Committee of Public Safety*
A. *(Georges-Jacques) Danton*

85 STARTER
A. *Alpha helix*
BONUS QUESTIONS
A. *Deacon Blue*
A. *Texas*
A. *Justin Currie*

86 STARTER
A. *Quetzalcoatl*
BONUS QUESTIONS
A. *Charles I*
A. *John Milton*
A. *Freedom of the press*

87 STARTER

A. *Margaret Thatcher/Baroness Thatcher of Kesteven*
BONUS QUESTIONS
A. *A statistic*
A. *Horace*
A. *Lamp posts*

88 STARTER

A. *Gray's* Anatomy (– descriptive and surgical)
BONUS QUESTIONS
A. *Richard I*
A. *Edward III*
A. *Edward, the Black Prince*

89 STARTER

A. Ulysses
BONUS QUESTIONS
A. *Rawalpindi*
A. *Lahore*
A. *Faisalabad*

90 STARTER

A. *F. Murray Abraham*
BONUS QUESTIONS
A. *Java trench*
A. Homo erectus
A. *Kapok*

91 STARTER

A. *Alexander Solzhenitsyn*
BONUS QUESTIONS
A. *They produce sound*
A. *Their wings*
A. *Cicadas*

92 STARTER

A. *St Agnes*
BONUS QUESTIONS
A. *Aga-saga*
A. *Bodice-ripper*
A. *Sex-and-shopping*

93 STARTER

A. *Switzerland*
BONUS QUESTIONS
A. *Pentimento*
A. *Lillian Hellman*
A. *Dashiell Hammett*

94 STARTER

A. *Cormorant*
BONUS QUESTIONS
A. *The Alcazar*
A. *(Francisco) Largo Caballero*
A. *The International Brigades*

95 STARTER

A. *Giotto (di Bondone)*
BONUS QUESTIONS
A. *'O worship the King all glorious above'*
A. *'With heart and hands and voices'*
(not 'with hearts', which is what most people sing!)
A. *'We plough the fields, and scatter'*

96 STARTER

A. *Cholesterol*
BONUS QUESTIONS
A. *Belfast*
A. *Mourne Mountains*
A. The Magician's Nephew
(1955)

97 STARTER

A. *Amethyst*
BONUS QUESTIONS
A. *Constantine I (the Great)*
A. *Buckingham Palace*
A. *Jean-François-Thérèse Chalgrin*

98 STARTER

A. *Soweto*
BONUS QUESTIONS
A. *George Harrison*
A. *Maverick*
A. *Prince*
(also known as the Artist Formerly Known as Prince/Symbol/Afkap)

99 STARTER

A. *Menander*
BONUS QUESTIONS
A. *Magic (Johnson)*
A. *The Red Dean*
A. *Pussyfoot*

100 STARTER

A. *LETS (Local Exchange or Economic or Employment Trading System or Scheme)*
BONUS QUESTIONS
A. *Trope*
A. *Heliotrope*
A. *Jerusalem artichoke*

101 STARTER

A. *Shorthand*
(also called stenography or tachygraphy or brachygraphy)
BONUS QUESTIONS
A. *Port*
(accelerated graphics port)
A. *Peripheral*
(peripheral component interface)
A. *Printer*
(printer control language)

102 STARTER

A. *The wrist*
BONUS QUESTIONS
A. *Hedy Lamarr*
A. *Vincent Price*
A. *Gina Lollobrigida*

103 STARTER

A. *The Somme*
BONUS QUESTIONS
A. *Hedge funds*
A. *Enid Blyton*
A. *Privet*

104 STARTER

A. *Cinema(tograph)*
(accept movies, film etc)
BONUS QUESTIONS
A. *Natural Law Party*

A. *Taliban*
A. *Pauline Hanson*

105 STARTER

A. *Infra-red telescope*
BONUS QUESTIONS
A. *Dungeons and Dragons*
A. Fidelio
A. *Monitor (lizards)*

106 STARTER

A. *Baroreceptors*
BONUS QUESTIONS
A. *The BBC*
A. Wallpaper
A. Loaded

107 STARTER

A. G
(conflagration; the descender is the stem below the g)
BONUS QUESTIONS
A. *Hindu*
A. *Karma*
A. *Yoga*

108 STARTER

A. *Hush*
BONUS QUESTIONS
A. Angst
A. *Martin Heidegger*
A. *Jean-Paul Sartre*

109 STARTER

A. *Vickers*
BONUS QUESTIONS
A. *Chicory Tip*
A. *Mellotron*
A. *Kate Bush*

110 STARTER

A. *Marie Stopes*
BONUS QUESTIONS
A. *(Rabindranath) Tagore*
A. *Hindu Reform Movement (Brahmo Samaj)*
A. *Amartya Sen*

111 STARTER
A. *The Seventeenth*
BONUS QUESTIONS
A. *The Venus de Milo*
A. *Vulcan*
A. *Magellan*

112 STARTER
A. *Secretary of State for Defence*
BONUS QUESTIONS
A. *Wilfred Owen*
   ('it is a sweet and glorious thing to die for one's country')
A. *Muriel Spark*
   (meaning 'remember that you have to die')
A. *Nicholas Poussin*

113 STARTER
A. *Sturm und Drang (Storm and Stress)*
BONUS QUESTIONS
A. *Paris*
A. The Ambassadors
A. *George Gershwin*

114 STARTER
A. *Criminal intent (of action)*
BONUS QUESTIONS
A. *Dodoma*
A. *Belize*
A. *Malawi*

115 STARTER
A. Blithe Spirit
BONUS QUESTIONS
A. *Feast days of patron saints of the British Isles*
   (David, Patrick, George and Andrew)
A. *Quarter days*
   (Lady Day, Midsummer Day, Michaelmas Day and Christmas Day)
A. *Queen's Birthday (actual and official)*

116 STARTER
A. *Poisson distribution*
BONUS QUESTIONS
A. *Richard Wagner*
A. *Joseph Haydn*
A. *Hector Berlioz*

117 STARTER

A. *St Kilda*
BONUS QUESTIONS
A. *James (the Greater, Boanerges)*
A. *Peter*
A. *Judas/Jude*

118 STARTER

A. *Alfred Waterhouse*
BONUS QUESTIONS
A. *Rupert Bear*
A. The Prisoner of Zenda
A. *James I of England, and VI of Scotland*

119 STARTER

A. *Psychosomatic*
BONUS QUESTIONS
A. Twelfth Night
A. *Field Marshall Montgomery*
A. *Hunter S. Thompson*

120 STARTER

A. *Catching trout*
BONUS QUESTIONS
A. *Gigolo*
A. *Richard Gere*
A. *Alistair Campbell*

SEMI-FINAL

1 STARTER
A. *Sphagnum moss (also called peat moss or bog moss)*
BONUS QUESTIONS
A. *Laurie Lee*
A. *George Orwell*
A. For Whom The Bell Tolls

2 STARTER
A. *The Norns or Nornir*
(in Norse literature sometimes called Disir. In some sources they are named individually as Urd, Verdandi and Skuld)
BONUS QUESTIONS
A. *The Arts and Crafts movement*
A. *Art Deco*
A. *Functionalism*

3 STARTER
A. *Triumph*
BONUS QUESTIONS
A. Sleeping Beauty
A. The Taming of the Shrew
A. *Sir Francis Drake*
(in the poem 'Drake's Drum')

4 STARTER
A. *Nigeria*
BONUS QUESTIONS
A. *A rosette worn in a hat or cap*
(although accept ribbon or a knot of ribbons, etc)
A. *At the neck (it's a frill of lace)*
(accept over the top/front of the shirt)
A. *Bertha*

5 STARTER
A. Ex cathedra
BONUS QUESTIONS
A. *'e' to the (power) 'x' or exponential (of) 'x'*

A. *sin (x)*
A. *sinh (x)*
(can also be pronounced 'sinch x' or 'sine h x' or 'hyperbolic sine x')

6 STARTER
A. *Bridge*
BONUS QUESTIONS
A. *French horn*
A. *New Orleans*
A. *Djibouti*

7 STARTER
A. *Cambridge University Library*
BONUS QUESTIONS
A. *Suffolk*
A. *Romney Marsh (accept Romneys)*
A. *Cheviot(s)*

8 STARTER
A. *Compiègne*
BONUS QUESTIONS
A. *Noah's Ark*
A. *The Tabernacle*
(the curtained tent containing the Ark of the Covenant)
A. *Solomon*

9 STARTER
A. *Australia*
BONUS QUESTIONS
A. *(The Battle of) the Falkland Islands*
A. *The Plate/Rio de la Plata*
A. *Midway*

10 STARTER
A. *Liquefied petroleum gas*
BONUS QUESTIONS
A. *The golden horde*
A. *Benvenuto Cellini*
A. *Samuel Johnson*

11 STARTER
A. *Felix Mendelssohn*
BONUS QUESTIONS
A. *Friedrich Nietzsche*
A. *Brendan Behan*
A. *J.M. Barrie*

12 STARTER

A. *Pheromone (or ectohormone)*

BONUS QUESTIONS

A. *Stars and bars*

A. *Star-streaming*

A. *Because the heads of the fish (usually pilchards) protrude through the crust as if staring at the stars*

13 STARTER

A. *Ekaterinberg*

BONUS QUESTIONS

A. *Viscount Palmerston*

A. *The Earl Derby*

A. *Viscount Melbourne*

14 STARTER

A. *Vauxhall*

BONUS QUESTIONS

A. *The South Sea Company*

A. *Namibia*

A. *Richard Rogers*

15 STARTER

A. *In a pack of tarot cards*

BONUS QUESTIONS

A. *Charles Dickens*

A. *Soames Forsyte*

A. *T.E. Lawrence*

16 STARTER

A. *The Shatt al-Arab* ('Stream of the Arabs')

BONUS QUESTIONS

A. *Politics*

A. *A statesman*

A. *Enoch Powell*

17 STARTER

A. *Raku*

BONUS QUESTIONS

A. *Q*

A. *Quebec*

A. *Armed vessels disguised as merchant ships*

18 STARTER

A. *St Boniface*
BONUS QUESTIONS
A. *Hungary (Hungarian Dances)*
A. *Italy (Italian Symphony)*
A. *Spain (Spanish Caprice)*

19 STARTER

A. *(Raw) silk*
BONUS QUESTIONS
A. *Franz Anton Mesmer*
A. *Bridey Murphy*
A. *Bloxham*
   (Arnal Bloxham)

20 STARTER

A. *Polyanthus*
BONUS QUESTIONS
A. *(George Stephenson's) The Rocket*
A. *At fairs*
A. *Queen's Bench (division)*

21 STARTER

A. *The Gaia Hypothesis (accept Gaia)*
BONUS QUESTIONS
A. *The puppet Pinocchio*
A. *The wooden horse of Troy*
A. *Thomas Bewick*

22 STARTER

A. *Michael Howard*
BONUS QUESTIONS
A. *(Gilbert N.) Lewis*
A. *Adduct*
A. *Heavy water (or D$_2$O)*

23 STARTER

A. *Thanksgiving Day*
BONUS QUESTIONS
A. *Discovery*
A. *Nostromo*
   (not Sulaco which is the craft in the sequel *Aliens*)
A. *Millennium Falcon*

24 STARTER

A. *The seed-vessel bursts open when ripe*
BONUS QUESTIONS
A. *Morocco*
A. *Toledo*
A. *Aragon*

25 STARTER

A. *Astronomy/astrophysics*
BONUS QUESTIONS
A. *Pyramus and Thisbe*
    (enacted in *A Midsummer Night's Dream*)
A. *Troilus and Cressida*
A. *Abelard and Heloise*

26 STARTER

A. *Selvage (or selvedge)*
BONUS QUESTIONS
A. *The Round Table*
A. *Seige*
A. *The Algonquin*

27 STARTER

A. Monty Python's Flying Circus
BONUS QUESTIONS
A. *J.M.W.Turner*
A. Bleak House
A. *George Bernard Shaw*

28 STARTER

A. *James Madison*
    (Madison, Madison Avenue, Madison Square Gardens)
BONUS QUESTIONS
A. *The Punjab*
A. *Isaac Walton*
A. *Rio Grande/Rio Bravo*

29 STARTER

A. *Low temperatures*
BONUS QUESTIONS
A. *Paul Cézanne*
A. *Pablo Picasso*
A. *Jean-Baptist Simeon) Chardin*

30 STARTER

A. *Jerome Robbins*
BONUS QUESTIONS
A. *Orion's Belt*
A. *General Sir Samuel Browne*
A. *Doldrums*

31 STARTER

A. *Wheel clamp*
BONUS QUESTIONS
A. *Bread*
A. *A volcanic eruption*
A. The Rubaiyat of Omar Khayyam

32 STARTER

A. *Speculum*
BONUS QUESTIONS
A. *Joseph*
A. *Florence Nightingale*
A. *Correggio*

33 STARTER

A. *Vespasian*
BONUS QUESTIONS
A. *Norway*
A. *Secretary General of the UN*
A. *Edvard Munch*

34 STARTER

A. *(Prince Grigori Aleksandrovich) Potemkin*
BONUS QUESTIONS
A. *Chief Justice William Rehnquist*
A. *The Watergate break-in*
A. *Chief Justice Earl Warren*

35 STARTER

A. *Cheese*
BONUS QUESTIONS
A. *The Bloomsbury Group*
A. *Smith Square*
A. *The Wallace Collection*

36 STARTER
A. Mastermind
BONUS QUESTIONS
A. *Foot and mouth disease*
A. *Pigs*
   (swine vesicular disease)
A. *Birds*
   (particularly domestic fowl, poultry)

37 STARTER
A. *Barry Goldwater*
BONUS QUESTIONS
A. *Basel*
A. *Basra*
A. *Baltimore*

38 STARTER
A. *William Boyd*
BONUS QUESTIONS
A. *(Jean-Baptsite de) Lamarck*
A. *Biology*
A. *(Trofim Denisovich) Lysenko*

39 STARTER
A. *Whitby*
BONUS QUESTIONS
A. *Brazil*
A. *Saudi Arabia*
A. *Belize*

40 STARTER
A. *Foehn (accept adiabatic)*
BONUS QUESTIONS
A. *Charlton Athletic*
A. *Bristol Rovers*
A. *Hampden Park*

41 STARTER
A. *Augurs or augures*
BONUS QUESTIONS
A. *Thomas Thorpe*
A. *Eighteen*
A. *The marriage of true minds*
   ('let me not to the marriage of true minds/admit impediments.')

42 STARTER

A. *Tripos*
BONUS QUESTIONS
A. *The eagle*
A. *Berchtesgaden*
A. *The Battle of Britain*

43 STARTER

A. *Panjandrum*
BONUS QUESTIONS
A. *Ajman*
  Sharjah
  Abu Dhabi
  Dubai
  Ras al Khaimah
  [al] Fujairah
  Umm al Quaiwain

44 STARTER

A. *Turmeric*
BONUS QUESTIONS
A. *Dorset*
A. *Lancashire*
A. *Somerset*

45 STARTER

A. *The heart of Robert the Bruce*
BONUS QUESTIONS
A. *The Pantheon*
A. *The Circus Maximus*
  (accept hippodrome; it was the largest of the Roman hippodromes)
A. *Coliseum/colloseum*

46 STARTER

A. *Eddie Rickenbacker*
BONUS QUESTIONS
A. *Hebrew*
A. *St Jerome*
A. *John Wyclif/Wycliffe*

47 STARTER

A. *Aniline*
  (also called phenylamine or aminobenzene)
BONUS QUESTIONS
A. *Margaret Beckett*
A. *Alan Beith*
A. *Sir Geoffrey Howe*

48 STARTER

A. *Diageo*
BONUS QUESTIONS
A. *The 'saucy' seaside postcard*
A. *Spy*
A. *Leonardo da Vinci*

49 STARTER

A. The Diary of Anne Frank
BONUS QUESTIONS
A. Voice Of An Angel
A. Björk (Gudmundsdottir)
A. 'Oh, For The Wings Of A Dove'

50 STARTER

A. *The Tour de France*
BONUS QUESTIONS
A. *Janus*
A. *Gray's* Elegy Written in a Country Churchyard
A. *André Gide*

51 STARTER

A. *Kent*
BONUS QUESTIONS
A. *Max Ernst*
A. *Gustave Courbet*
A. *Louis-Philippe*

52 STARTER

A. *Henry W. Fowler*
BONUS QUESTIONS
A. *Hera*
A. *Ceres*
A. *Athene*

53 STARTER

A. *Natterjack toad*
BONUS QUESTIONS
A. *The Atlantic Charter*
A. *The* Bismarck
A. *New Jersey*

54 STARTER

A. Grease
BONUS QUESTIONS
A. *Freedom* [7]

A. *Eleven*
A. *Voyager(s) (one and two)*

55 STARTER

A. *Commonwealth*
BONUS QUESTIONS
A. Labyrinth
A. *Daedalus*
A. *Bobby Sands*

56 STARTER

A. *Dilbert*
BONUS QUESTIONS
A. *Candela*
A. *Siemens*
A. *Steradian*

57 STARTER

A. *Chequered*
   (flag in motor racing)
BONUS QUESTIONS
A. *The black widow*
A. *Rudyard Kipling*
   (in 'The Widow at Windsor')
A. *Judith*

58 STARTER

A. *Wolfgang Pauli*
BONUS QUESTIONS
A. *Dance of death or dance macabre*
A. *Hans Holbein (the younger)*
A. *W. H. Auden*

59 STARTER

A. *Fuzzy logic*
BONUS QUESTIONS
A. *Arianism*
   (from Arius)
A. *Burning*
A. *Anabaptists*

60 STARTER

A. *Honcho*
BONUS QUESTIONS
A. *War of the Three Henrys*
A. *Everlasting League*
A. *Austria-Hungary*

61 STARTER

A. *A chain*
BONUS QUESTIONS
A. *Devon*
A. *Kent*
A. *Henry Addington*

62 STARTER

A. *Grampian*
BONUS QUESTIONS
A. *The Ambassadors*
A. *George Bush*
A. *Eric Cantona*

63 STARTER

A. *Halcyon days*
BONUS QUESTIONS
A. *Tycho Brahe*
A. *Speed of light*
A. *(Ejnar) Hertzsprung*

64 STARTER

A. *Raymond Poincaré*
BONUS QUESTIONS
A. *The British Petroleum Company plc*
   (accept BP or British Petroleum)
A. *Standard Oil Company (Ohio)*
A. *Amoco*

65 STARTER

A. *Persepolis*
BONUS QUESTIONS
A. *Kilimanjaro*
A. *Mount McKinley*
A. *The Andes*

66 STARTER

A. *Ausgleich*
BONUS QUESTIONS
A. *Quenching*
A. *Geiger counter*
A. *Love*

67 STARTER

A. *Manchurian Candidate*
BONUS QUESTIONS
A. *Squall*
A. *Aneurin Bevan*
A. *Shark*

68 STARTER

A. *Ming*
BONUS QUESTIONS
A. *'Sgt. Pepper's Lonely Hearts Club Band'*
A. *'Yellow Submarine'*
A. *'Lucy In The Sky With Diamonds'*

69 STARTER

A. *Corkage*
BONUS QUESTIONS
A. *(William Thomson) Baron Kelvin of Largs*
A. *Daniel Fahrenheit*
A. *Réné-Antoine Ferchault de Réaumur*

70 STARTER

A. *Vanilla*
BONUS QUESTIONS
A. *Egyptians*
A. *Ladybird*
A. *Thomas Huxley*

71 STARTER

A. *Glass lizard*
BONUS QUESTIONS
A. *Arthur Conan Doyle*
A. *Anton Chekhov*
A. *Doctor Finlay*

72 STARTER

A. *Meander*
   (Phrygia being an area of west-central Anatolia)
BONUS QUESTIONS
A. *Noël Coward*
A. *Queen Victoria*
A. *W.S. Gilbert*

73 STARTER

A. The Gondoliers
BONUS QUESTIONS
A. *Factorial*
A. *Imaginary part (of the unknown)*
A. *Product (of the sequence of unknowns)*

74 STARTER

A. *Abyssinia*
    (*The History of Rasselas, Prince of Abyssinia*)
BONUS QUESTIONS
A. *Bulgaria*
A. *Yugoslavia*
A. *Romania*

75 STARTER

A. *It is drinkable*
BONUS QUESTIONS
A. *Austria*
A. *Eastern Kingdom*
    (i.e. Osterreich)
A. *Kurt Waldheim*

76 STARTER

A. *Point of inflection*
BONUS QUESTIONS
A. *Manchester*
A. *(Ancient) Rome*
A. *Shrewsbury*

77 STARTER

A. *Sapporo*
BONUS QUESTIONS
A. *Ankara*
A. *Damascus*
A. *Calico*

78 STARTER

A. *Saprophytic or saprophyte*
    (also called saprobe/saprovore/saprozoite)
BONUS QUESTIONS
A. *Borrowdale*
A. *National Trust*
A. *Britain's wettest place*

79 STARTER

A. *Grenade*

BONUS QUESTIONS

A. *Hawk*
A. *Accipiter/Accipitridae*
A. *(Australian) Labor Party*

80 STARTER

A. *Sequestrate*

BONUS QUESTIONS

A. *Pulpit*
A. *Mimbar*
   (accept the Arabic minbar)
A. *Bimah/bema*

81 STARTER

A. *Pax Britannica*

BONUS QUESTIONS

A. *Stagecoach*
A. *John Wayne*
A. *William Hazlitt*

82 STARTER

A. *Poste-restante*

BONUS QUESTIONS

A *They were the dates of royal weddings*
A. *Pieter Bruegel (the Elder)*
A. *(Sir) Michael Tippett*

83 STARTER

A. *Shinto*

BONUS QUESTIONS

A. *They both suffered injury to their ears*
A. *Spain*
A. *Ted Hughes*

84 STARTER

A. *Magnetic levitation*

BONUS QUESTIONS

A. *Threadworm*
A. *Whitworth*
   (after Sir Joseph Whitworth)
A. *Ariadne*

85 STARTER

A. *Frank Lloyd Wright*
BONUS QUESTIONS
A. *Sun Myung Moon*
A. *Giovanni Domenico Cassini*
  (Cassini's laws)
A. *Bette Davis*

86 STARTER

A. *Septicaemia*
BONUS QUESTIONS
A. *Thomas Tallis*
A. *Johann Sebastian Bach*
A. *Malcolm Sargent .*

87 STARTER

A. *7 January*
BONUS QUESTIONS
A. *Poland/Hungary/The Czech Republic*
A. *Finland/Sweden/The Republic of Ireland/Austria*

88 STARTER

A. *Glengarry*
BONUS QUESTIONS
A. *Edgar Allan Poe*
A. *Rupert Brooke*
A. *Richard II*

89 STARTER

A. *Helga*
BONUS QUESTIONS
A. *Reynard*
A. *(Foxe's)* Book of Martyrs
A. *Lillian Hellman*

90 STARTER

A. *Shaka or Chaka*
BONUS QUESTIONS
A. *Dioxin*
A. *Chlorine*
A. *Agent Orange*

91 STARTER

A. *Simnel cake*
BONUS QUESTIONS
A. *Presbyterianism?*
A. *Jean Calvin*
A. *Geneva*

92 STARTER

A. *Totalizator*
BONUS QUESTIONS
A. *Five-year plan*
A. *The Schlieffen Plan*
  (Alfred, Graf Von Schlieffen)
A. *Sherlock Holmes*

93 STARTER

A. *Skunk*
BONUS QUESTIONS
A. *George I*
  (1721)
A. *Victoria*
  (1886)
A. *Charles II*
  (1665, 1666)

94 STARTER

A. *(James) Gordon Bennett*
BONUS QUESTIONS
A. *Apollo*
A. *St Martins*
a. *Gielgud*

95 STARTER

A. *Tired and emotional*
BONUS QUESTIONS
A. *Truth*
A. *Neville Chamberlain*
A. *A. J. P. Taylor*

96 STARTER

A. *Samuel Taylor Coleridge*
BONUS QUESTIONS
A. *The Pleiades*
A. *Middlemarch*
A. *Corr*
  (They and their brother Jim make up the band The Corrs)

97 STARTER

A. *Hydroponics*
BONUS QUESTIONS
A. *Sir Walter Scott*
A. *Arlington*
A. *Alexander Pope*

98 STARTER

A. *Nick Hornby*
BONUS QUESTIONS
A. *Land*
A. *Mayhem*
A. *Twelve pence/one shilling/one-twentieth of a pound*

99 STARTER

A. *Nicene Creed or Niceno-Constantinopolitan Creed*
BONUS QUESTIONS
A. *Vienna*
A. *Amsterdam*
A. *Brussels*

100 STARTER

A. *The Body Shop*
BONUS QUESTIONS
A. *(Sir/Saint) Thomas More*
A. *The Birdman of Alcatraz*
A. *John Bunyan*

101 STARTER

A. *Sir Henry Havelock*
BONUS QUESTIONS
A. *Asgard*
A. *Lyoness*
A. *Tir na noc (or tir-nan-og)*

102 STARTER

A. *Tribeca*
(triangle below canal)
BONUS QUESTIONS
A. *The Civil List*
A. The Mikado
A. Schindler's Ark/Schindler's List
(by Thomas Keneally)

103 STARTER

A. *Phenol or carbolic acid*
BONUS QUESTIONS
A. *Longman*
A. *A thistle*
   (it first appeared in Edinburgh)
A. *Macmillan*

104 STARTER

A. *George Mallory*
BONUS QUESTIONS
A. *Gérard Depardieu*
A. *Robin Williams*
A. *Rick Moranis*

105 STARTER

A. *Ben Jonson*
BONUS QUESTIONS
A. *Recusants*
A. *Latitudinarians*
A. *Broad Church*

106 STARTER

A. *A diamond is forever*
BONUS QUESTIONS
A. *Mark Elder*
A. *Sambuca*
A. *Drambuie*

107 STARTER

A. *Scored the first ever World Cup Goal*
BONUS QUESTIONS
A. *House of Keys*
A. *The Salem witch trials*
A. *Madness*

108 STARTER

A. Terra Nova
BONUS QUESTIONS
A. *Nullification doctrine*
A. *Slavery*
A. *Homestead Act*

109 STARTER

A. *Brigade of Guards*
(accept any of the five individual regiments, Grenadier, Coldstream, Welsh, Scots, Irish Guards)

BONUS QUESTIONS

A. *Nine*

A. *Innisfree*
(in his poem 'The Lake Isle of Innisfree')

A. *Lord Peter Wimsey*

110 STARTER

A. *Ourselves alone*

BONUS QUESTIONS

A. Lost Horizon
(by James Hilton)

A. *Sir Arthur Sullivan*

A. *Pandemonium*

111 STARTER

A. *Pina colada*

BONUS QUESTIONS

A. *Leander*

A. *Niagara Falls*

A. *Field Marshal Lord Kitchener*

112 STARTER

A. Bild (Zeitung)

BONUS QUESTIONS

A. *Catalan*

A. *Formentera*

A. *Minorca/Menorca*

113 STARTER

A. *Mary Quant*

BONUS QUESTIONS

A. *Glaucoma*

A. *Greensands*

A. *Gulls*

114 STARTER

A. *540 degrees*
(formula = (2n – 4) x 90 where n = number of sides)

BONUS QUESTIONS

A. *The Trent*

A. *The Wye*

A. *The Tay*

115 STARTER

A. *René Descartes*
BONUS QUESTIONS
A. *Turquoise*
A. *Sinai*
A. *Turkish*

116 STARTER

A. *Modulator and demodulator*
BONUS QUESTIONS
A. *Spherical abberation*
A. *Astigmatism*
A. *Coma*

117 STARTER

A. *Love Hearts*
BONUS QUESTIONS
A. *Bulgaria*
A. *Austria*
A. *Iran*

118 STARTER

A. *(Literary and artistic) copyright*
BONUS QUESTIONS
A. *(Edwin) Hubble*
A. *Red shift*
A. *Barred spiral*

119 STARTER

A. *Nemesis*
BONUS QUESTIONS
A. The Third Man
A. La Ronde
A. *(Giant) ferris wheel*

120 STARTER

A. *He was born in Hiroshima on 6 August 1945, the day the atomic bomb was dropped there.*
BONUS QUESTIONS
A. *Molière*
A. *Colette*
A. *Françoise Sagan*

FINAL

1 STARTER
A. *Buttercup*
BONUS QUESTIONS
A. *The medieval clock*
A. *Doctor Faustus*
A. *Caesium*

2 STARTER
A. *Saltire*
BONUS QUESTIONS
A. *Edinburgh*
A. *Tunbridge Wells*
A. *Butchery*

3 STARTER
A. *(Serum) albumin*
BONUS QUESTIONS
A. *The Three Graces*
A. *Antonio Canova*
A High Noon

4 STARTER
A. *St Benedict (of Nursia)*
BONUS QUESTIONS
A. *Walt Whitman*
A. *Ted Hughes*
A. *R.S. Thomas*

5 STARTER
A. *Mrs Patrick Campbell*
  (born Beatrice Tanner)
BONUS QUESTIONS
A. *Nantes*
A. *Kuala Lumpur*
A. *Astrakhan*

6 STARTER

A. *Robert Schumann*
BONUS QUESTIONS
A. *The Fair Maid of Kent*
A. *Norway*
A. *Snowdrop*

7 STARTER

A. *Moving the goalposts*
BONUS QUESTIONS
A. *Bicuspids*
A. *Eye teeth*
A. *Syphilis*

8 STARTER

A. *Fiscal drag*
BONUS QUESTIONS
A. *Almayer's Folly*
A. *Oliver Goldsmith*
   (part of a song from *The Vicar of Wakefield*)
A. *History*

9 STARTER

A. *Iroquois*
BONUS QUESTIONS
A. *Burma*
A. *Lord Mountbatten*
A. *Isle of Wight*

10 STARTER

A. *Fathom*
BONUS QUESTIONS
A. *Dame Janet Baker*
A. *Forth (railway) Bridge*
A. *George Bush*

11 STARTER

A. *Magnetic flux density/magnetic induction*
BONUS QUESTIONS
A. *Christianity*
A. *The celestial city*
A. *Mary Baker Eddy*

12 STARTER

A. *Tabloid newspapers*
BONUS QUESTIONS
A. *Junges Deutschland (Young Germany)*
A. *Charles Edward Stuart, the Young Pretender*
A. *German war reparations*

13 STARTER

A. *[Andean] condor*
BONUS QUESTIONS
A. *The Act of Supremacy*
A. *The (first) Test Act*
A. *The Act of Settlement*

14 STARTER

A. *Australia*
BONUS QUESTIONS
A. *Doctor (James) Kildare*
A. *Richard Gordon*
   (real name Gordon Ostlere)
A. *A.J. Cronin*
   (Archibald Joseph Cronin)

15 STARTER

A. *Jack and Jill*
BONUS QUESTIONS
A. *Anne Bancroft*
A. *Filariasis*
A. *Canon law*

16 STARTER

A. *Lemma*
BONUS QUESTIONS
A. *The Party of Wales*
A. *The Democratic Left*
A. *Alliance*

17 STARTER

A. *Anton Chekhov*
BONUS QUESTIONS
A. *Creep*
A. *Walter de la Mare*
A. *Radiohead*

18 STARTER

A. *Psephology*
BONUS QUESTIONS
A. *Islay*
A. *Bute*
A. *Kyle of Lochalsh*

19 STARTER

A. *Currant*
BONUS QUESTIONS
A. *Napoleon (Bonaparte)*
A. *Byron*
A. *Antonio Canova*

20 STARTER

A. *Circumference of the earth*
  (accept radius/diameter)
BONUS QUESTIONS
A. *Austria*
A. *Anschluss*
A. *(Kurt von) Schuschnigg*

21 STARTER

A. *Falls Road*
BONUS QUESTIONS
A. *Cobalt, nickel, gadolinium*
A. *(Magnetic) domains*
A. *(Pierre) Curie*

22 STARTER

A. *The wind of change (is blowing through this continent)*
BONUS QUESTIONS
A. *Mozart*
A. *Stravinsky*
A. *Sir Kenneth MacMillan*

23 STARTER

A. *Gnocchi*
BONUS QUESTIONS
A. *Hieronymus Bosch*
A. *Hydrogen*
A. *Spark plug*
  (NB also in 1902, Honold developed high voltage ignition)

24 STARTER
A. *Charing Cross*
BONUS QUESTIONS
A. *Calypso*
A. *John Denver*
A. *Saturn*

25 STARTER
A. *Tosca*
BONUS QUESTIONS
A. *Pidgin*
A. *Franglais*
A. *George Orwell (in 1984)*

26 STARTER
A. *Cerebellum*
BONUS QUESTIONS
A. *Iechyd da*
   (pronounced 'yachy da')
A. *Prosit*
A. *Skoal*

27 STARTER
A. *Many questions fallacy*
BONUS QUESTIONS
A. *Sicily*
A. *Guiseppe Verdi*
A. *Vincenzo Bellini*

28 STARTER
A. *Alice B. Toklas*
BONUS QUESTIONS
A. *Arrow (head)*
A. *Spear*
A. *Shield*

29 STARTER
A. *Observatories*
BONUS QUESTIONS
A. *Jamie Shea*
A. *(Charles Stewart) Parnell*
A. *New York Mets*

30 STARTER

A. Dreams
BONUS QUESTIONS
A. Lux
A. Liquid oxygen
A. Salmon

31 STARTER

A. Canute (the great)
BONUS QUESTIONS
A. Isadora Duncan
A. De Lorean
A. Thunderball

32 STARTER

A. St Andrews
BONUS QUESTIONS
A. Duke Ellington
A. Piano
A. William Shakespeare

33 STARTER

A. William Hogarth
BONUS QUESTIONS
A. Sedge
A. 'And no birds sing'
A. (Newton) Aycliffe

34 STARTER

A. House or domestic cat
BONUS QUESTIONS
A. Sucre
A. Simon Bolivar
A. Colombia/Gran Colombia

35 STARTER

A. Aromatic (compounds)
BONUS QUESTIONS
A. Sir Barnes Wallis
A. John Cowper Powys
A. Thomas Cook

36 STARTER

A. *Semi-quaver*
BONUS QUESTIONS
A. *Sec x × tan x or sine x over cos squared x or tan x over cos x*
A. $\dfrac{1}{1+x^2}$ or $\dfrac{1}{x^2+1}$
A. *-cosech²x*
(pr: cos – zetch)

37 STARTER

A. *Blip*
BONUS QUESTIONS
A. *An earthenware cooking vessel/stockpot*
A. *Persil washing powder*
(although the name derives from the key ingredients, perborate and silicate)
A. *Rizla cigarette papers*

38 STARTER

A. *Colour vision*
BONUS QUESTIONS
A. The Rape of the Lock
(Alexander Pope)
A. *Gaza*
A. *Bill Clinton's*

39 STARTER

A. *Missal*
BONUS QUESTIONS
A. *The sten gun*
A. *(General Henry) Shrapnel*
A. *(John J.) Pershing*

40 STARTER

A. *Acrostic*
BONUS QUESTIONS
A. The Lady
A. *Alfred Hitchcock*
A. *Jane Austen*

41 STARTER

A. *Pluto(n)*
BONUS QUESTIONS
A. *James II (VII of Scotland)*

A. *The reassertion of the supremacy of the Church of England (over Protestant Non-Conformity)*
A. *Henry II*

42 STARTER

A. *(Horse's) oats*
BONUS QUESTIONS
A. *(Horace Walpole's)* The Castle of Otranto
A. *Udolpho*
A. Northanger Abbey

43 STARTER

A. *Piezo-electricity*
BONUS QUESTIONS
A. *Vita Sackville-West*
A. *Harold Nicholson*
A. *Sissinghurst (Castle)*

44 STARTER

A. *Philip Larkin*
BONUS QUESTIONS
A. *Louisiana*
A. *Cajuns*
A. *The pelican state*

45 STARTER

A. *Oblate (spheroid)*
BONUS QUESTIONS
A. *Giuseppe Mazzini*
A. *Enver Pasha*
A. The Nation

46 STARTER

A. *Babylon*
BONUS QUESTIONS
A. *Dorothy Lamour*
A. *Carroll Baker*
A. *Diane Keaton*

47 STARTER

A. *The hovercraft*
BONUS QUESTIONS
A. *Symbiosis*
A. *Nest-sharing*
A. *Endoparasites dwell* in *the host : ectoparasites live* on *it*

48 STARTER

A. *Rafflesia*
BONUS QUESTIONS
A. *(Sadi) Carnot*
A. *Isothermal and adiabatic (or isothermal and isentropic)*
A. *50 per cent*

49 STARTER

A. *Winnie the Pooh*
BONUS QUESTIONS
A. *Paraguay*
A. *Ethiopia*
A. *Afghanistan*

50 STARTER

A. *The miniature/miniatures*
BONUS QUESTIONS
A. *Paris*
A. *Ariane*
A. *Huygens*
(named after Christiaan Huygens)

51 STARTER

A. *Industrial stock indexes*
BONUS QUESTIONS
A. *Joe Orton*
A. *Defacing library books*
A. What the Butler Saw

52 STARTER

A. *Pre-eclampsia*
(accept eclampsia, which is a more severe condition; accept also gestational edema-proteinurea hypertension, or GEPH. also accept toxaemia (of pregnancy) as a term sometimes used to refer to pre-eclampsia and/or eclampsia)
BONUS QUESTIONS
A. *Art Nouveau*
A. *Liberty*
A. *(William) Hamley*

53 STARTER

A. *Neva*
(Alexander Nevsky)
BONUS QUESTIONS
A. *Daniel*
A. *Bel*

A. *Portia*

54 STARTER

A. Jane's Fighting Ships
BONUS QUESTIONS
A. *Alexander von Humboldt*
A. *Peru (the Peru/Peruvian current)*
A. *Saul Bellow*

55 STARTER

A. *Bowman*
   (Sir William Bowman, 1816–1892)
BONUS QUESTIONS
A. *Hephaestus*
A. *Ares*
A. *Aeneas*

56 STARTER

A. *Sir Edward Elgar*
BONUS QUESTIONS
A. *Forty minutes*
A. *Alan Bennett*
A. *Lizzie Borden*

57 STARTER

A. *Acre*
BONUS QUESTIONS
A. *The Heptarchy*:
   (Northumbria, Mercia, Wessex, Sussex, Essex, Kent and East Anglia)
A. *Offa*
A. *Winchester*

58 STARTER

A. *Sabbath day's journey*
BONUS QUESTIONS
A. *Thomas Hobbs*
A. *Socrates*
A. *Jean-Paul Sartre*

59 STARTER

A. *Hamburg*
BONUS QUESTIONS
A. *Vertigo*
A. *Tinnitus*
A. *Meniere's disease*

60 STARTER

A. *Oblomov*
BONUS QUESTIONS
A. *Alma Mater*
A. *Brain*
A. *(Franz Joseph) Haydn*

61 STARTER

A. *Seventeen [units]*
(8 squared is 64, plus 15 squared [225] is 289, which is 17 squared)
BONUS QUESTIONS
A. *Porcupine*
A. *William Cobbett*
A. *Flying boat*

62 STARTER

A. *Monica Lewinsky*
BONUS QUESTIONS
A. *Feathering*
A. *Bantamweight*
A. *Cock feather*

63 STARTER

A. *Ibiza*
BONUS QUESTIONS
A. *Lytton Strachey*
A. *Hot water bottles*
A. *Think of England*

64 STARTER

A. *Christopher Columbus (Cistobal Colon)*
BONUS QUESTIONS
A. *Glasgow*
A. *Scouse*
A. *Oxford*

65 STARTER

A. *Command economy*
BONUS QUESTIONS
A. *(Australian) aborigines*
A. *(Papua) New Guinea*
A. *Faroes/Faeroe Islands*

66 STARTER

A. Bildungsroman
BONUS QUESTIONS
A. *New Year*
A. *Hsin Nien*
A. *Vietnam*

67 STARTER

A. *Lighthouses (and signal lights)*
BONUS QUESTIONS
A. *Angina*
  (accept heart disease/cardiovascular disease)
A. *Lack of oxygen at altitude/altitude sickness*
A. *Baldness (specifically male pattern baldness)*

68 STARTER

A. *George Wallace*
BONUS QUESTIONS
A. La Mer
A. *Also Sprach Zarathustra*
A. *Academic Festival Overture*

69 STARTER

A. *Hardness*
BONUS QUESTIONS
A. *John Irving*
A. *Chet Baker*
A. *Hotel California*

70 STARTER

A. *The method/method acting*
BONUS QUESTIONS
A. *Trombone*
A. *Piano*
A. *Flute*

71 STARTER

A. *Why is the night sky dark?*
  (i.e. if the universe is infinitely big and full of stars, then each line of
  sight would end on a star and the night sky would be bright. However,
  the universe is simply too young for light to reach us from distant stars)
BONUS QUESTIONS
A. *Dada(ism)*
A. *Jean Arp*
A. *Francis Picarbia*

72 STARTER
A. *Niagara Falls*
BONUS QUESTIONS
A. *Mahogany*
A. *Hickory*
A. *Sycamore*

73 STARTER
A. *Nitrates*
BONUS QUESTIONS
A. *Revenge*
A. Kind Hearts and Coronets
A. *Byron*

74 STARTER
A. Buenas noches
BONUS QUESTIONS
A. *Million Instructions Per Second*
A. *Garbage In, Garbage Out*
   (GIGO)
A. *Musical Instrument Digital Interface*

75 STARTER
A. *Emmanuel Swedenborg*
BONUS QUESTIONS
A. *Voortrekker Monument*
A. *Henry the Navigator*
A. *Santiago*

76 STARTER
A. *Legion d'honneur/the legion of honour*
BONUS QUESTIONS
A. *Oedipus*
A. *Blindness*
A. *Antigone*

77 STARTER
A. *He was the first person to queue for* Star Wars: The Phantom Menace, *six weeks before the film was due to open*
BONUS QUESTIONS
A. *Thomas Hardy*
A. *Guy Fawkes*
A. *The executioner's axe*

78 STARTER

A. *Segue*
BONUS QUESTIONS
A. *Beaufort Sea*
A. *Valdez*
A. *Prince William Sound*

79 STARTER

A. *Colouring*
BONUS QUESTIONS
A. *Cable Street*
A. *Clay cross*
   (the act prohibited councils from providing subsidized housing for the poor)
A. *The Curragh*

80 STARTER

A. *The pineal gland*
BONUS QUESTIONS
A. *Neptune*
A. *Venus*
A. *Saturn*

81 STARTER

A. *(Edward) Chad Varah*
BONUS QUESTIONS
A. *Standard time*
A. *The atomic second*
A. *Rugby*

82 STARTER

A. *Paul Gauguin*
BONUS QUESTIONS
A. *Anton Chekhov*
A. *Jonathan Miller*
A. *Giorgio Armani*

83 STARTER

A. *The Antarctic Circle*
BONUS QUESTIONS
A. *Car number plates*
A. *1963*
A. *The yearly letter was used as a prefix/moved to the front*

84 STARTER

A. *Dick Tracy*

BONUS QUESTIONS

A. *The price of the object being taxed*
(as opposed to a specific tax, imposed at a rate per unit of quantity, regardless of price)

A. *Fossil fuels*

A. *Gift tax*

85 STARTER

A. *Cambodia*

BONUS QUESTIONS

A. *100 metres hurdles*
Shotput
Javelin
High jump
Long jump
200 metres
800 metres

86 STARTER

A. *Icon*

BONUS QUESTIONS

A. *Amides*

A. *Urea*

A. *DEET*

87 STARTER

A. *Absinth(e)*

BONUS QUESTIONS

A. *-plicate*
(e.g. triplicate)

A. *-ceps*
(e.g. biceps, triceps)

A. *-reme*
(e.g. trireme)

88 STARTER

A. *Grizzly bear*
(accept Alaskan brown bear)

BONUS QUESTIONS

A. *Klaus Kinski*

A. Love At First Bite

A. *Anthony Hopkins*

89 STARTER

A. *(Gilles de la) Tourette*
   (Tourette's syndrome)
BONUS QUESTIONS
A. French Without Tears
A. The Winslow Boy
A. Separate Tables

90 STARTER

A. *(Regular) pentagons*
BONUS QUESTIONS
A. *John Jellicoe*
A. *Molotov*
   (Vyacheslav Mikhailovich Skryabin)
A. *Ramsay MacDonald*

91 STARTER

A. *The Chancery*
BONUS QUESTIONS
A. *Peppercorn*
A. *Star anise*
A. *The Royal British Legion*

92 STARTER

A. *Pelion and Ossa*
BONUS QUESTIONS
A. *Radio waves*
A. *Paraboloid*
   (accept parabolic)
A. *Very Long Baseline Interferometry*

93 STARTER

A. *George IV*
BONUS QUESTIONS
A. *Bathos*
A. *Assonance*
A. *Antithesis*

94 STARTER

A. *(William) Heath Robinson*
BONUS QUESTIONS
A. *Chicago*
A. *John Hancock Centre*
A. *Bob Fosse*

95 STARTER

A. *Omphalos*
BONUS QUESTIONS
A. *Conisbrough Castle*
A. *Ravenglass*
A. *Norfolk*

96 STARTER

A. *Hildegard*
BONUS QUESTIONS
A. *The battle of flowers*
A. *Flodden*
A. *Thumbelina*

97 STARTER

A. *Macrobiotics*
BONUS QUESTIONS
A. *Oberon*
A. *Pansies*
A. Love's Labour's Lost

98 STARTER

A. *Leonard*
BONUS QUESTIONS
A. *Tennessee*
A. *The Bible Belt*
A. Inherit the Wind

99 STARTER

A. *Ostia*
BONUS QUESTIONS
A. *Caravaggio*
   (Michelangelo Merisi da Caravaggio)
A. *Velasquez*
   (Diego Rodriguez da Silva)
A. *Murillo*
   (Bartolome Esteban Murillo)

100 STARTER

A. *Lilith*
BONUS QUESTIONS
A. 24
A. *Upsilon, omicron*
A. *Stars (in a constellation)*

101 STARTER

A. *Faraday (cage)*
BONUS QUESTIONS
A. *Cameroon/Togo*
A. *Republic of Congo*
 (which became Zaire, before the name was reinstated)
A. *Sudan*

102 STARTER

A. *Albanian*
BONUS QUESTIONS
A. *Prostitute*
A. *Silversmith*
A. *Tax collector*

103 STARTER

A. *Peacock*
BONUS QUESTIONS
A. *Claret*
A. *Entre-Deux-Mers*
A. *Sauternes*

104 STARTER

A. *Battle of Bosworth (field)*
BONUS QUESTIONS
A. *Rudyard Kipling*
A. *C.S.Lewis/Aldous Huxley*
A. *Cervantes*

105 STARTER

A. *A crooked cat*
BONUS QUESTIONS
A. *Decimal currency*
A. *Lord Denning*
A. *The inchmaree clause*

106 STARTER

A. *The future*
BONUS QUESTIONS
A. F
A. *14*
A. *Actinides*

107 STARTER

A. *Queen Victoria*
BONUS QUESTIONS
A. *Helvellyn*
A. *Snowdon*
A. *Kinder Scout*

108 STARTER

A. *Gout*
BONUS QUESTIONS
A. *Sweden*
A. *Philip V*
A. *Italy*

109 STARTER

A. *Leonardo di Caprio*
BONUS QUESTIONS
A. *Expedition of a thousand*
A. *Mille Miglia*
A. *Finland*

110 STARTER

A. *4*
BONUS QUESTIONS
A. *Liechtenstein*
A. *Luxembourg*
A. *Andorra and Monaco*

111 STARTER

A. *Cafetière*
BONUS QUESTIONS
A. *Geoffrey of Monmouth (or Galfridi Monemutensis)*
   (*History of the Kings of Britain* (c.1136). Not the first to refer to Arthur
   [ref. in ninth-century Nennius and others] but the one on which later
   romances were based)
A. *Leir (Lear)*
A. *Aeneas*

112 STARTER

A. *Bedbug*
BONUS QUESTIONS
A. *Golden horde*
A. *Henry James*
   (not his last completed novel, which was *The Outcry*)
A. *Do to others what you would have them do to you*

113 STARTER

A. *Jane Austen*
BONUS QUESTIONS
A. *Salary*
A. *Stipend*
A. *Purse*

114 STARTER

A. *Game Boy*
BONUS QUESTIONS
A. *Benjamin Disraeli*
A. *(14th) Earl of Derby*
   (Edward George Geoffrey Smith Stanley)
A. *Suez Canal*

115 STARTER

A. *A person who pursues a civil action on behalf of another who cannot*
BONUS QUESTIONS
A. *Fibrillation or atrial fibrillation*
A. *Thrombin*
A. *Collagen*

116 STARTER

A. *'The Flight of the Bumble Bee'*
BONUS QUESTIONS
A. *Jargon*
A. *Argot*
A. *Cant*

117 STARTER

A. *Igneous rocks*
BONUS QUESTIONS
A. *Qwerty*
A. *Dvorak*
A. *The quick brown fox jumps over the lazy dog*

118 STARTER

A. *Transom*
BONUS QUESTIONS
A. *Imprisoned (for life)*
A. *Drowned (in the Thames while trying to resist arrest)*
A. *Transported (to Australia)*

119 STARTER
A. *Ascension (day)*
BONUS QUESTIONS
A. *Carbon, hydrogen, oxygen and nitrogen*
A. *Sulphur*
A. *Iodine*

120 STARTER
A. *'The Game of Life'*
BONUS QUESTIONS
A. *Technically Advanced Civilizations*
A. *Mars*
A. *Albert Einstein*